POWER AND EVERYDAY LIFE

For my daughters Shola and Liana

Power and Everyday Life

*The Lives of Working Women in
Nineteenth-Century Brazil*

Maria Odila Silva Dias

Translated by Ann Frost

Rutgers University Press
New Brunswick, New Jersey

First published in Brazil as *Quotidiano e poder em São Paulo no seculo XIX – Ana Gertrudes de Jesus* by editora brasiliense, © Maria Odila Leite da Silva Dias, 1984.

First published in the United States by Rutgers University Press, New Brunswick, New Jersey, 1995.

First published in Great Britain by Polity Press in association with Blackwell Publishers, 1995

ISBN 0-8135-2204-8 (hardcover)
    0-8135-2205-6 (paperback)

Library of Congress Cataloging-in-Publication Data

Dias, Maria Odila Leite da Silva.
    [Quotidiano e poder em São Paulo no século XIX. English]
    Power and everyday life : the lives of working women in nineteenth-century Brazil / Maria Odila Dias : translated by Ann Frost.
        p. cm.
    Includes bibliographical references and index.
    ISBN 0-8135-2204-8. – ISBN 0-8135-2205-6 (pbk.)
    1. Poor women–Brazil–São Paulo–History–19th century.
    2. Women–Brazil–São Paulo–Social conditions. 3. Poor women–
    Brazil–São Paulo–Social conditions.   I. Title.
    HV1448.B72S26413   1995
    305.5'69'082–dc20
                                                        94-47497
                                                        CIP

Typeset in 10½ on 12 pt Times
by Joshua Associates Ltd., Oxford
Printed in Great Britain by T. J. Press, Padstow, Cornwall

This book is printed on acid-free paper.

Contents

Preface: The Other Witnesses

These pages bring together for us very valuable areas of study: work, recollection, the work of women, the work of recollection, the evocation of the dead. They present us with the situation of the working woman – of yesterday – of today? – and moreover, the situation of all those who survive in a hostile world. They show us the risky, hazardous existence of those who pursue their daily life with stealth, people who venture tentatively into the social jungle, to steal one more day, one more spark of life from the closed fist of Fortune.

There are works which offer us the drawing room of history, with its framed portraits on the walls, its stylish furniture, everything on show and beautifully set out. There are some investigations, however, which go straight to the core of the house, to its kitchens and its offices; they search through those plots of wasteland where rubbish is dumped, and where minor figures secretly come and go. There in the sheds and the basements, in the domestic jungles, these shadows hide, cover their faces with their hands and run away. They have no faith in historians, or in anyone who approaches them vested with the insignia of power.

But let us sit by the well, pick up a forgotten piece of earthenware, and wait ... in the bushlands, for someone who can recognize the sound of returning footsteps, of clothes being beaten on the boards, of a spoon in a bowl, a lament, perhaps a song ...

Reconstructing history like this does not require an abstract ability to deal with the past, but an evocation, rather like a religious evocation, or rather, an invocation. While events were taking place that deserve to be recorded for the next generation, the people we are invoking were working for the leftovers of other people's lives: they dusted, swept, washed dishes, emptied ashtrays, shook the crumbs, made beds, waited at table. We have picked up these leftovers and given them preferential treatment.

It was the common people who lived a subordinated, dominated existence, one which sank without trace and disappeared into the lives of the ruling classes and their History. They were the witnesses of oppression; their testimony, if we could put it together, would provide the most genuine evidence of the past. As the history of civilization unfolds like a pact of destruction, the victims have to be forgotten. If remembering the dead is painful, remembering these small testimonies, recounting a history in reverse, is even more so, for it is a horrifying history. Let us then approach Maria Odila's book with the knowledge that the ground we tread is hallowed by invocation.

The main theme of this book is the struggle for survival of women who lived on the fringes of the system, who settled in the cracks of society, on the margins of officially recognized work. They moved around with stealth and cunning amid formal, repressive ranks. These women, selling from their trays and washing clothes in the rivers and public fountains, are as clever as chameleons, small animals who do not aspire to defeat others, since they themselves have already been defeated, but simply to stay alive. Without any official know-how or written culture, all they have is their skill, their ability to improvise, and the knowledge that comes from experience, which is so disdained in the elderly and in women. Theirs is the daily round, which begins each and every morning, without hope, in their attempt to stay alive; such is the humble work of these women, hounded by the police, hiding away in back alleys, in basements and back rooms, on barren lands.

Has their work on the fringes of society undergone any change?

Maria Odila describes women who took on the role of men, women warriors and household providers.

Popular stories – which the great master of folklore, Xidieh, perceives so clearly – recall brave young girls like Cinderella, overcoming the obstacles of unending toil. They also call to mind those fierce old women, who struggled all alone in a world that was so prejudiced that they were seen as witches.

One section of her chapter on 'The magic of survival' is particularly powerful:

> Surviving under the harsh conditions of daily life was an exhausting job, and was achieved through magical contacts and supernatural interventions. Metaphors of hunger and images of the struggle to survive are embodied in the figures of old, domineering women: their foul forms could be seen fishing

in rivers of empty waters; as ghosts on lonely paths, they were seen bending over bundles of firewood, which they put together and then undid, in a compelling, deadly spell. There were little old women who drew water from a well with a worn-out rope.

I recalled once again the records of Dona Alice, during the 'Spanish flu' in São Paulo, records which I had the honour to put together:

There was no running water; there was a well in the middle of the grass, between the factory and the wire fence. At that time, one night ... the well cable was very old, mended with bits of wire. Families would hang out their clothes on the fence, and they were soon frozen stiff, and looked like ghosts. I can still remember, even now, that the water in the butt was frozen solid. How could I wash clothes in ice? Drawing water was difficult too, in that cold. I couldn't make up my mind, but ended up breaking the ice in the butt and drawing water from the well.

I was very moved by Rosalía de Castro's epigraph in the chapter on 'Ladies and women slaves at a price':

I am turning brown,
like a little Moorish girl,
daughter of dark people.

Like the children to whom this book refers, the children of forsaken women, the great Galician poetess was also a child who was abandoned on the wheel of fortune, on the night of her birth in Santiago de Compostela. Rosalía lived at a time when only white-skinned women were highly valued, did not have to work hard, or look like the sunburnt Moorish girls in the poem ('the burning heat has left me dry as a leaf').

I thought of my grandmother, Maria da Conceição, the mother of Antonio Federico, my father. She spent her youth living at a point in the road where it meets Avenida Rebouças, which was called Dona Hipólita when I was a child, and is now known as Gabriel Monteiro da Silva. When she married, she went to live on her husband's estate, in the backwoods of Santo Amaro, where she was widowed very young. That lady, Maria da Conceição Correa, must have had a hard time, for in her struggle she became known as 'tough as old leather' (perhaps it was a rejected suitor who gave her this name because she chased him away with her broom when he asked for her hand). My family used the phrase as an insult: whenever I did something wrong in my childhood, someone would immediately say to me, 'It's clear she's as tough as old leather!'

I think of that grandmother when I read Rosalía's poem, and I remember her stern, brown old face:

> I am growing old and withered
> like a rose in winter,
> I am growing weak,
> I am turning brown,
> like a little Moorish girl,
> daughter of dark people.

But daily life is not just a matter of economic survival, and I believe that those women were cheerful, in the way that people who live within a network of solidarity have to be brave: 'Among the stallholders there were some who became very popular because of their cheerfulness, their loquacity and inexhaustible hilarity . . .'

I thought the last chapter very beautiful, the most concrete and the most visionary, peopled as it is with women who travel through it on foot, with their baskets of clothes or their trays with green corn and hot pine seeds, or in carts, laden with grapes, milk and firewood.

Through her historical research, which is also an invocation, Maria Odila Silva Dias has opened up the way for these women to reach us.

Ecléa Bosi

Acknowledgements

This research was partially financed by the Fundação de Amparo à Pesquisa do Estado de São Paulo (Foundation for the Support for Research of the State of São Paulo). It was this financial aid which allowed me to spend a period at the University of Texas, where its preparation was begun.

I am grateful to Odila and Candinho, my parents, for the time spent together and for their unfailing support.

I cannot but remember with gratitude twenty years of conversations with the historian Sergio Buarque de Holanda, teacher and friend, to whom I am greatly indebted.

I am also grateful to Professor John Gledson, of the Institute of Latin American Studies of the University of Liverpool, for his careful revision of the English translation of this book; to Professor John Monteiro, of the University of Campinas in the State of São Paulo, for helping me with the notes for the British public; and to Peter Burke, Reader in Cultural History at the University of Cambridge, for having first suggested the book for translation and publication by Polity Press.

All the photographic reproductions included in this book are from the collection in the Instituto de Estudos Brasileiros da USP (Institute for Brazilian Studies, University of São Paulo).

Translator's Note

The author's *mulheres sós* – which can be translated as 'women on their own', 'single women' or 'lone women' – include women in all sorts of family circumstances, unmarried or not legally married, single mothers, widows, women living as mistresses, women in and out of relationships. What they have in common is that they cannot look permanently to anyone else to support them and must fend for themselves and their dependants.

Introduction

The assumption of a feminine condition, an abstract, universal ideal, which is ahistorical by definition, forces women of any period into mythical, sacred areas, where they carry out appropriate work on the margins of reality, and ignored by history.

The reconstruction of the social roles of women as mediations which allow their integration into the overall historical process of their time would seem to be a promising way of resisting myths, precepts and stereotypes. Their special way of participating in the social process can be discerned through the reconstruction of the totality of social relationships.

This work is a contribution towards the knowledge of the historical roles of women who belonged to the oppressed classes, whether free, slaves or freedwomen, during the first stages of urbanization in the city of São Paulo, between the end of the eighteenth century and the dawn of the abolition of slavery in 1888; I am not referring to official or prescribed social roles, but to improvisations which were continually adapted in the course of the tensions and conflicts which make up the organization of commercial production, the system of domination and the structuring of power relations.

The social memory of their lives is becoming lost, more for ideological reasons than through any real lack of documentation. It is true that the information is difficult to find, for it is scarce and fragmentary, and implicit rather than explicit in the documents. This work tries to collate widely scattered data and to examine their implications.

The historiography of the last few decades favours a social history of women, for we are turning to the records of those groups of people who were excluded from power. New approaches and more appropriate methods are freeing historians from their atavistic prejudices, and are opening the way for a microsocial history of everyday life. The perception of different historical processes occurring simultaneously, the relativity of the dimensions of history, of linear time, of ideas like progress and evolution and of the limits of possible knowledge, are all leading historians to spread their attention more widely, and no longer to limit themselves to the study of the process of the accumulation of wealth and power, and to institutional political history. In a moment of compassionate irony, Machado de Assis noted how the march of time was at variance with human lives: 'How many contingencies there are in life, reader! Some things originate from others, become entangled, confused and are lost, yet time goes on, exactly the same ...'[1] The limitations of methods and sources concerned with the system of power make us reflect on the limits of a certain type of history – of a learning which does not include the everyday life of those social classes marginalized by the institutions of power.

The lives of craftsmen in England, inevitably overtaken and dismissed by the Industrial Revolution, were painstakingly reconstructed by a historian studying the process of the formation of the social consciousness of the working classes: E. P. Thompson, as someone who has worked with manuscript sources on the history of oppressed social groups, made the astute comment that lost causes do not exist in history, and that what appears to be of minor importance in one set of circumstances can turn out to be decisive in others.[2]

Always relegated to the field of obscure routines, everyday life has been revealed by social history as an area where there was an improvisation of informal roles – often new, potentially conflictive and confrontational, and where special forms of resistance and struggle multiplied. The aim is to reappraise public activities in the field of the social history of everyday life. The French historian Emmanuel Le Roy Ladurie, in his book on *Montaillou*, brought to light a whole chain of informal social roles, of links and interventions in the system of power; the work revealed a whole organization of solidarity and neighbourhood co-operation, and of a resistance which is unorthodox, challenging, silent and obstinate.[3] In the same way, the study of the everyday life of slaves unveils a cumulative experience of improvisation, of cultural adaptation, and of resistance to the authorities which is something new in historical research, and which is transforming the social history of slavery.[4]

Incorporating the social stresses of everyday life into history means reconstructing the organization of survival for groups who were marginalized by power, and at times by the actual process of production. This is principally so in the initial period of urbanization in the town of São Paulo,[5] which was deeply marked by the slavery system, and by the export economy – of sugar, followed by coffee – which was of no immediate advantage to the town and did not encourage the expansion of internal supplies, or the formation of a free labour market. Under the circumstances, the town bulged rather than grew, its poverty increasing and providing a structural availability of manual labour; poor women, on their own and as heads of families, survived precariously by doing temporary work, acting independently rather than as wage-earners. Their integration into São Paulo society involves the study of transitory, intermediate, social structures or formations rather than that of actual participation in the production process.

The urbanization of São Paulo did not immediately mean the social rise of a Europeanized bourgeoisie, or the formation of a class of free, salaried people. Nevertheless, the increase in women in poverty, both slaves and freedwomen, surviving off the homecraft industry and small-time itinerant trade forms part of the consolidation of the slavery-based economy and of the concurrent process of concentration of properties and rents.

In the town, they survived in the blurred margins and shadows of incipient commercialization, playing an important part in the structural continuity of our history and even today they still continue to challenge the development policies designed by economists and anthropologists.

The production and commercialization of foodstuffs, of secondary importance from the point of view of the economic system of large-scale farming, remained structurally disorganized, dogged by the feeling of social contempt which was directed towards domestic or retail activities. Social prejudice against the organization of production aimed at the consumption and production of essential commodities, which was deep-rooted in the colonial system itself, seemed to grow worse in the initial stages of urbanization. Finally, slave-owning society did not anticipate the supply and the production of a workforce *in loco*, since it was imported from Africa.

This was the social milieu of these *paulistas*, São Paulo women in a kind of limbo and exile from anything of social value in the economy of their period. They lived a life of precarious poverty as they gradually commercialized their domestic production, evolving from inside their households towards the more central streets in the city, which they occupied for several decades. The organization of their livelihood depended on very strong links of solidarity and neighbourhood cooperation, which were continually being created and adapted.

Some of the prejudices that declassified them socially arose from the chauvinist, misogynist values that were deeply established in the slave-owning system, reinforced by the scorn that was felt for manual labour or any job involving subsistence living. Apart from this, they were also affected by the prejudices that arose from the organization of the family and the system of inheritance within the ruling classes, which relegated them to the category of social dregs, these single mothers and mistresses, who were an integral part of the system of domination itself.

Although their presence was institutionally non-existent and socially held in low esteem, it was conspicuous in the town. The fact that they did not participate in political or administrative history did not diminish the importance of the role they played.

Their social sphere was one of disorder and confusion, between public and private sectors – a necessary part of the system of power based on slavery, and one which had many repercussions on the process of establishing the state, taking place at the same time as the urbanization of the city.

The same process of increasing poverty that had produced them came in the end to drive them away from their improvised space in the central districts of the town, well within the limits of bourgeois possibilities, between the opera house and the shops. They were driven out by the growth of bourgeois attitudes in the town, by urban improvements, lighting, the reorganization of housing, the raising of municipal taxes, and, finally, by the railways.

They were also swept away in confusion by the final crisis of the abolition of slavery; they were turned out of the urban area that they were occupying, only to re-emerge in the outer districts of the city. There they remained during the first decades of the twentieth century, still on the fringes of the capitalist system, making up the masses of unemployed women, a reserve force of unused manual labour, living precariously from the same expedients of homecrafts and the initial commercialization of foodstuffs.

This piece of research is a beginning, which I hope will produce cumulative results in the course of time; the documentation is especially difficult, because of the widely scattered nature of sources, and also because, in general, like all written sources, they are compromised by domination and power, and extremely uncommunicative about the daily life of poor, illiterate women. This is a history of implications, a history without sources, a history constructed by reading between the lines.

ONE

Daily Life and Power

These characters, who long before their birth did not yet appear in the
Scriptures (since there were not yet any Scriptures), when they were
written, over the many centuries that followed, became a part of them
and appeared with the same continuity, albeit with dark shadows and
faint colours, for the life they were to live was still a long way off . . .

Antonio Vieira, *Sermões*

In the city of São Paulo, the area of survival for women in poverty,
whether they were white, slaves or freedwomen, lay within the boundaries of the relative autonomy allowed by the authorities to social out-
casts. Since it was difficult, if not impossible, to control effectively, this
area of autonomy grew with urbanization, creating more opportunities
for the improvisation of unconventional roles. In the city, poor women
circulated throughout the public areas – at the fountains and washing
places, in the streets and squares – where there was constant inter-
mingling between local inhabitants and outsiders, minor civil servants
and small, clandestine traders, the fringes of slavery and free trade.

With regard to their regular means of livelihood, which is unreliably
documented in written sources, we come across disparate yet simul-
taneous fragments of discourse and events, which both complicate and
negate each other: on the one hand, a whole repressive system of legislation which could not be implemented on a daily basis; on the other,
traces of an autonomous existence pervading the city, offering women
no opportunity for employment, and forcing them to create their own
means of survival. It is both difficult and complicated to unravel the
facts about daily routines which were not even regulated by the chiming

of the church bells; we are forced to reflect on the limitations of written documents as sources for social history.

With their usual grumbles and protests, the women would carry out small transactions and commissions in a variety of verbal arrangements and deals, which were complicated by family ties and domestic relationships between relatives and neighbours; few traces of these have survived in documents after the censorship of clerks, sheriffs, orderlies and weights and measures inspectors. Their day-to-day methods of survival involved the continual exchange of information and gossip, and a whole network of personal contacts and favours, including protection, relations with godparents and concubinage. All these were to their advantage, and they knew how to exploit and use them in such a way that it became impossible for the authorities to exercise control, so forceful were these people's demands – insistent, personal petitions, and constant, persistent claims. There were a great many complaints, numerous disputes and a great deal of quarrelling, much of which has been lost in the official documentation. When the women came to submit their claims at the town hall in person, they were not allowed into the presence of the officials unless they were escorted by two soldiers. Even in the seventeenth century it was being observed how they used to mutter and gossip about the authorities, who took the places that they usually occupied in church.[1]

There are odd pieces of information which have survived, faint echoes of their tense relations and confrontations with the system of domination, filtering through the hegemonical consciousness of written sources, which are yet another reminder of the protests of the poor women street vendors.[2]

The spoken word was an essential tool for survival among illiterate women, but when their words were transcribed at second hand they lost their force, and hardly figure in any of the documents. Almost nothing has survived of what was a principal element in their way of life: the endless gossip in doorways, and the collusion that went on around the selling trays, in the streets and on the bridges:

> When women get together
> It is to gossip about others,
> Beginning at the new moon,
> They go on until the moon is full . . .[3]

The smells, the shouting and the street cries, their gesticulations, their songs, many of the intonations and mannerisms of the women vendors, as they sat on their mats, pipe in mouth, or travelled along the roads, all form part of the communication involved in their survival and have been lost for ever. Up until 1765, when the job of female judge for petty offences was abolished in Lisbon, the town hall would pay a woman to administer public thrashings to women traders and vendors who shouted and screamed obscenities in the streets and markets of Lisbon.[4] In the police records of the city of São Paulo in the last century, there is plenty of evidence of the imprisonment of wild, rebellious women, who shouted out, using foul language. In a document dated 20 September 1834, the Justice of the Peace in Santa Ifigênia pronounced the beatings and harsh treatment administered to Anna Francisca da Conceição to be well deserved:

> since she has made a nuisance of herself in the neighbourhood by her disgraceful behaviour, and since she is a troublemaker and a rebellious woman, and has been the cause of several fights, which I have tried to settle with the parties, as I have real sympathy for the supplicant, bearing in mind the wretched state to which she finds herself reduced, perhaps as a result of her mutinous nature and liking for arguments . . .[5]

There are numerous legal documents and records concerning disturbances which arose from affronts to the authorities, the wealthy, and the name of the emperor: obscene language in the streets, in processions and in church.[6] There were several lawsuits concerning moral defamation, and imprisonments of women who were accused of being insurgent and causing riots in the streets, like Anna Benedita do Espírito Santo, a seamstress, known as Cascafina, Quitéria Caetana, an African washerwoman from south of the cathedral, Vicência, an ironing woman of twenty years of age, and so on.[7]

Apart from hearsay concerning wild women and the reports of troublemakers, little has reached us regarding the importance of swear-words and their magical powers of sorcery in relation to the tasks and chores of everyday life. They have gone down in history as a reflection of the cantankerous old crones of Gil Vicente or of Fernando de Rojas;[8] here and there the Branca Anes, the Inez Pereiras, the Celestinas. Or they appear in the proceedings of the Inquisition as the blaspheming of women who were exasperated by training black women from the country, or angered by some unforeseen circumstance.[9]

As far as their daily routine is concerned, little has survived in written documents – which are, by their very nature, the opposite of the everyday life of illiterate women.

Scattered pieces of evidence of the presence of poor women

experiencing the process of urbanization in the city of São Paulo found their way through oral sources into the town hall registers, which do not so much record their presence, but rather present picturesque sketches of their fleeting passage through life and through history, as though they had been immortalized by the names of remote corners and odd hiding places: creole Josefa's hill, Inés Vieira's lane, Catarina Dias's bridge, the spinners' street, the straw hut of Quitéria Maria de Jesus, by Zunega's pond, close to the little church in Ifigênia.[10]

Outside the noise and bustle of the more central streets, some of the picturesque stereotypes in travellers' journals carry all the hallmarks of preconceived ideas, with emphasis placed on local colour, and bearing all the subsequent abstract idealization of figures removed from their historical context.

Zaluar remarks on the latent tension within the population between the bohemian way of life of the Europeanized students and the secrecy of the local people: neither seemed suited to the other, nor did he think that they could ever live in harmony.[11]

This traveller, like others before him, presents a picture of life which has little to do with either students or the wealthy: one of pious women in their coarse shawls or black lace mantillas, walking along the streets, rosary in hand, or saying a prayer in the chapel on the corner.

> . . . where pious women
> Run into each other in the badly paved streets,
> Rosary in hand . . .[12]

Contemporary observers also described black women selling from trays, sitting on the pavements of the Rua da Quitanda Velha, by day or night, in the smoking light of dark, wax candles which they fixed to their trays, or which they secured in their turbans as they went slowly on their way, throwing shadows along the route.[13]

They make constant reference to the presence of poor women in the streets, where upper-class ladies hardly ever appear, or in the churches, sitting on mats on the ground. They talk in terms of dark shadows, wrapped in black cloth,[14] and say almost nothing about their living conditions. Because of their preconceived ideas, they refrain from comment, or deliberately omit any information about where they lived, or how they survived.

Nevertheless, reading between the lines of the official documentation from the town hall, or the various documents of the governors, there is plenty of casual information, which appears frequently, albeit in a very scattered fashion. Poor white women, slave women and freed women dealt in the poorest and humblest kind of trading, the selling of foodstuffs, vegetables, bacon and tobacco, in the streets around the town hall: in the cottages of Rua da Quitanda Velha, in the Ladeira do Carmo, the hill called the 'big hole', and in Rua do Cotovelo ('street of the elbow') (1800).[15] The women streetsellers would spread their wares on the ground, between the churches of Misericórdia and Rosário, and carry on a penny trade for slaves. Any itinerant business went to the few who took over the alleys and passageways between the Rua do Rosário and the Rua do Comércio: hell alley, Beco Cachaça . . . to the extent that the tradesmen in Rua Direita, who had established shops there, were driven to protest, mainly about the filth, the mosquitoes and the smell.[16]

Women were not allowed as assistants in the shops,[17] and only the odd wealthier woman ran an established business, such as a general store, or a wine merchant's.[18]

The town had an abundant female workforce which the traders did not need, and which the few factories did little to exploit. Some of the cloth factories distributed orders to seamstresses and women spinners, who were hired by the day, and who would usually work in their own homes. Frei Velloso, a local botanist and writer, commented in 1822 that the town was overrun with poor women;[19] they were living in rented houses and rooms, in small, low-ceilinged, mud-walled buildings, with crumbling roofs and floors of trodden earth, in the poorest parts of streets like São Bento, Ladeira de São Francisco, roads like Rosário and Boa Vista. In this last street, which runs parallel to Rosário, the houses were built so far below street level that one could see over the top of them, from one street to the next, and watch the statues being carried on their biers in the Ash Wednesday processions.[20]

Anna Francisca, a mulatta seamstress and an unmarried mother, lived to the south of the cathedral with two small grandchildren and her daughters, also seamstresses and also single mothers (Joaquina Maria, twenty-seven years old, and Rosa Maria, thirty-one); D. Maria Amália, a white spinster of thirty, also lived to the south of the cathedral, employing five slave women as seamstresses in her house. Anna Benedita do Espírito Santo, a mulatta seamstress, who was arrested in the streets with a knife in her hand, lived in a small, rented room in Ladeira do Carmo in 1853. In Ifigênia, near the Luz Convent, six young mulatta women spinners lived together in the same house, with their small children . . .[21]

They were everywhere, both within the city bridges and beyond them. They were not often seen in the better class streets, like Carmo and Santa Teresa, but they did not, nevertheless, live segregated lives.

Many of them were the poor neighbours of large mansions, like the one belonging to the Toledo spinsters, on the corner of Rua do Rosário and Travessa do Colégio, or Senator Vergueiro's house in Rua Direita.[22]

In the early decades of the last century, the urban area within the bridges was just those parts which extended from the Convento de São Bento to the Campo da Forca, to the Capela dos Aflitos, near the cemetery of the same name, to Tabatinguera, which was then still a precipice, and the farm belonging to the English. Outside this nucleus of dark, potholed streets, there were wretched hovels which alternated with remote patches of dense thicket, a refuge for escaped slaves, or with blank walls that marked the boundaries of the private orchards of the wealthier farms. These were dotted over the city to the south of the cathedral, in Ifigênia, in the Braz,[23] and outside the bridges, on the main access routes into the city.

In their comings and goings, the poor women of the city used to congregate in the more crowded places, where they could offer their services to students and foreigners as washerwomen or cooks, and where they also had better opportunities to make small business deals or to find odd jobs to do (selling wax, decorating the streets for a procession, making soap, and so on).

In 1822, Auguste de Saint-Hilaire would watch the road to Penha from one of the windows in the governor's palace, and he described the activities of a group of washerwomen on the flat area around the Carmo. Ferrão bridge, which was the next stage on the road to Penha, was another meeting place for women vendors and washerwomen. Here the countrywomen who grew their own crops brought small surplus goods to sell in the city; they refused to pay any tax, claiming that they were dealing in staple commodities.[24]

Other places where the presence of washerwomen was more noticeable were the bridges of Lorena, in Piques, Bexiga, near the lodge of the same name, and Acu and São Carlos, in Ifigênia. With their children on their backs, they would untie bundles of clothes on the river bank, wash them in the river and often hang them out to dry on the railings of the bridge. These were busy meeting places in general, where tolls were collected, and where businessmen and clerks would meet to have a chat and to eye the washerwomen. In 1848 it was forbidden to hang washing on the bridge railings or to rinse out clothes at public fountains.[25]

In 1854, Ferreira de Rezende noticed countrywomen going past his house on the road to Ó, selling eggs, vegetables and fresh fish 'for next to nothing'. In 1839, Kidder described the women sellers carrying jars on their heads, full of sugar cane brandy from Ó.[26]

Their comings and goings indicated the harsh struggle for survival for the many women who were single parents. Some of them figure in the census of 1836: Joaquina Maria de Andrade, a native of Santo Amaro, had a small place in Ifigênia, where she lived with six small children. 'She has no decent means of survival,' the registrar observes.

Lining the access roads outside the city, their wretched huts attracted the attention of the tax officer, as well as the stares of passers-by. Florinda Maria, a young widow of twenty-two who was from Rio, lived in a hovel on the road to Penha, the district to the north of São Paulo, with two tiny children, the younger a baby of six months; Anna Joaquina had a tiny plot for growing manioc in Ifigênia, where she lived with her only son: 'She is very poor, and', say the neighbours, 'she doesn't bother about her son's upbringing . . .'[27]

The documentation in the town hall pays detailed attention to the small taverns and wretched grog shops on the sides of the roads. Although they were very poor, they had to pay the tax levied on brandy. In 1819 a scrupulous survey was carried out of all the small, clandestine grog shops.[28] On his way to Penha, Saint-Hilaire was struck by one of these small stores, whose counter was a narrow little window: 'No one is allowed to go into the room where the food and brandy are kept.'[29] It is significant that it was much the same almost half a century later, whether in the way these shops along the edge of the highway were described, or in the very fact of their poverty. On his way to Porto Feliz, Zaluar spent the night in 'a filthy, disgusting hovel of a room belonging to an old creature who, by her dress, appeared to belong to the female sex'.[30] She gave him some maize bread and rum.

Countrywomen and vendors would roam around, kept within sight by the local authorities, who maintained a watchful eye on their constant presence in the trading places and on the bridges over which foodstuffs were brought into the city. They were to be found in the trading places in Juqueri and Barro Branco, on the Atibaia road, in Piques, in the remote corner of Bexiga, on the borders of the Anhangabaú, on the road to Luz, selling small quantities of chickens, eggs, flour and cheese.[31]

Some of them would come in ox carts, on the pretext of bringing small amounts of surplus goods from their pieces of land, but in fact, according to a succession of complaints registered at the town hall, carrying illegal goods to sell clandestinely and thereby evade tax. Other women would bring stones in their carts for building works in the town, or firewood for the inhabitants to use: those who came from Freguesia do Ó travelled along the borders of Santa Ifigênia and, from there, came across the Acu and Constituição bridges, driving their carts towards Largo de São Bento at the heart of the old commercial centre of São Paulo.[32]

There is a whole kaleidoscope of small, scattered but frequent references, trickling in from the most unlikely sources. They vouch for the fact that the women's presence was conspicuous, though the information is fragmented and provides very little insight into the way in which they integrated into the society of their day.

One of their favourite meeting places was the embankment on the flat area around the Carmo, along which they brought their foodstuffs into the town from Guarulhos, Nazaré and Moji das Cruzes. A document of 1821 tells of preparations in progress here for the arrival of Prince Dom Pedro, on his way from Rio.[33]

From this date onwards, documents are concerned with the process of the independence of Brazil from Portugal, with the building of the state at local level: potentates and political parties struggle for power through constitutional reforms restructuring institutions and the organization and control of local trade. From 1828 onwards, after the election of a new town council, tensions remain high between the followers of the old council and the provincial or governmental authorities nominated by the central powers, as witness a continual series of orders and counterorders. In the mesh of animosities between the Bernardo and Andrade factions, we get glimpses of the women in poverty, struggling for a precarious livelihood. In anonymity they experience the lot of the common people, the fight for survival of the oppressed, and they are quite removed from the problems of patriarchs and leading statesmen. They learn of political independence through the conversations of their neighbours, and their life continues, ruled by family and neighbourhood relationships, which remain barely affected. In fact, their lives gradually get harder, and their confrontations with the authorities over tax, land, hygiene and public morality become increasingly painful.

In the documents of this period many facts overlap each other in an intricate web of small matters. In 1822, for example, the Toledo spinsters tried to come to some agreement with the council authorities to prevent the expropriation of the tenement houses which were next door to the mansion where they lived. This became the pretext for a great deal of discussion over the limits of ownership, and the municipal authorities appeared to sympathize with their demands; in the meantime, Martim Francisco and Brigadeiro Jordão, a member of the Provisional Council, were determined to oppose them.[34]

Remote from the interests of the ruling classes, the small-time women leaseholders, threatened by the concessions of new allotments of land to settlers or by the demarcation of lands leased by the council, had to defend and fight for their newly cleared land, which was their only means of survival. A large extension was closed off on the Tamanduateí embankment, which was land for common use, to serve as pasture land for pack animals; in Pari, in Santo Amaro, they were threatened with eviction by the seizure of lands for redistribution to settlers.[35]

It is not political events or the framework of institutional reforms that define the history of these women. Their daily life was complicated more by continual crises over provisions, brought about by high prices and the shortage of foodstuffs in the city. The memory of the famine of 1818 was still vivid in their minds, and the same crisis threatened to repeat itself in 1823, again in 1826, and yet again in 1828.[36] It was during these times of acute crisis – when, as the municipal authorities put it, 'the people threatened to rebel' – that they appear in written history, albeit with veiled references, since from the point of view of the authorities their practices of clandestine trade and small-time itinerant contraband were of debatable significance. They grumbled about those in power; they protested over taxes; they felt very remote from the local elite conflicts which fill the written sources of the period, with their intrigues between political leaders and rich merchants, fighting amongst themselves. According to the constitution of 1824, women were not even eligible to vote in the first ballot, and even if they had been, only a minority among them would have had the minimum income of 100$, which was the necessary requirement to be a voter.[37]

Other concerns marked their days. In January 1823, Anna Gertrudes de Jesus, an inhabitant of Santa Ifigênia, requested 8$ from the council for removing an ant hill from her property. In March of the same year, Governor Oeynhausen attempted to have Martim Francisco and Brigadeiro Jordao exiled.[38] In March 1822, arrangements were made for restricting the area for the women street vendors, allowing them to congregate only in the Beco do Alferes José Fernandes as far as the Brigadeiro gates. In 1826, Gertrudes Rodrigues do Espírito Santo, Perpétua Gertrudes, the widow Ana Joaquina and Maria Antônia do Rosário, all street vendors from Santo Amaro, testified that the council clerk was collecting unjustified payments.[39]

They were disregarded as a group of people, marginal to history books and even to everyday life, their existence barely perceived. Never in a supposedly European society, writes the historian Gilberto Freire, did men appear in public always without their wives as did ordinary Brazilian men at the time of the empire.[40]

Anonymous figures in the process of survival during the early years of the Empire, women appeared infrequently and as if by chance in the documents of the time. In 1824, the Santana embankment was flooded, and passers-by had to wade through water which came up to their knees: 'it was especially embarrassing for the women, as it was both difficult and shameful for them to tuck up their clothes in public, especially as many men lingered there out of curiosity, making fun of the stumbling of the women and their confusion.'[41] Independence had no effect on disease, malaria or the pollution of the Tamanduateí river, which were responsible for the deaths of many infants. These figures rarely emerge in the chronicles of everyday life. They appear only in times of crisis, during the epidemics of cholera morbus or of smallpox, which struck in 1823, in 1828 and again in 1831. Then the women appeared on the scene like good Samaritans; they received a small stipend from the Council so that they could nurse sick slaves and freedmen in their homes; they also took part in the preparations for the arrival of the statue of Our Lady of Penha, patroness of São Paulo.[42]

In 1831, when feelings were running high against Portuguese merchants and civil servants (as, incidentally, had been the case in 1824), tension increased between the women street vendors and the salesmen from the better quality shops; women emerged in the censuses also in anonymity, since they declared themselves as Brazilian but the majority would not declare their family names.

The solid presence of women in the population of the city – of women on their own, with their husbands away – had been an integral element of the town's traditions since the seventeenth century. It only began to attract the attention of the authorities, in their letters and reports sent back to Portugal, during the last decades of the eighteenth century, with the influence of more enlightened attitudes and Europeanizing reforms affecting the ruling classes.

The settling of the mining towns of Minas Gerais (1698–1730), of Goiás from 1726 onwards, and Mato Grosso in 1730, saw an even greater increase in the itinerant habits of the men from the town who were mineworkers, tradesmen and muleteers. Gone were the times when Maria Castanho was the only Portuguese woman in São Paulo. During the eighteenth century, women dominated urban life, although it is true that they were more notable for their poverty, as a result of their precarious and needy existence, than for their social standing. The itinerant menfolk were socially more prestigious than the women who stayed behind in the town, the rearguard of the population. The clearing of small crops, small-time trade and activities connected with consumption and subsistence could never compete in the colony with the aura of risky enterprise with which the business ventures of the *paulistas* were associated, earning their living on the roads as muleteers.[43]

During the independence period it was known that almost 40 per cent of the inhabitants of the city were single women, heads of families, many of them in relationships but not married, and many of them unmarried mothers. Their contemporaries gradually became aware of their presence in an uncomfortable and prejudiced way. In the years that followed 1822 there was almost as much suspicion concerning poor women's sexual habits as there was about revolutionaries. In August of 1822, Europeanizing, reformist fashions were becoming extreme, and the municipal authorities applied for measures against common law marriages, widespread among the population; in the same year they decided to set up a shelter for foundlings and undertake a scheme of assistance for abandoned babies.[44]

The phenomenon of single women who are heads of families is both common and intricately involved in the structure of colonial society. It is a phenomenon characteristic of urbanization in the colonies of Brazil, and has been a theme of research, for recently several studies have come out concerning single-women households in Vila Rica, as well as other mining towns of colonial Brazil; the subject has also been studied for Salvador and Rio de Janeiro.[45] In the first decades of the last century, multiple factors helped to keep it alive.

It becomes impossible to determine precise causes for it, since it is part of a vast all-embracing process that concerned social change in a very complex society. Basically it was an important feature of social control as exercised by the ruling classes, for family structure was a strategic instrument used by them to maintain their acquired social privileges. Social roles were prescribed which were difficult for men and women of the less favoured social classes to maintain, though some of their chauvinistic values such as masculine social roles permeated the whole colonial society. In the meantime, the ideological norms and values relating to marriage and the organization of the family which were enjoyed by the upper echelons of society did not extend to the poorer spheres of free men who had no properties to hand down. Poor girls who had no dowry remained unmarried, or tended to establish a succession of consenting partnerships.

In the registers of 1804 and 1836, 40 per cent and 36 per cent respectively of urban households were made up of single women who were heads of families. From these records of the population we can identify a sample of households headed by single women in different districts of the city. We concentrate the survey on the areas north and south of the cathedral square and on Ifigênia, these being the most central districts, and then on two peripheral districts which are strategically placed at entry points to the important commercial routes: Penha, on the road to Rio de Janeiro, and Freguesia de Nossa Senhora do Ó, which is the approach road for the muleteers coming from Goiás to the city. They also happened to be the access routes into the city for foodstuffs.[46]

From this selective sample of households headed by single women (see tables 1.1 and 1.2), we will go on to attempt to derive as much information as possible about their living conditions, the work situation and the domestic organization of the female population of the city. In spite of the subtle differences peculiar to more commercial districts, like the cathedral square, the phenomenon was common to the city as a whole: its main characteristic was a predominance of older women as heads of families, widows and also unmarried women.[47]

Table 1.1 Women heads of households in districts of São Paulo in 1804

Districts	Total households in district	Women heads of households	Women heads as % all heads
1st	506	206	40.7
2nd	378	169	44.7
3rd	301	146	48.5
N. S. do Ó	165	61	37.0
Total	1,350	582	43.1

Source: DAE, Maços, 1804.

Table 1.2 Women heads of households in districts of São Paulo in 1836

District	Total households in district	Women heads of households	Women heads as % all heads
North of cathedral	340	147	43.2
South of cathedral	570	173	30.3
Ifigênia	442	135	30.5
N. S. do Ó	183	47	25.7
Penha	208	81	38.9
Total	1,743	583	33.4

Source: DAE, Maços, 1836.

In these essentially female households, 64 per cent of dependent daughters remained unmarried, as did 77 per cent of the domestic maidservants and 82 per cent of the slave women.[48] About 40 per cent of births in the city were illegitimate,[49] and a great many of these were in households of single women.

Although they were unmarried, many of these women had children: 25 per cent of the women who were heads of families were single mothers, a figure which increases if one takes into account the dependent daughters who were single mothers in 60 per cent of the households of single women.

There was a predominance of white women among unmarried mothers, although there was a steady increase in the mixed race population after 1830, primarily among dependent ex-slave domestic maids and secondly as mulatta heads of households.[50] It is not surprising – since this was the casual and usual way in which these matters were considered – that contemporaries did not take a more objective view of the phenomenon as a whole, one which in São Paulo involved mainly impoverished white women, the overflow from the colonizing ruling classes. In the state of Minas Gerais a predominance of mulatta and mulatto former slaves had been established, for initially there had been an almost total absence of white women in the pioneering movements that populated the area.

This surplus of single women in the population was not the result of any one isolated factor, but of a multitude of reasons which were peculiar to the social and economic system of colonial society as a whole. Above all, it was related to an overwhelming process of increasing poverty which, especially in the towns, went hand in hand with the autonomous growth of the population, against a backcloth of economic stagnation. In São Paulo, more specifically, it derived from the numbers of white women who had no dowry and were living in common law marriages or in successive temporary relationships, many of them as single mothers.

Table 1.3 Ethnic identity of women heads of households in São Paulo

	1804 *(no. and %)*		1836 *(no. and %)*	
White women	351	61.9	333	58.9
Mulatta women	177	31.2	187	33.1
Black women	39	6.9	36	6.4
Indian women	0		9	1.6
Total	567	100.0	565	100.0

Source: DAE, Maços.

From 1830 onwards, there was an increase in the city of the mixed race and freed population, and the phenomenon of temporary absence from the city was particularly noticeable among mulatto men (see table 1.4).

In the meantime, the overall tendency was one of a predominance of single, white women, in a process which was only partly explained by the absence of men. By 1830 the population was more or less equally balanced; the presence of men, however, was intermittent, a situation which was made worse by customs which underlined the instability of marriages and relationships succeeding one another in shortlived partnerships.

In 1768, the Morgado de Matheus[51] became worried about the Crown policy concerning marriages. He attributed the surplus of unmarried women in São Paulo partly to the lack of a bureaucratic element in the religious ceremony and to the charges imposed by priests; he even suggested that the recruitment of men of marriageable age into the army was a possible cause and also that it should be borne in mind that men's business dealings meant they were often away from their homes.[52]

During the reign of Dom Pedro I (1822–31), this custom of travelling away from home persisted, and was aggravated by continual military recruitments for the wars in the River Plate area,[53] which depleted the male population and threatened the daily life of women who were poor. From this point of view, Independence simply exacerbated the ills they had suffered since the time of the captain generals; now and again, vicars and parish priests would intercede on their behalf, and would forward to the authorities their requests for their sons and husbands to be exempted from military recruitment.[54]

However, it was not just the removal of men from the population or the fact that their presence was intermittent which explains the phenomenon of single women as heads of families. A crucial factor must also

Table 1.4 Balance of the male and female population according to ethnic type, São Paulo, 1829

	Women	Men	Total	% of women
White	1,778	1,591	3,369	52.8
Mulatto	1,210	803	2,013	60.1
Black	133	152	285	46.7
Total	3,121	2,546	5,667	55.1

Source: DAE, Maços, 1829.

have been the rigid division between the areas of activity of the sexes, which could be seen as both cause and effect at the same time. It became more obvious with the increase in marriages between partners who were very unequal in age: the fact that men were usually ten or twenty years older than their wives or mistresses led to an increase in widows and women left on their own.[55] The situation was intensified, basically, by the instability of successive partnerships and the poverty of men accustomed to leading itinerant lives; they did not have the wherewithal to maintain their families, and therefore moved to the pioneering areas of the province in search of a livelihood, ending up by forming new relationships ...

> I am going to make my little boat
> of little guapé leaves,
> so as to carry my love
> from Santos to Taubaté
>
> I am going to make my little boat
> of Jataí bark,
> to carry my beloved
> over to the river Mogi side.[56]

The population of single women in the city was mainly from the locality: in 1804 about 27 per cent came from places away from the city, and in 1836 only 7 per cent.[57] Nevertheless, within the city there was a strong shift towards the more central districts, as the seamstresses and women stallholders who had been born in villages on the outskirts, such as Santo André, Penha, Juqueri and Cotia, moved in to live in the more central parts of the town.[58]

These women had the significant custom of dropping their family names and using their first names, which the registrar would sometimes prefix with a respectful 'Dona'. About a third of them retained their family names, sometimes the well-known one of a landowning family. However, the great majority would be named after saints of local devotion, like Ana Gertrudes de Jesus, Maria da Cruz, Madalena de Jesus, Gertrudes do Espírito Santo, Joaquina Josefa da Anunciação. They did this possibly because they had been born illegitimately or had lived as mistresses, but more probably because they did not have any decent means of survival to live up to local standards.

A small percentage of these single women heads of family possessed more than ten slaves: in 1804 only 19 out of 557; in 1836 only 18 out of 589.[59] Over 80 per cent of them declared that they made a living from their own work, and many of them, who had no slaves, said that they had no decent means of survival. The way they did survive was nonetheless unreliably documented by official sources such as censuses, registers of permits from the town hall, or the numerous legal proceedings and hearings in which they became involved. It is true that there was more information about their bad habits than about the way in which these poverty-stricken women really organized their lives. It should be kept in mind that the registers of the population had the express purpose of bringing about social improvement; they were put into effect 'the better to civilize and keep the inhabitants obedient . . .'[60] The women of São Paulo figured further in hearings involving the church, in the Easter dispensation lists, and on the bishops' visits, when they were accused of 'living in sin', or denounced as witches or panderesses.[61] The legal proceedings in which they appear offer no concrete information, such as names, occupation or age, but are full of vague judgements and generic references: 'vagrant women', 'unruly', 'troublemaker', 'degenerate', 'of ill repute', 'behaved with depravity', 'was deceitful', 'was arrested for being a concubine'.[62]

Written documentation in general, whether from administrative, judicial or police sources, when dealing with matters concerning the female sex, falls into the symbolic and mythical domain of the great cultural archetypes. It lists examples circumscribed by the paradigms of Judaic and Christian religions: angels, devils, saintly matrons who have led honourable lives, fallen women, down-and-outs . . . It exists in a vast domain which involves everybody, not just official sources, for the world of myths is an inherent, universal basis of language and culture.

For countrywomen and freedwomen in the streets of São Paulo, royal personages took on a mythical air rather than the aura of political personalities. The Empress D. Leopoldina,[63] faithful wife and devoted mother, assumed the legendary charisma of these popular stories, which dealt with female imagery: saintly women who have been wronged, Genevieve of Brabant, Inez de Castro,[64] Boccaccio's Porcina, the Griseldas of the stories of Trancozo. The Marquesa de Santos, the Emperor's ex-mistress, who was a local figure, and very real as a woman and a powerful lady, living in her mansion at number ten, Rua Alegria, took on the mythical proportions of a repentent Magdalene: chosen through the love of Jesus, she was able to act as intermediary in the cause of those who were suffering and in need of guidance.[65] The dashing Emperor himself took on the guise of Jean de Calais, or of Robert le Diable, heroes in local folk tales from medieval French popular literature.

In this way, age-old stereotypes, fitting each and every kind of historical circumstance, keep appearing in written documentation, which is, by nature, less flexible and innovative than the spoken word.

Metaphors and imagery handed down from writer to writer get repeated through the ages.

The image of the good woman, devoted to her family yet also hospitable, generously giving her time to the poor and needy, exists simultaneously, like a link, both in popular imagery and in the declarations of the chroniclers and genealogists of the ruling classes, connecting the different classes of the slave-owning system. This is the cult of Saint Isabel, queen and charitable lady, celebrated in learned hagiology: for example, in the sermons of Antonio Vieira[66] and of Montalverne, and in popular stories, where the poor but religious stallholder is applauded for her readiness to share what little she has with anyone who knocks at her door.[67]

Learned literature is full of references to model female roles, the kind that can be preached about from the pulpit and shown as examples of what is correct, conventional and desirable.

> I will not point out that she was a virgin, renowned for her innocence and for the holiness which glorified her when she was twelve years; I will not remind you of the eighteen years in which she was a wife and mother; I will omit this whole series of memorable events which in these two important periods of her life testify to the strength of this woman . . .[68]

The same message emerges from the words of Brother Gaspar da Madre de Deus, the eighteenth-century chronicler, when he describes D Maria I: 'She is a woman, I will confess, but a strong woman; she is a woman, but with the attributes of a man and chosen by God, like Deborah, to be the Redeemer of Portugal.'[69]

Almost all the women we examine in this work were illiterate, which in a way underlines the role of stereotypes and conventions to be found in written sources. They never revealed themselves directly or objectively. Their declarations were collected by a third party, and inevitably distorted by the standardizing values of institutional sources. According to documents and records of the town hall, third parties had signed for them 'on request', and when they made a petition to the authorities they usually did so through a solicitor. In his book, Alcântara Machado recalls that among the 450 inventories consulted, only two of the women could read.[70]

It is this element that reinforces the air of convention and myth in the official documents, and turns them into compilations of archetypal situations: rape, incest, adultery, crimes of passion . . . In São Paulo, the newspaper *Publicador Paulistano* carried an article in its issue of 5 August 1854 about a slave woman in São Pedro do Sul, a district of

Angussu, which repeats the story of Medea: 'in a moment of madness, a slave woman belonging to Duarte Medina Martins slit the throat of a woman companion and her two children, as well as her own son, then promptly hanged herself.'[71]

Whenever feelings are dominated by the fury of instinct, it seems that the inherent values of written sources tended to reinforce the stereotypes relating to female roles in general. Apart from this, there were strong prejudices which limited woman's access to the world of culture:

> A girl who knows too much
> Becomes a woman confused
> To be the mother of a family
> Better to know little or nothing.[72]

These are deep-rooted prejudices among Iberians in general, and also found among learned Frenchmen in the seventeenth century, in a famous polemic concerning 'les femmes savantes'. In São Paulo on 16 March 1835, as the result of an inspection of the Seminário for orphaned girls, a report was made to the president of the province denouncing the misconduct of the woman teacher who, instead of teaching needlework and embroidery, was teaching literature from difficult books.[73]

In a letter to his sister in 1814, Marrocos, a minor civil servant in the court of D. João VI, boasted about the limitations of his bride:

> This little mistress of mine is not demanding about her wardrobe; she cannot dance or play an instrument; she serves no decorative purpose at the window with fan or handkerchief, she does not know how to receive visitors in the drawing room, or discuss matters of war; yet she knows how to satisfy in everything that concerns the running of the house, both for her comfort and mine, for herein lies her talent and her upbringing; in spite of the fact that there was a large number of slave women in service in her mother's house, the daughters were made to carry out the same weekly duties, and the old crow (*sic*) saw that it was done to the letter, to the tune of the whip and the bat, and these will always be useful to her, as if they were her court assistants.[74]

Nearly four hundred years of the ABC of female behaviour lay behind the court's resistance to the intrusion of Europeanized customs. At the end of the sixteenth century, the stories of Trancozo put forward the following pieces of advice for a married woman, urging her to desist from learning to read and to content herself with needlework:

the A means she should be Attentive to her household
and the B Beloved in the neighbourhood
and the C Charitable to the poor
and the D Devotee of the Virgin
and the E Earnest in her duties
and the F Firm in her faith
and the G Guardian of her property
and the H Humble towards her husband
and the I Inimical towards gossip
and the L Loyal
and the M Meek
and the N Noble
and the O Honourable
and the P Prudent
and the Q Quiet
and the R Reasonable
and the S Sensible
and the T Tireless in her work
and the V Virtuous
and the X Christian
and the Z Zealous in matters of honour
And once she has mastered all these, and let them become second nature to
her, then she has truly become wiser than all Philosophers . . .[75]

In a popular eighteenth-century story which is well known among São
Paulo women, a female slave faces a circle of learned men and outdoes
them with her strange kind of wisdom; it is a combination of prophecy
and memory, more in the line of orphic cults and the mysteries of Eleusis
than of learned wisdom. The tales of the slave Teodora and Saint Catherine, both of Eastern origin and rewoven into Iberian tradition, concern
two mythical figures whose inherent inferiority as women is suddenly
transformed into an unexpected strength, but into a peculiar strength,
different from and complementary to the masculine power of the wise
men of Alexandria who represent male culture.

In the case of Teodora's story, all her powers of wisdom – 'I know the
heavenly book by heart and can interpret it in seven different ways'[76] –
are devoted to saving the possessions of her young master. These are
the female qualities which are best known in popular stories, women's
dedication and devotion and their capacity for supporting their
masters or companions. There is a deeply rooted misogynist tradition,
as much in learned literature as in popular Portuguese stories, which
stems from a common source in the sixteenth century; it was probably
introduced into the colony through the Jesuit religious theatre, and
perpetuated itself in traditional festivals, songs and customs. In his

book on women and the maritime expansion of the Iberians,[77] the historian C. R. Boxer studied the misogynist attitudes in books on etiquette and moral guidance, mainly for what they reveal about the chauvinist ethics with which they discriminate against adulteresses and prostitutes, from the *Espelho de Casados* ('Mirror of married men') by João de Barro of 1540, to the 'Way to talk to the world so as to avoid scandals' of 1552, to the 'libertines' of the eighteenth century.[78]

The subject does not end at the level of sources and literary evidence. Several historians reveal the same incapacity to deal with the participation of women in the process of the formation of Brazilian society. They get lost in value judgements and cannot rid themselves of idealizations and stereotypes which prevent them from seeing more clearly the historical context with which they are dealing. In his book *Retrato do Brasil*, Paulo Prado refers to native women as mere tools of pleasure or instruments of work in the rough, rural homes of colonial times. He emphasizes also the childlike passivity of black African women.[79] Even Gilberto Freire, a scholar concerned with the study of colonial customs and daily routines, sees the white woman as 'man's servant, and a flesh and blood toy for her husband'.[80]

Even among social scientists there is a tendency to define the female domain in functional terms, as the opposite, or the ideal alterity, of an essentially male culture.[81] In official documents and sources, objective information is obscured by symbolism and metaphor; deprecatory, generic imagery masks references to women slaves, freedwomen and poor white women; all these criteria belong to the Manichaeism of the Counter Reformation, to which classical nuances get added, referring to the female body as an object of sexual conquest and pleasure. Women rarely possess the individuality of historical characters. They represent different, mysterious, unknown and often dangerous forces.

Few judicial proceedings or police hearings record information about poor women, directly or indirectly, without some sort of moral bias. On 15 September 1834, Domitildes de Trindade, a mulatta woman vagrant, who had neither a passport nor a begging permit and with a babe in arms, was arrested in the Braz quarter. When she was interrogated, her incoherence amounted to a continuous delirium: 'for this reason I ordered her to be sent out of the district.'[82] In spite of everything, legal proceedings and police hearings provide a rich and fascinating terrain for the work of the historian. Scattered, random documents offer a genuine source of valuable information. An example is the case of a hearing over the body of a black woman, Catarina Lopes, who was found dead in the Tamanduateí river in January of 1821.[83]

Even a simple death certificate can say a great deal about neighbourhood relations among poor women in the city of São Paulo: 'deceased, around 25 February 1844, Rosa Maria das Dores, an outsider, origin unknown, nor known whether married or single . . .'[84]

The urge to reform and the preoccupation with building a more systematic rationality which characterizes the chroniclers and genealogists of the eighteenth century prevents them from describing everyday customs without colouring them with normative presumptions and moral judgements about the instinctive passions that they imputed to a certain kind of female primitivism.[85] In the bourgeois literature of the urban novels of the nineteenth century, there is constant tension between the female world of vital forces – of the heart, of instinct, of biological continuity, of the linking of generations – and those of reason and of history, essentially the domain of men. For Machado de Assis, in *Iaiá Garcia*, the main difference between biological nature (the sphere of women) and social nature (that of men) is the greater capacity of the latter to dominate their own kind.[86] The abstract female ideal is always stronger than the individuality of the characters. In *Memorial de Aires*, by the same novelist, Fidélia experiences the tension between the individual and her species. It is in women, above all, that the force of instinct lies, the biological and vitalist cycle of eternal rebirth, like the *ouroborus* of the cult of the Great Mother. Women and music, 'something outside time and space, a pure ideal.'[87]

José de Alencar, another nineteenth-century Brazilian novelist, who deals with the subject of the rebellion of women and their struggle for the right to their own individuality, very often sees female characters as a mere 'diaphanous image of a dream that takes on the graceful form of a woman.'[88] Strong female personalities like Aurélia or Diva end up by yielding to their chosen companion and surrendering themselves as 'possessions'.[89]

On the other hand, even in scholarly works that try to analyse and study the domain of the feminine, there persists an interest in the symbolic and in the allegories of the 'female condition'. By insisting on the study of female myths which belong to the field of learning, of tradition, of literature, and which support each other in an unbroken vicious circle, they avoid the study of a specific historical context. Yet this is an important step if one is to eliminate the ideological content, and it is a *sine qua non* for revealing women as social beings who complete systems of power relations, networks of domination and neighbourhood links.

The historical study of their lives in society reveals informal roles, as part of a process of change and transformation, which has nothing to do with the domain of myths and cultural norms. Historical reconstruction shows female spheres which are in opposition to cultural norms; informal roles that women have taken over, and not those prescribed to them; for this reason, they were often concealed or omitted from written documents. The real historical roles of women can be apprehended in the tensions, interventions and essentially social relationships which integrate women in history and the social process; they can only be read between the lines, from the omissions and from all that is implicit in written documents. Because of this, patient reading is needed, a discerning search for information that is left out, for data very sparingly distributed, for that which appears by chance, or which is marginal to the context or to the formal contents of the document. This is true of wills, where there are references in the margins to small gifts left to poor female cousins or nieces, to servant girls or slave women, who had been living-in companions in their daily lives; small quantities, derisory amounts, but loaded with symbolic meaning and allusions to specific relationships belonging to the organization of domestic work.[90]

The same thing happens in divorce papers, where the names of poor women from the surrounding areas of São Paulo appear unexpectedly. In 1834, Francisca Maria, a mulatta seamstress of twenty-five, was living in the parish of N. S. da Boa Viagem (Our Lady of Travellers), though she had been born in the cathedral district; she lived off her farming and her sewing, and came forward to testify what she knew 'from hearsay' about the relationship between her neighbour, who was also a seamstress, and the husband who had abandoned her. Similarly two seamstresses from Atibaia came forward to testify in a lawsuit of 1836: Maria Gertrudes, a twenty-one-year-old black freedwoman, married, and Manoela do Espírito Santo, a widow of twenty-three.[91] These are just pieces from a multitude of patchwork remnants waiting to be assembled, glimpses of the vast neighbourhood network, fragments of life situations in an extensive system of relationships which need to be pieced together from scattered information about colour, occupation, sex and age, to be placed in a wider, specific sequence of events still to be sorted out . . . Women in poverty in the initial process of urbanization in São Paulo were socially unacceptable; they belonged to the sphere of informal and improvised roles and areas which can be interpreted as symptoms of new needs and structural changes. It is not surprising that they should have been forgotten in the official sources, with their bias towards recording prescribed roles and normative values which were in keeping with the control and maintenance of the established social order.

If it is difficult for less observant anthropologists to notice these informal roles in their field research,[92] how much more so will it be for historians, who are limited to written sources. There is for the historian of working-class women a special need to be aware of what can be read between the lines of documents, to know what to look for, and how to look for it.

Finding out about the structure of everyday life at the level of the organization of household, family, relatives and neighbours is a difficult terrain, one which is on occasion penetrated by historians with brilliant results, yet always with enormous difficulties of documentation.[93]

It is impossible for historians to tread these paths if they are preoccupied with methods which presuppose balance, functionality, stability, conservation and the status quo; whether they like it or not, they find themselves caught up in the official, normative content of their sources – laws, values, instructions, data which express what ought to be done, ideological and moral systems which control and maintain the established social order.

If they start from these parameters, historians inevitably interpret informal roles as atypical or pathological, rather than as symptoms of change in the prescribed social order. The predominance of households headed by women in the towns is a case in point; some historians see this not as an organization for survival, dictated by new circumstances, but as a symptom of anomie and of domestic disorder.[94]

These women were not integrated into the institutions of power: they were not salaried, nor did they own properties; they did not enjoy civil rights, nor did they have access to political citizenship. Nevertheless, they sustained their system of organization of family life, of survival, of relationships and community life.

In a study of the informal roles of the Igbo women of Nigeria, Judith Allen has done interesting work on the ideological blindness of the British civil servants and their administrative reforms.[95] Brought up in the *mores* of Victorian England, they studied the local political organizations, with a view to integrating them into the new colonial administration they had come to establish. Discerning the male hierarchy of leadership, they immediately tried to apply it to the new local administration. What escaped their notice completely was the parallel and complementary organization of the Igbo women, who had their own political leadership. The women would meet periodically in the public squares of their villages, where they would take decisions and control local business, which was their area of activity in the community. Occasionally they would attack the men in rituals of traditional reprisals, which were accepted by local custom, but which the British

functionaries attempted to repress with police violence, treating them
as unexpected outbreaks of disorder, rowdiness or drunkenness!

Informal roles, by their very nature, are not officially recognized, nor
are they highly valued in society, although they may be important in the
tangible processes of everyday life.

In the colonial system of Brazil, many of the informal roles were
related to the consumption and distribution of foodstuffs. This was an
area of activity of little importance from the point of view of the function-
ing of the colonial system, and normally relegated to the slaves as
degrading work. Plantation workers, stallholders and pedlars were
socially despised, and their work had pejorative connotations. Those
who were socially prestigious in the colony were the owners of the sugar
plantations, farmers of export products, capitalists, bankers, merchants,
bureaucrats and administrative or ecclesiastical functionaries.

During the Mascates war,[96] the main victims of the shooting in
Recife were the black fisherwomen, who were sent to the beach to collect shellfish. This was a minimal source of basic food for every family
at that time, since foodstuffs were cut off from the city by the state of
siege. As this was a daily exercise, and often twice daily, the women
were seldom able to take shelter without a few of them getting caught –
poor, anonymous victims of a fight that had nothing to do with them.

In the slave-based society of Brazil during the colonial period, the role
of household provider[97] was unbecoming for men. When they did not
have slaves to carry out degrading tasks, they did not want to lower themselves to looking after the fields and the domestic animals, and to selling
small surpluses. According to oral tradition and custom, it was the
women who took on these jobs, which were vital for the support of their
families.[98] Yet it is still only with the greatest difficulty that one can disentangle references to their daily work as providers of their own subsistence.

These informal, improvised roles have an important significance in
unravelling the much-discussed patriarchal system in Brazil. According to customary and traditional interpretation, the division of labour
and of activities between the sexes was clearly demarcated, and the two
were kept rigidly apart; this established areas of activity which were
complementary yet neatly separated. In fact, the absence of the menfolk, or their intermittent presence, frequently brought about an alter-
nation or exchange of jobs, rather than a division: it was not at all
exceptional for women to assume masculine roles.

The censuses themselves indicate that about 35 to 40 per cent of
women assumed the role of provider for their families; as heads of
households they declared that they lived from their own work.[99]

The independence of women and their role as provider or supporter of the family seem to have been accepted as the norm by legal authorities; thus they frequently refused them their requests and ignored their pleas for assistance in their normative roles as helpless orphans or abandoned widows. In 1810, Francisca das Chagas protested about the recruitment of her son, a tailor and, according to her, 'her only support in her poverty'. The judge refused her petition: 'The supplicant lives from her businesses and not from the work of her son Gonçalo Silva, for in truth the supplicant is a hardworking, active woman, and has a slave who is called Joana; she is constantly making odds and ends to sell from trays, from which she makes enough money to live in comfort and in keeping with her position.'[100]

There were protests in divorce hearings against husbands who denied maintenance to their wives, who found themselves 'forced to buy their basic clothing at their own expense, and having to find employment to this end in the manufacture of objects fitting for their sex'.[101]

Documentation confirms the traditional division of labour which exists from the beginning of colonization. Chroniclers like Gabriel Soares de Souza had already projected their own views on to the savages: 'The mothers teach their daughters to adorn themselves like Portuguese women, and to spin cotton and do most of the household chores, according to custom.'[102]

In São Paulo, at the end of the seventeenth century, apart from the rural properties already mentioned, a home crafts industry began to develop, based on native labour. The making of cotton cloth, felt hats and marmalade required the active leadership of women, for the men were more involved in the transportation and commercialization of the end products.[103] The sudden prosperity in the mining industry brought about the decline of this business in the eighteenth century, as soon as people in São Paulo began to import English products, which were in competition with local crafts. However, for the beginning of the nineteenth century there are documents in which are testimonies and specific traces of work done by São Paulo women in place of their husbands:

Luzia Angélica de Sá, from the small town of Faxina, says that because her husband is absent, having travelled to the court in Rio de Janeiro, she finds herself in charge of a drove of pack animals and herds of cattle, to be traded, as determined by the said husband; and so the supplicant came from Taubaté to arrange for the transportation of a new herd of oxen, which was in Itapetininga, and brought a foreman with her for this purpose, called José Manoel de Siqueira; it happened that, in the same place, he was enlisted forcibly as a soldier in the town's local forces; and so the supplicant is left

without a foreman for the transporting of said oxen, and is now in great
difficulties.[104]

For a man to dress up as a woman was a ritual reserved for masquerades and carnival time, and it was even punishable by law. Frei Vicente
do Salvador tells how some individuals escaped from English pirates in
Rio de Janeiro 'by wearing women's cloaks': 'the bishop, so that their
punishment should serve as an example to others, put one of them to
shame on the pillory, with a basket holding a spinning wheel on his
belt.'[105] There were many references to women dressed as men,
however, not so much with mythical connotations, but more as a means
of defence in everyday life, whether it was to travel incognito and safe
from violence in the streets, or to make it easier to carry out men's
work, such as that of carpenter.[106] The eighteenth-century Brazilian
poet Tomàs Antônio Gonzaga makes reference to a sensual mulatta
woman, dressed as a man so as to show off the beauty of her body to its
best advantage, singing a bawdy song.[107]

In São Paulo, where work took the men off on expeditions into the
hinterland, female roles took on their own special connotations, which
were strengthened in the nineteenth century with the persistent
absence of menfolk, who enjoyed a roving existence as the middlemen
for commercial firms, between Rio de Janeiro, the south of Minas,
Mato Grosso and Goiás.[108]

The colonizing process itself, the growth of the population, the
imbalance between the sexes, the tendency to explore new frontiers in
the hinterland where there was an absence of white women, and the
increase of a largely female population, sometimes of mixed race and
sometimes of poor whites, in the rearguard, so to speak, and in villages
where the men were absent – all these are circumstances peculiar to the
colony, which modified Iberian customs and traditions and gave a
special improvised quality to social relationships as a whole, and, more
specifically, to those between men and women. Officially, according to
the conventions of documents rather than to the reality of everyday life,
there was persistent emphasis on the traditional separation of the func-
tions of either sex: in the registers, for instance, it was assumed that little
boy orphans would learn to read and write, and the girls to sew and
embroider. Some Iberian, Mediterranean or Moorish traces might still
continue perhaps, but only as superficial elements in a new social
process full of contradictions.

The separation of the areas of activity of men and women corresponded less to the norms and conventions inherited from Portugal
than to a concrete reality, that of the redistribution of the necessities of

life with the growth of the population; the specific tasks of each sex in the different social classes in the process of colonization were not complementary but alternative: the system grew out of the substitution for and the improvisation of the duties of men who were absent. Because of the temporary or permanent absence of their menfolk, women were forced to play many 'masculine' parts, among them those dealing with the administration of possessions, including plantations and stud farms: 'The women are beautiful and masculine, and it is the custom for their husbands to leave them to run the house and property, for which job they are well fitted.'[109]

Many women were forced by circumstances to assume masculine roles. This was the case with herdswomen who travelled the roads to bring their oxen to sell or barter. This was doubtless an exception to an old rule, but it was broken more frequently than expected. Lists of herdswomen appear from time to time in the *livros de barreira*, or customs books, which register the payment of traffic taxes on the main highways. In April 1847, Joaquina Ferreira de Alvarenga went through the Caraguatatuba pass with nineteen animals, and had to pay 3$800 réis; Beralda Iselinga Pereira paid 7$400 with fifteen animals; Quitéria Lopes Moreira, with eighteen animals, paid the sum of 3$600.[110] In 1795, in Goiás, near Vila Bela, there is a report of women who were permanently herdswomen: Ana Lopes sold dried meat, Ana Felipe from São Romão sold small portions of salt.[111]

In the outskirts of the city of São Paulo some women made a living by using their ox-carts to transport things, bringing firewood or stones into the centre; others did business in wood. In 1825, the town council paid Maria Joaquina da Silva for nine cartloads of building stones at 640 réis each (5$700). In 1830, in Penha, a woman paid tax on her delivery cart.[112] On 17 December 1830, fines were imposed on some women who had not paid the tax for transporting cartloads of stones for the paving of the roads. There was an account on 9 March 1844:

> Yesterday, I had dealings with Rita de Ral, the owner of a stone quarry in the same place, in the district of Pary, and speaking to her on behalf of the town hall I asked for her permission for a few cartloads of stones to be removed for the building of roads and for a few other works that the town council needed to carry out for the benefit of the public. She hesitated to agree unless the town hall could give her some compensation; an agreement was reached by which the town council would give her 80 réis for each cartload of stones that was taken from her quarry.[113]

In São Paulo there was a chronic shortage of men to work as day labourers on public buildings and road repairs, where slaves and free men usually worked side by side. In the town hall documents of 1825 the majority of day labourers registered are women.[114] Referring to this problem of the lack of male day labourers in Salvador, Katia Queiroz Mattoso comments on how common it was to find women working as building labourers.[115] In the novel by Domingos Olympio, Luzia Homem laboured as a stone worker on the construction of the penitentiary of Sobral, in Ceará.[116] On 23 December 1884, the newspaper *Diário Popular* of São Paulo carried a report about some women who made their living from piece work, clearing thickets, and dressed like men: 'and they do it as well as the best of workers.'[117]

In the town of São Paulo the public area in which poor women found their livelihoods was gradually taken over by the process of urbanization, giving way to a prolonged period of confrontation between public authorities and working women, who opposed each other with mutual protests and resistance. The women washed their clothes at public fountains, they reared pigs which they left untethered, they allowed their young animals to invade neighbours' lands; since they had no slave to take away their rubbish, they dumped it in public places.[118] In order to survive, women in poverty had to have access to the common lands, and defend precariously occupied fields and shacks, often built outside the allocated areas permitted by municipal laws. They demanded access to the brushwoods and wastelands of the city, claiming land to build houses and yards 'in view of their poverty'.[119] At times they anticipated concessions and built houses on public land: in 1846, Gertrudes das Dores Barbosa fenced in some land on the road to Penha, through which there was a public right of way.[120]

They put up a stubborn resistance to municipal regulations affecting their living areas, to measures for the division of streets, road reforms and the alignment of houses on the streets. On 5 May 1836, Anna Gertrudes asked for permission to keep her house which was outside the proper part of the Rua da Boa Vista.[121] In 1831 the authorities succeeded in collecting the urban tithe tax only from the houses which were situated in the most central parts of the city. In 1835, the same Dona Gertrudes had asked the town hall for a second revision of the demarcation limits for the payment of this tax, so that it would exclude the road on which she lived, 'which leads to Moóca . . .'[122]

Friction with the town hall was constant. The women stubbornly resisted the custom, which was deeprooted in the ruling classes, of being asked to participate in repairs and public works. They alleged that 'they had not been informed in time': 'In view of the tenacity with which Dona Maria Anna Jacintha and her sister are opposed to paying their share of 16$100 towards the cost of the canal and the fountain . . .

let the tax inspector find the sum, since it was through neglect that the women involved were not warned about it.'[123]

Whenever there was a shortage of foodstuffs or of water in the fountain, there were riots and brawls involving quarrelsome women and street rioters.[124]

They were combative women, and had to be very inventive and 'improvise their affairs from day to day'. They had a vital, miraculous way of inventing informal roles, and they would not have been able to survive without it. There are popular stories which recount the playing of roles for which there was no instruction, preparation or training; there was only the everyday routine, along with the experience of life, following the example of classic female personalities whose wisdom was based on artifice and cunning, worshipped by the Greeks as the goddess Metis, as opposed to reason and erudite learning.[125] Everyday dealings demanded an astuteness which was adapted to the turnings of the wheel of fortune, and of *apoiké*: the fortuitous interruption of routine by unexpected chance or fortune, a challenge which cannot be met with science, but simply the art of invention.

The spoken word held a magic force for these women; this is clearly illustrated in a story of African origin, in which the sorceress tries to remember a word – pleasure – that she had forgotten, and which gurgles through the neck of a bottle: 'que vim vinim vinim . . .'[126] There were words for casting spells, for blessings and cures, sorcery against stealing,[127] superstitions and amulets gathered from oral tradition, or even from the lawsuits against witchcraft which appeared at times in the records of the Inquisition, or bishops' inquiries.[128] The power of the evil eye, insults and threats, like those made by watersellers at the fountain against the slave girls from the wealthy houses, are not just limited to the meetings and dances of the slaves, but reflect the tensions of society as a whole. Domestic labour, which spilled over from the houses into itinerant street trade, has a story of magic and endurance all of its own, politicized to some extent in the confrontations of everyday routine work: the committing of petty theft, the odd witchcraft ritual, the cursing of the master's house – all these were typical and appeared frequently in the annals of urban slavery in colonial Brazil.[129]

It appears difficult to reconstruct the rituals of a popular, auto-nomous culture from written sources, as Mikhail Bakhtin did for the period of Rabelais.[130] In Brazilian society, relationships between social classes were deeply embedded in different popular cultures, forming a melting pot of everyday coexistence, with a variety of ways of entry into a slave-owning society which was rigidly hierarchical.

Scattered elements of African culture were conserved by the very nature of the authoritarian paternalism of the masters, who might tolerate a wide range of tribal rituals, meetings, drum-beating ceremonies, guitar-playing groups, challenges and *capoeiras*.[131] Different accents and well-differentiated tempos and rhythms characterized the processes of day-to-day lives in the São Paulo districts, as different historical ages coexisted in opposite rituals of profound social distance. This social abyss between heterogeneous neighbourhoods affected them deeply, throwing together slave women, freedwomen and poor white women to live side by side in an enforced and tense contact, from the Rua de Santa Teresa to the 'big hole', from Rua Direita to the Beco da Cachaça, from Rua do Carmo to the Rua da Boa Vista . . .

TWO

Bakerwomen and Women Stallholders: Survival and Resistance

> ... and in the same way, the women stallholders must not sell flour, maize or beans from their trays, either retail or by the penny trade, because all these aforementioned are the preserve of the innkeepers, who pay duties on their businesses.
>
> Registro da Câmara Municipal (town hall records), 1803

Female social roles were entangled with economically less prestigious jobs in the city of São Paulo. Women in poverty tended to make a living in the less profitable sectors of the economy, which the tax office had difficulty in controlling. There had long been a confrontation between the colonial system and everything which concerned the basic needs of the local population, an area disregarded by chroniclers and authorities, as being part of the domestic sphere which was opposed to the interests of the *res publica*. It is in this context that female roles were defined through the disagreements within the colonial system itself; caught up in the precarious organization of the provision of foodstuffs, the women frequently became angry and clashed with the authorities, because they lived off this contraband.

Their presence in the city was characterized by a permanent state of tension with the authorities, arising out of the structural contradictions of the colonial society itself. Sometimes the women were almost forgotten in a process of mutual distancing and through the relative tolerance of the authorities; at other times they were more obviously aggressive and troublesome, in open conflict, and would almost reach the point of dispute and violence. This was the case among the bakerwomen in the second half of the eighteenth century, and the same was to occur again with the women stallholders during the course of the last century.

In the second half of the eighteenth century, one crisis in the city followed another, centring on high prices and shortages of food – as much of local produce as of goods from Portugal, which were the monopoly of the Crown. Each time, public discontent found an outlet through the protests of the bakerwomen. In spite of the fact that they took place within the limits of town neighbourhoods and guilds, their protests had wide repercussions in the city.

Once a year, on the occasion of the Corpus Christi processions, bakerwomen were called together, along with the women stallholders, to organize a 'ball' dance,[1] to be put on in the trade corporations' pageant, with carpenters, cobblers, tailors, etc.

The bakerwomen, who were poor whites, born locally or in Portugal, had slave women who sold their penny loaves from trays in the street each day. They were well-known figures in the city: Angela Vieira, who gave her name to the Beco, spent her life at variance with the authorities; Isabel Peres Teixeira, Josepha de Moura, Anna da Silva, Escolástica and Catarina Vellosa . . . there was only one black freedwoman among them, Josefa de Souza, who faced them in an equal competition.[2]

Once a year they were called together by the town council to buy permits for their women slave vendors, and to present their weights and measures for inspection by town council officials. In the official documents there is an almost continuous list of accusations, denunciations of fines and imprisonments of slave women for selling without a permit or below the weights fixed by the town councillors. These disagreements were sometimes aggravated by the crises produced by high prices, shortages and hunger in the city. Over and above the expense of making special ovens[3] and buying copper pots, the bakerwomen had to contend with the added difficulties of the supply of flour, maize and salt.

More often than not, when there was a shortage, well-known profiteers from the city, together with suppliers of flour from Atibaia and Nova Bragança, would intervene and would misappropriate cargoes bound for the city of São Paulo, to resell them at higher prices in Minas Gerais (1739, 1794) or in the nearby port of Santos.[4]

According to the abundance or the scarcity of produce, the town hall would fix the price of the penny loaf at 6 onças, when times were good, lowering it to 4 or 5 onças at times of scarcity.[5] The instability of supplies and of prices made it very difficult for the hard-pressed bakerwomen, who were the weak links in a long chain of intermediaries who interfered continually by raising the prices of the produce; apart from this, they were bound by the prices rigidly fixed by the town council. Their disobedience provoked fines, threats and imprisonments. On the one side there were petitions and claims from the bakerwomen against the orders of the town hall, and on the other judgemental attitudes and violence from the fiscal authorities. The women were accused of buying wheat flour in bulk, of adulterating the bread with mixtures of irregular ingredients, like wood shavings, or with different kinds of flour.[6] It was a silent struggle of rumours and mutual provocation, which left them a certain margin of resistance: the bakerwomen tried to control the price of bread in their own way. They continually replaced their women slave vendors, they forgot to pay for their permits, resulting in fines of $6 and even thirty days in prison. They sold the bread well below weight and they used mixtures which, according to the town councillors, caused illness in the city.[7] In more difficult times they resorted to strikes and refused to bake bread. This was what happened in 1734, and again in 1739.

In this latter year, although they had already been fined once, the bakerwomen insistently defied the town council, in an act of retaliation which the authorities overlooked.[8] Since the weights and measures inspectors did not respect the decisions of the town hall, new officials were called up, sworn in, and advised to 'watch the bread situation'. The town councillors threatened the bakerwomen with permanent cancellation of their permits. The bakerwomen ended up paying double fines, and being thrown into prison twice.[9]

In 1746 there was another shortage of wheat flour, and the town council refused to review the weights. The bakerwomen went on strike again, but this time a strike *sui generis*, stalling for time, out of malice: as a gesture of protest, Ignácia de Jesus Caminha gave formal notice from her job as a baker.[10] The others, with the tacit agreement of their neighbours and connections in the trade, went to the town hall one by one, explaining that at that moment they had no flour, that they had ordered it from Santos, and that 'once it had arrived, they would continue to bake the said bread as always, to sell to the people.'[11] In their declarations they all assured the town hall that 'they were not challenging their orders, notwithstanding the increase in the weight of the bread; that they would be happy to continue as bakerwomen ...' The town hall decided to grant them eight days, at the end of which 'whether the flour in question arrived or not, they must bake the bread to deliver to the people.'[12]

The predicament continued, amid numerous complaints provoked by both sides, with obstinacy on the part of the bakerwomen and defiance from the town hall. In March the town councillors decided that the permit which had been paid for the slave women was no longer valid: 'if the said women want to have bread made, they must take out new permits in their names, each one of them giving guarantees in respect of the rules and penalties of this Senate.'[13]

The bakerwomen were divided in their opinions, and this gave rise to different local factions. In 1747, Pedro Taques filed a law suit against the municipal authorities over a young slave girl who had been fined for selling underweight loaves.[14] In 1748, Angela Vieira's slave women were arrested for walking the streets and selling loaves without permission. On 18 April 1798, records were still showing the imprisonment of the bakerwomen's slave women, as well as the same resistance to the prices fixed by the town hall.[15]

In Lisbon there were also tense relations between the bakerwomen and the municipal authorities, and they resorted to the same unofficial expedients over the control of prices. The bakerwomen resorted to strikes (in 1718, 1719, 1724, etc.), petitions, protests and lies, and had to contend with the additional problems of suppliers, intermediaries, women measurers and vendors.[16]

A more effective protest in 1744 was an official refusal by the bakerwomen of São Paulo to put on the traditional dance in which they moved and turned with little girls on their shoulders; this dance was usually their responsibility in the Corpus Christi processions, at that time the most important festival of the year. In São Paulo, in the eighteenth century, the masquerades, carnival and burning of Judas were spontaneous festivals, for which it was necessary to get permission each year from the authorities; other festivities, such as the *congadas* and drum-beating ceremonies of the slaves were officially forbidden.[17]

The Corpus Christi procession was carefully planned and organized by the municipal authorities along traditional lines, on a pattern which had been common to the cities of Europe since the Middle Ages and to the Portuguese colonies.[18] It was imposed on the people every year like a rite of obedience and servitude, by means of a formal, compulsory summons backed by threats, fines, punishment or imprisonment. It was as if everybody must conform to a great, collective act of deference to the higher authorities. The procession involved scrupulous preparations, and the costs were shared between the main authorities of the town. Everyone had to attend, carry the canopy and appear in the correct hierarchical order, so that the procession would present all the links in a great chain of beings, thereby representing the ritualization of the social order of the king's vassals. Great and small were summoned, under threat of punishment, a threat which weighed heavily on the poorer people, but was a matter of indifference to the rest. Rich merchants offered wax candles; artisans, bakerwomen and women stallholders paraded in floats and put on dances that they financed themselves. The festival was repeated in all the cities of the colony, with the same ceremonial and the same preparations.

It provided an opportunity to clean and sweep the streets, to paint and decorate.[19] Everything was controlled by a military division of the army and the cavalry, which was there to try to prevent any disorder or violence from either side of the procession, and especially any outburst of drum-beating from the slaves on the flanks, who often interrupted the established solemnity of the occasion.[20]

Traditionally the artisans put on the famous parade of Saint George,[21] and the bakerwomen and women stallholders their traditional girls' dance, with elaborate costumes brought from Portugal.

In 1741, the authorities chose the black girl, Paschoa, belonging to Maria da Siqueira, to be in charge of the bakerwomen's dance, and Mariquinha Viegas to organize the dance of the women stallholders.[22] In 1743, the black freedwoman Josepha was elected in the name of the bakerwomen, and Quitéria, the slave girl who worked for the brother of the Reverend Padre Angelo de Siqueira, was chosen in the name of the women stallholders.[23]

In 1744 it was the turn of Suzana, the slave girl who worked for the bakerwoman Isabel Paes, and of Ursula, the slave girl belonging to Margarida de Oliveira, to organize the stallholders. However, the city was in difficulties. A serious drought hit the harvest, profiteers came on the scene and there was the threat of hunger from high prices and shortages of foodstuffs. Amid a great deal of violence, scapegoats were sought. In May some fugitive negro slaves at loose on the highways were blamed for the food crisis; armed, and in groups of ten, they had raided the planters and stolen cargoes of maize, beans, bacon and game.[24] The weights and measures inspectors, in their turn, imposed heavy fines on the bakerwomen, and there were imprisonments and arguments. When they summoned the procession, the authorities seemed to foresee disturbances, imprisonments and the usual results of disobedience. At the last moment the bakerwomen refused to put on their annual dance. This serious, official protest was made symbolic in a scandalous manner, and the authorities ordered their imprisonment.[25]

Relations between the women stallholders and the municipal authorities had been equally tense from the start, albeit less symbolic on great public occasions. Their whole way of life involved freedom of movement throughout the city, since they depended on an active circuit of information, of small talk, reporting back and verbal agreements. The repressive measures devised by the colonial system involved permits, curfews, passports and safe conducts, which would affect the women's ability to earn their living quite drastically if they were to be strictly enforced. As the urban area grew, a small trade was established between poor women, in which they were both sellers and buyers, in this way constituting their own clientele; women vendors and stallholders were agents for both supply and demand, managing to survive with a relative degree of autonomy because of the difficulties involved in any effective police vigilance or control. Growing urbanization created more opportunities for the commercialization of domestic services and itinerant selling, without the control of taxes.

Their means of livelihood was based on tense relationships between women slaves, free women and freedwomen within the neighbourhood and in society as a whole, a society was characterized on the one hand by the need for mutual help, and on the other by the forced inclusion of its members, because although they were socially disqualified, they were links in a chain of human beings who belonged to a slave-based society that was highly hierarchized. Everything was permeated by a system of domination, of patriarchal authority, in which public and private areas became confused; laws, administration, legal and police authority, all became mixed up and intertwined in a process which alternated between violence, protection, force and common law marriage. A thick web of personal relationships protected and covered the women's area of autonomy, since for a good part of the last century it was possible to avoid the attention of the fiscal authorities.

Little by little, small-time innkeepers and established merchants started appealing to the authorities in a persistent persecution of the itinerant women street vendors. By means of orders and preventative measures, they managed to limit the free circulation of the clandestine women stallholders and vendors, and of the slave women and freedwomen; they restricted them to demarcated areas of the city, and established a system of fairs or open-air markets.[26] It was a century-long struggle, which involved both the destiny of free women and urban slavery itself in a single process.

Many of the women who had few slaves survived by keeping stalls, taking commissions and running 'their businesses'. They resorted to a multitude of activities that were linked to local trade: as intermediaries in small transactions, as profiteers and agents on commission for household surpluses. Near the small cottages marketplace they set up stalls to sell local agricultural products retail. They also had a trade going in the more central streets, dealing in sweetmeats and household wares, fruits and juices, *aluá*,[27] coffee and sugar cane juice. They followed the movements of the city, attracting as their customers the population of herdsmen on the move, minor trade officials and government employees.

Dona Maria Joaquina 'lives from her stall-selling', a fifty-six-year-old white widow, she lived north of the cathedral district with her unmarried daughter and five slaves; Maria Antônia da Fonseca, a 'stallholder', a white widow of fifty, lived in Santa Ifigênia, with five servants and ten slaves; Antônia Maria, also a 'stallholder', was a white, unmarried woman of sixty-three, living north of the cathedral square with four servants.

Maria Rita 'lives off her business', a single, white woman of forty-seven, she lived south of the cathedral district with two slaves; D. Joaquina Eufrazia 'lives off her business', a white widow of twenty-nine, she lived south of the cathedral square with one servant and one slave. Maria do Carmo 'lives off her jobs', single, white, thirty-three years of age, she lived south of the cathedral district with two slaves; Bernardina Luiza, 'a pedlar', a single, white woman of thirty-nine, lived all alone in the second block south of the cathedral district.[28]

Local trade in foodstuffs was heavily burdened by surcharges and duty, whether it was trade in local produce or goods from Portugal. Because of this, it was manipulated by a whole hierarchy of authorities, important and minor civil servants and local bosses, mainly merchants who had the wherewithal to buy up salt, flour and brandy in bulk so that they could speculate at times of acute shortage. The dispute between rival factions of the ruling classes for political and economic control of local trade, which lasted from 1821 till 1828, left the way wide open for disorder and contraband dealings, and under its camouflage vast sectors of the poorer people in the urban population were able to establish a precarious form of survival.

Clandestine trade was not an activity that brought in much profit. Competition was considerable, since small intermediaries proliferated on the fringes and margins of bulk transactions. Starting from the small women slave owners, the system unfolded in a chain of smaller and smaller operations; a symptom of widespread poverty, they symbolized the machinations of social domination. Only a sparse living was to be had from building up a stock of the cheaper goods in small quantities and selling them piecemeal or in the form of household odds and ends. However, as an alternative to the exorbitant prices of essential commodities, further increased by speculation and excessive taxes, this small contraband trade fulfilled an important social function in the city, for it redistributed foodstuffs at cheaper prices than those permitted by the established stores and groceries.

The supply and the circulation of foodstuffs among the poorer consumers in the city were almost all through contraband: they did not declare how they were acquired or where they came from. An air of magic and secrecy clung to them. Some very essential commodities such as salt, tobacco, oil for lamps, and brandy were heavily taxed and became the monopoly of the few. Household luxuries such as fish oil, castor oil and bacon were also sold piecemeal, but only appeared rarely and at a high price. Primary products were easy to find among slave women vendors or in the established groceries; the household goods were more accessible among the neighbourhood saleswomen; there was bacon, candle wax, honey ... soap, home-made cotton cloths, eggs, chickens.

It was household products that figured most prominently in the popular stories which portrayed small-time trade: Pedro Brum would sell clay pots, honey on credit and a little salt; Mariazinha, in order to escape from hell, resorted to 'a little soap, some pins and ashes'.[29] Local candle wax was much in demand on the eve of the Corpus Christi processions, and the municipal authorities tried to get it donated by wealthy individuals.[30]

A few of the women rural workers in Penha and Freguesia do Ó had small sugar mills, where they made local brandy to sell retail; they also made *catimpuera* or maize brandy, though this was prohibited from the middle of the eighteenth century.[31]

In 1767 the authorities were concerned about the credit and retail trade, not only because it was impossible to effect any proper collection of the taxes due, but also because they considered the distribution of produce in small amounts to be economically harmful, since it was decimated without producing profits. They planned reforms which would make the economy more commercialized, and tried to stamp out 'backward' practices.

For women who were fighting for survival rather than profit, their marginal position helped them to penetrate the complicated web of laws, municipal orders, bribery and speculation, and to infiltrate the hierarchical chain of a thousand and one small intermediaries who made up the network of street trading. Small transactions passed from hand to hand, from the workers and farmers of the surrounding districts to the small established tradesmen, and the women who were poor and without slaves had their own way of fitting in as itinerant vendors of 'bacon by the pound, tobacco by the yard, brandy by the measure, fish by the ounce, eggs and chickens piecemeal'.[32]

The expression *quitandeiras* (stallholders) used in official documents was imprecise in its social connotations, since it included ladies, women slaves and black freedwomen, covering a whole social hierarchy of urban trade.[33]

> Catarina Siqueira 'lives from her stall', a white spinster of fifty-four, she lived with three slaves in the south of the cathedral district; Maria Benedicta, 'stallholder', a single, black woman of forty, also lived south of the cathedral square with one slave girl; Joana Maria 'lives from her stall', a mulatta widow of sixty-three, she lived with her two young daughters and a servant girl, north of the cathedral district; Quiteria Dias, 'stallholder', a black widow of seventy-two, lived in Santa Ifigênia with two servant girls, one black, the other white; Francisca 'lives from her stall', a black, single woman of twenty-five, she lived north of the cathedral district with two small sons.[34]

In the legal records of the town hall there were frequent references to the stallholders, who were the targets of ambiguous complaints, both persecuted and protected by the powerful people in the town. Accusations, probably with ulterior motives, were levelled against the stallholders who bought in bulk in order to speculate. It was impossible, however, to police them effectively. Under the protection of the powerful houses, who were fighting among themselves for control over local trade, the area of activity that belonged to the survival of the underprivileged grew without restriction, and would continue to do so in spite of the gradual constrictions of orders, preventative measures, laws, policing and taxes.

Making a living from a stall presupposed, above all, having a reliable means of access, albeit surreptitious, to a supply of foodstuffs which could be obtained more cheaply and which could be accumulated to build up a stock. It was a fairly widespread urban occupation, greater than was officially declared in the censuses, since if it remained anonymous it could evade taxation. One of the most popular means used by the ladies was a continual rotation of slaves, who took turns to sell clandestinely in the streets. In Salvador at the end of the eighteenth century, Vilhena noticed that the slave women from the wealthier houses managed little by little to sell retail goods freely, without needing permits to sell foodstuffs like dry goods, odds and ends or any kind of merchandise:

> and so no one interferes with them, or asks them to account for themselves, out of respect for the powerful houses from which they come; this is a real safe conduct which frees them from any kind of danger; and woe betide anyone who interferes with them. Black women, however, who do not belong

to upper-class houses, must get a permit from the Senate in order to be able
to sell, and remain immune to the treachery of the ever-vigilant inspectors.[35]

In São Paulo, the divisions between families heading rival factions, and
the remote and rather precarious inclusion of women property owners
into the fringes of the ruling classes, would explain the high number of
fines incurred throughout the century.

The women stallholders lived in the shadow of a much more
prosperous trade, which was run by more powerful merchants and
intermediaries: the commercialization of fluctuating harvests and of
the small surpluses of countrymen and farmworkers was an area open
to speculation, and precariously controlled by rival groups within local
politics. Since some sectors of this local trade constituted monopolies
and political protection groups, they were more lucrative than others.
Among the former, notoriously, were the ones dealing in salt, meat and
oil, which was also used to light the city.[36] The bulk of the manual work
done by slaves was concentrated on these profitable products, making
fortunes for men like the Barão de Iguape, the Visconde de Antonina
and the Conselheiro Vergueiro, wealthy local politicians of nineteenth-
century São Paulo. As well as having interests in the so-called commercial firms, the richest businessmen held strategic posts either in politics
or the Treasury, for example as weights and measures inspectors at the
town hall; these posts were much coveted by cattle dealers and traders
as a way of making a fortune, for they included the responsibility for
organizing local trade, and for collecting taxes and fines.[37] They also
longed to get jobs collecting important taxes, such as the ones on
brandy, drinks and flour.[38]

Apart from municipal taxes on essential commodities, there were
also heavy duties to pay to the Crown, collected for the most pressing
needs of the time: subsidies for Queen Catherine II's dowry, for the
rebuilding of Lisbon, for the installing of the court in Rio de Janeiro, or
for the maintenance of the troops who were fighting in the River Plate
area. There were plenty of complaints and local writs, such as the one in
1823 protesting against the tax surcharge on essential foodstuffs.[39]

This excess of taxes imposed on essential goods encouraged small-
time contraband, which in its turn guaranteed a better circulation of
food and an itinerant retail supply of produce in penny trade. When tax
was imposed, the produce was removed entirely out of reach of the
purchasing power of the main urban population. In 1799, in the documents of the town hall, there was open discussion about the competition between the trading of the poor and the 'big-time commerce' of the
town hall.[40]

Chains of small intermediaries ran a number of operations success-ively, each one with its own network of personal contacts within the community, involving collusion, information and exchange of mer-chandise, at a level closer to mere subsistence than to one of accumula-tion or of profit. In this way, stretching over the vast social area from the authorities and the speculative traders to the poor farmers who had small surpluses at their disposal, they operated in the central streets or from the small cottages themselves, sometimes sending their women slaves out beyond the bridges to trade with a third party, who ended up with the major part of the profits.[41]

There was a whole hierarchy of shops and groceries serving the wealthy population in the city. They were, on the whole, fairly modest, and not very different from the small jerry-shops and the wretched huts which catered for the small consumer needs of the slaves and freed-men. In an inventory of 1840 there appeared an order of merchandise from one of the grocery stores in the city.[42]

½ box soap	6$000
4 measures of maize brandy	2$500
2 measures of Portuguese brandy	1$600
2 pounds of anise	$960
2 cheeses	$600
2 arrobas of bacon	4$480
2½ arrobas of sugar	2$560
½ arroba of coffee	1$120
1 pestle	$320
3 measures of small potatoes	$450
30 candles made of local wax	$280
19 tallow candles	$280
7 half barrels of cornflour	70$000
2 white china basins	$280
1 ferrule for spiking tobacco	$200
1 coffee grinder	$480

There were few women owners of grocery stores or modest businesses. This one was among them – on the records, in fact, for being in debt. Other examples appear in the records: 'In 1836, Dona Gertrudes Thereza, businesswoman, a white widow of fifty-one, lived in the south of the cathedral district with six slaves; Anna Francisca de Jesus, businesswoman, fifty years old, white spinster, lived south of the cathedral district, with three slaves; Gertrudes, 'with a dry goods and grocery store', a white spinster of fifty-two, lived in the north of the cathedral district with a servant girl.'[43]

The nineteenth-century writer Vieira Bueno described the retail trade in the first decades of that century as being all in the hands of men who were small-time Portuguese traders:

> there was a tiny retail trade in dry goods, drinks and groceries, supported by a poor population of fifteen to twenty thousand inhabitants. There would be at the most about twenty shops selling everyday goods, with the peculiarity that almost all of them belonged to individuals with extraordinary surnames, which the people were very clever and imaginative in making up, like Good Smoke, Good Night, Maneco, Ribs, Stumbling Domingos, etc. There was only one hardware shop in the Rua Direita, belonging to Hardware Maneco. There was also only one chinaware store, which, as an exception, belonged to a Brazilian called Teco.[44]

Better known in the city were the black women stallholders and itinerant vendors; Vieira Bueno recalled one in particular: 'Among the stallholders there were some who became very popular because of their cheerfulness, their loquacity and inexhaustible hilarity, like the orange seller whom the medical students carried round the streets in triumph.'[45] Others, like Nha Maria Café and the 'cabbage seller', were also remembered in the city.[46] However, the surnames of the more notorious women in the city, sticking in the memory, recalled the machista values of jokers and students rather than the struggle for survival of working women. A whole folklore of names of working women was recorded in the city streets, whether they were prostitutes or beggars: Ritinha Sorocabana (Little Rita from Sorocaba), Antoninha Bela (Little Antonia the Beautiful), Bellona (Beauty, Bellona, Goddess of War), Anna Perula (Anna the Leaf Bud), Isabelinha Onça Paraguaia (Little Isabel the Paraguay Tigress).[47] Other famous women who were remembered from those times were Catarina Arde-lhe o Rabo (Catarina Hot Tail), Maria Salta Riacho (Maria the Stream Jumper), Maria Ocê me Mata (Maria You're Killing Me), Jurity a Onça (Jurity the Tigress), Maria Garangão (Stout Maria), Zefa Balanço (Zefa the Wobbler), Marianna Fogo de Vista (Marianna Love at First Sight).[48]

The poor women of São Paulo only dealt in small-time clandestine trade, selling retail and by the pound, remaining on the margins of trade that sold in bulk, and of foodstuffs from the small houses or the shops. Their work was above all itinerant: Vieira Bueno did not say much about them, but in his memoirs he recalled clearly the local situation in which the women streetsellers had their place:

> There was no market for the sale of foodstuffs, vegetables, fruits, etc. Everything was sold on the streets by the black women selling from trays, or by the

countrywomen (from the interior) who came with their muleteers from the neighbouring areas. The same applied to the droves of horses loaded with provisions, coming from further afield, places like Cutia, Juquery and Nazareth, etc. . . . that is when they were not waylaid by profiteers outside the city. It was only the cargoes of bacon and salted pork that went to the small houses, on the road to the small cottages, marketplaces which took up one side of the alley opposite the Little Market – because of this it was called the Street of the Cottages.[49]

The area where they operated was made socially unacceptable by the competition from slave labour, which debased and lowered its tone, reducing the small farmers and pedlars, the women vendors and stall-holders to the status of real social pariahs.

In the inventories of countrymen and small-time local tradeswomen there are references to the compulsory weights and measures demanded by the municipal regulations:[50]

2 pairs of scales	1$440
1 set of three cake tins for soaking food	1$000
1 set of three wooden measures for dry goods	2$000
1 set of three lead weights	$800
1 half alqueire measure	$320
1 eighth alqueire measure	$160
1 iron spit	$120
1 small box with lock	$960
1 weighing hook with pound weights, all of iron	1$000

From the middle of the eighteenth century there were inspections by employees of the town hall, who checked the weights and measures as well as the cleanliness of the stalls: in 1741 an edict was read out in the streets and posted up 'in the usual place', reminding the stallholders that they must periodically sweep the dirt or the rubbish from the place where they were selling; they must also respect the prices fixed by the town hall: 'They should not sell eggs for less than three to the vintém, nor should oranges or bananas be sold without a price being agreed . . . nor must they buy up tobacco, game or eggs in bulk in order to resell from their stall.'[51]

The struggle between the factions trying to gain control of trade dated back to the time of Pombal, who managed to wrest it from the duties of the municipal council and hand it over, in 1765, to the domain of the governors and central authorities of the Crown.[52] In 1772 public stores and depositories were built to centralize the operations of local trade within the precincts of the jurisdiction of the governors.[53] In

1812 justices of the peace and weights and measures inspectors were
still confronting one another with contradictory arguments regarding
speculation and the export from the city of goods which were intended
for the consumption of its inhabitants.[54] Orders and counter-orders
followed one another – the defence of free trade, against fixed prices
and the collectivism of the Senate – which determined the freedom of
movement of the women stallholders in the city. Trade monopolies
were abolished in March of 1821, and by October of the same year the
provincial assembly had taken over the subsidies and new taxes which
had previously been controlled by the town council.[55] This was the
beginning of a battle that resulted in the reorganization of the rights of
the municipality in 1828, and numerous attempts to monopolize fiscal
control of street trading at a provincial level.

It was as mediators and intermediaries, small secondary links under
the protection of big business, that women stallholders and vendors
assiduously played their part in the operations of local trade; the resale
of plots of land and foodstuffs was certainly less lucrative than the meat
or brandy business, in which small-time officials and cashiers from
established shops took an intense interest.

The local network for the collection of taxes, like the operations for
intercepting small producers, demanded a whole system of support
and information at neighbourhood level, involving family and personal
relationships. Ladies who had few slaves had their own interests in the
system, taking part in the operations of the more powerful profiteers,
and being left with some supplies of goods like beans, maize, cassava
and bacon, which they tried to sell retail, depending on their own needs
and the contacts they had in the neighbourhood. Their business was
mostly itinerant trade – the sale of small local crops or odds and ends –
but a minority of small-time women owners of slaves had stores or
shops, that is, small businesses.[56] Then their activities were more concerned with the redistribution of foodstuffs in small quantities; because
of this they were rather disliked by the innkeepers and small businessmen, who protested that the competition was unfair since they themselves were obliged to pay taxes, while the women vendors usually
managed to avoid them.[57]

When salesmen and small shop owners took measures against the
women stallholders and vendors, there were rarely any voices raised in
their defence. A political faction might take sides when there was in-
fighting over the precise margin of speculation for the distribution of
goods for local consumption. Traditionally, homemade goods and
those for consumption did not have a fixed price. However, from 1738
onwards rice was included among certain foods such as beans, flour,

bacon and maize which could not be sold without a permit from the council, which also had to fix the prices.[58]

Between 1765 and 1821, when the monopolies and exclusive trading privileges of the Portuguese Crown were suspended, the authorities argued over the issue of free trade, and over the control which the council as a corporation exercised over prices. In 1797 innkeepers and small businessmen brought pressure to bear on the governor in an attempt to abolish the privileges of auctioning and of sales monopolies on drinks, foodstuffs, salt, whale oil and brandy.[59] They also turned on the small itinerant trade that was such a threat to them, finally managing to achieve some measures which directly affected the movements of the women stallholders. From then onwards any itinerant sales were forbidden in the city:

those who come from the bridges of Penha to the edge of Santa . . . and from the areas of Santa Anna and N. S. . . . to the edge of N. S. da Lapa . . . In the same way, nobody will be allowed to sell eggs on the streets or at the entrances to the city, but must bring them straight to the edge of the Bexiga, and only there may they sell them to the people, and not to the women stall-holders, or to any other people who buy in order to resell, until two in the afternoon; from then onwards they can sell them to anybody . . . No cabbage seller shall be allowed to sell cabbage to the women stallholders without first taking them throughout the city, and only then may they dispose of them. No woman stallholder may buy rice in bulk so as to sell in small quantities from trays, just as those who sell the said rice shall not sell it to the aforementioned stallholders; similarly, the women stallholders will not be allowed to sell flour, maize or beans in small quantities very cheaply from their tray, as all this merchandise here stated is reserved solely for the innkeepers, who pay taxes on their businesses.[60]

Once the colonial monopolies were abolished, there was a drive to reorganize local trade, renewing privileges and again increasing the burden of taxes. In 1814, as if to show how inefficient these measures were, the wine store owners once more attacked the competition the itinerant women vendors represented, quoting their own poverty, which was doubtless aggravated by the new taxes but which they believed was 'brought about by the fact that the women stallholders were selling those goods which were meant for the shops, as were rice, eggs, distilled brandies, cheeses, beans and flour, which they were buying so as to resell, without any expenses, even that of a permit.'[61] They wanted to limit the stallholders to trade in drinks and homemade sweets and 'somehow avoid the monopoly that the same women stall-holders have in game, so it is said, and the way they come and go in the

city with rice, flour and other goods . . . that should be exclusive to the
wine shops and licensed inns . . .'[62]

In 1821 the municipal by-laws turned directly against the practice of
neighbourhood clandestine trade, and they tried to prohibit shop
goods from being sold from houses 'with an open door and no counter',
for which a permit would be needed; they also specified for the authorities 'what kinds of goods they should be selling'. Nevertheless, they
made an exception for the country farmers, 'who may sell their goods in
the streets or in the shop if they are under the measure of half a coarta.'
This cancelled out any kind of effectiveness in the regulations, since it
would be very difficult to distinguish poor farming women from poor
tradespeople in the streets of the city.[63]

This open conflict with the authorities never ceased. Even on the
occasions of religious festivals and pilgrimages, like the one for Our
Lady of Penha, women vendors continued arguing over the right to sell,
defying the monopolies on the one hand, and the perennial competition between themselves, on the other.

After 1828, when municipal government was finally reorganized,
their situation became gradually worse, for as the city grew, so repression increased. The fines imposed on itinerant sales without permits
became more and more prohibitive, considering the degree of poverty
that characterized the everyday life of free women in the city. These
repressive measures lost their force by the very frequency with which
they had to be repeated.[64] However, after the legislation against itinerant trade in 1828, the women stallholders and vendors began to
declare themselves in the censuses in a vaguer, more furtive way, as living 'from their business' or 'from their activities'.[65]

In 1829 regulations began to charge a fee of 6$400 for a tray seller,
and a fine of 8$000 for anyone caught without paying the due sum. The
income of ladies who lived from their businesses or activities varied
between 8$ and 12$ a month. The majority of their customers, however, who were poor seamstresses, women spinners, washerwomen
and street vendors, only made from 3$ to 5$ a month.[66] Custom came
from their own neighbours, whose purchasing power was very low, and
who lived in rented rooms or wretched hovels.

As second-class citizens, poorly off, with incomes often below 150$
a year, the women stallholders were treated as scapegoats; in the
municipal annals they were used by third parties to cover up clandestine operations on a larger scale. It is this which explains the continual protests against them, and the fact that they were able to survive
them, if the occasion demanded it.

There were some speculators with capital who took part in clandestine trade. In 1828 the town hall legislated against people who had been put into circulation by commercial firms to sell dry goods from trays, as a way of evading tax. Occasionally the wealthier owners of country houses and small farms around the city also took advantage of this small-scale trade in order to sell their surpluses without paying taxes.

There were few speculators in the retail trade as a whole, however, which began to share the character of the generalized poverty of the city and almost imperceptibly started to merge with the penny trade of the poorest people. Street trade which was not very lucrative was characterized by a process of decreasing mobility: between 1804 and 1836 the increase in poverty persisted and the women owners of just a few slaves gradually diminished in number during the course of the century.[67] Small-scale trade barely provided a living, much less the exorbitant profit which had been suggested by ambiguous accusations.

THREE

The Myth of the Absent Lady

A las longas terras	(To far away lands
En traz vos me irey;	I shall follow you;
Las compridas vias	Long roads
Eu as andarei;	I shall walk;
Lingoas d'Arabias	Languages of Arabia
Eu las fallarei;	I shall speak;
Mouros se me vissem	If the Moors see me
Eu los matarei.	I shall kill them.)

'Cancioneiro do Conde de Marialva', in Theophilo
Braga, *História da Poesia Popular Portuguesa*,
p. 228.

In his memories of the city of São Paulo, Vieira Bueno refers in passing to the existence of a furtive, cunning stratum of the population of the city. It was one of 'concealed poverty', where women would go out into the streets by night:[1] 'beautiful women without a dowry', impoverished white women, unmarried girls and old spinsters, concealing their poverty under black wool cloaks inherited from better times. Living on the fringes of the growing bourgeoisie that was the new elite of the coffee boom, they were like surplus sectors of impoverished white women, rejected by the society that had been their cradle. They were the target for prejudices, some of which had deep roots in the very system of populating and colonizing in previous centuries.

Mário de Andrade collected some popular verses and presented them in a short essay on the theme of the 'absent lady'. A famous São Paulo modernist poet and writer of the first half of the twentieth century, he put a great deal of thorough research into the question of the lack of white women in the colony, as the handwritten notes in his archive testify. In a 'distressing survey' which took over ten years to put together, he collected ballads and popular verses about the absent lady, to whom the sailor or the colonist travelling the world should be faithful. In a masterly, pioneering attempt at investigating Luso-Brazilian machismo, he collected folkloric evidence of the yearning for the figure of an ideal woman, who was always unattainable. Popular ditties reveal a succession of the difficult situations a man faced, expressing a perpetual search, different variations on the theme of impossible love and of the Don Juan story, embodied in the concrete, historical pattern of the process of the colonization of Brazil. Some women appear as sexual objects of passing conquest:

> Little mulatta women are cockle boats
> Black women are narrow fishing boats:
> What beautiful vessels
> For sailors to board . . .[2]

Such women are seen as passing temptations during the time in port, unworthy of that yearning for the absent lady carried by men in their hearts, or used as an excuse for man's never-ending soul-searching:

> She has yet to be born
> who will be my love.[3]

Through the study of a complex of maritime elements, that 'in Brazil became elements of the land as well',[4] Mário de Andrade hinted at the sublimating function of a lyrical process which corresponded to the historical experience of a navigating and colonizing people.

The step from the paradigm of impossible love to the idea of the absent lady as an ideology of domination seems an easy one to make. Personified in the social plan of the Portuguese for colonization, she would have her historical role in the politics of the mixing of different races, and in the perpetuation of privileges. Like a form of romanticism pervading metaphors about fleeting liaisons,[5] the absent lady would underlie the social values of domination in colonial society.

In different ways, the stereotype of the white woman established unattainable standards that were impossible for women of other social classes to achieve. The more ritualized social conventions became concerning ostentation in social status, the more evident the latent tensions became, surfacing in the form of offences and disorders, both in documents and in everyday life.

The myth of the absent lady is part of the apparatus of repression of attempts to make the act of concubinage with women of other races formal or public. The social roles of women, conventions and patterns of ostentation are all loaded with evocative, ambiguous nuances which involve the basic relationships between sex, status and colour. Norms which are an inherent part of the hierarchy of a slavery-based colonial society led to practices of extraordinary behaviour and display, which can be seen repeatedly in the descriptions of festivals, whether civic or religious.

In the varied series of events which made up the populating process, the myth of the absent lady gradually gained historical credence, both with historians and in official documents. The references were coloured with racist connotations, their violence depending on the intensity of the process of miscegenation. It was already implicit in the texts of the Jesuits and the São Paulo settlers who mingled with local native Indians,[6] but it doubtless took on a clearer connotation in the context of the mining society. In the eyes of Frei Vicente do Salvador, the bastard, illegitimate children of the Portuguese with Indian women tended to inherit more 'from the common background of their mother than from the lineage of their father'.[7] Similar comments were repeated about the mixing of races in Minas Gerais in the second half of the eighteenth century: 'the children of well-to-do men, who had the misfortune to be born and brought up in Brazil, do not inherit the incentives of honour [of their fathers], but happily adopt the customs of the black people, the mulattos and savages and the other absurd people of this land.'[8]

São Paulo settlers lived in the very core of the growth of the gold towns and chroniclers like Pedro Taques recorded the experiences of the pioneering fronts. Few women went with their husbands, unlike the wife of Pedro Taques de Almeida, who travelled to Goiás with his family: 'the great majority of white miners, who are unmarried men, have casual relationships with black and Indian women, unions which could not be legalized because of the nature of their caste.'[9]

Frei Gaspar and Pedro Taques place strong emphasis on the value of the absent lady in their genealogies, condemning unrestrained passions and carnal appetites as 'the common affliction to which one is driven through lust over the heat of years'; 'João Pires de Campos, driven only by the inexcusable appetite and unhappy destiny of his kind, heedless of the obligations of his noble blood . . .'[10] As far as Pedro Taques is concerned, the women with Indian blood, even those with the lightest complexion, appeared in a very pejorative light.[11] The exaltation of the virtues of white women of pure stock, as opposed to 'women from corrupt, reprobate nations', was implicit in his texts. In documents from the second half of the eighteenth century it was made clear how low the estimation was of dark-skinned freedwomen. They appeared with the ambiguous aura of sexual objects, suspected of prostitution and evil ways, to which was usually added the inevitable matter of their doubtful descent and a parenthood which was always difficult to prove:

> if the aforementioned mulatta woman, as she is called, has more children, if one accepts that they are all of the same claimant; if the mother has the reputation of dishonouring herself with men other than the claimant, especially at the time of conception, for which reasons she will be questioned to make sure about the baptism, much caution will be exercised – or if, at the time, the claimant is away from the city of Rio de Janeiro, and for how long . . . or became seriously ill and with what; and if he had maintained the said mulatta woman at his own cost, or if she, because of his casual treatment of her, was used to taking advantage of other men, and if the said mother were to tell other people who was the father of the child, it became publicly and widely known that the claimant was the father, or if there was any doubt or divergence of opinions on this matter . . .[12]

In Salvador and on the sugar coast, generally speaking, steps were taken from the middle of the seventeenth century to discriminate more clearly against the clothes worn by slave women and domestic servant girls, with the aim of emphasizing the social distance of the white ladies:

> Considering the extravagance of the Brazilian slave women, and the need to eliminate this excess and the bad example that it could set . . . The King was pleased to decide that no slave woman anywhere in Brazil or in any of its captaincies should wear a silk dress, or one of cambric or holland cotton, with or without lace, on any occasion, nor, in addition, should they wear any ornament of gold or silver on their dresses.[13]

In 1701, Antonil criticized the extravagant attire of mulatta women of ill repute, loaded with strings of beads, earrings and other gold trinkets, demonstrating the impossibility of maintaining a law against a custom which was becoming more and more ingrained.[14]

In 1705 more steps were taken against excesses of attire 'in which women often go about at night, and because it is necessary to forbid slave women to wear silks . . . Do not allow slave women to wear them, so as to prevent them inciting to sin with the expensive adornments with which they clothe themselves.'[15] There were numerous prohibitions, frequently repeated in Salvador, in Rio de Janeiro and in the small mining towns.[16]

The ladies were criticized for encouraging prostitution among the slave women. It was a rite of passage that became more and more common in the eighteenth century, occasionally determining the acceptance of mulatta women who had become wealthy and had become noble ladies. There was the scandalous case of Chica da Silva, the diamond contractor's mistress,[17] and that of Mariana Baptista de Paracatu, who in 1798 offered D. Maria I a bunch of bananas cast in gold in exchange for a noble title and for permission to attend Mass in the company of white women – where, according to legend, the priest waited for her to arrive before starting Mass.[18]

The narrowness of the social ambience in São Paulo made such excesses inconceivable there. The Jesuits criticized the slack way in which Indian women dressed, going about the town half naked. In their wills, São Paulo women counted among their good deeds that of making sure that the Indian women they brought to their houses were always dressed in rustic cloth, which they had woven themselves.[19] There were many cases of relationships between Portuguese colonists and Indian women, and of Indian women 'kept indoors'; very occasionally there would be an unequal marriage, which caused scandal and disapproval.[20] Excesses of social behaviour and occasional lapses were concealed beneath thick cloaks: hooded felt cloaks of barracan, shepherds' hoods and fine woollen black fabrics, fine Indian cotton cloths, felts from São Paulo and Sorocaba, English baize ... under which slave women, women living with their lovers, prostitutes and impoverished white women were hidden. It was the very antithesis of the excessive ostentation with which the colonizers from Bahia or miners from the gold district dressed their favourite household slave women, to show them off in church. In São Paulo the principal fortunes were made by methodical businessmen, with a struggle, and they were more concerned with winning the social approval of the important people of the land than with scandalizing them with malicious behaviour. Theirs was not the easy wealth of the gold or diamond speculators; in the middle of the eighteenth century, the proof of poverty which had always predominated in the São Paulo area was still the same as ever, as described by Frei Vicente do Salvador in 1598: 'men and women would dress in dyed cotton cloth, and if there was the odd baize cape and serge cloak, it would be lent to the couple getting married, for getting to the church gates.'[21]

It was what the Morgado de Matheus, the Portuguese governor of

São Paulo, heard in 1767 about a member of the church: 'that when he went to confess last Lent, in the district of São Roque, which is in the parish of Cotia, thirty or forty men, or probably more, a very considerable number, went to confession with him, with only one jacket between them, which they took turns to wear, one after the other.'[22]

Linens and silks, velvet and lace were the perquisites of absent ladies, and rarely seen.

With their business profits from provisioning the mining areas, the *paulistas* began to import red and blue baize, and coloured silk stockings from England;[23] after that, homespun cloths were in fierce competition with raw burlap and even striped linens, and imported rustic cloths.

The social rise of the *paulistas*, who became rich from mule breeding for transportation and trade, made them anxious for social recognition – for titles; paramilitary honours and noble status – which manifested itself more in the desire to imitate the great than in the temptation to scandalize.

Rivalry and competition in dress were consumerist tendencies which were sharply criticized by the magistrates of the Crown, who were conscious of the poverty of the social milieu: 'The splendour of their dress is at variance with the means of these people: if the goods were made in Portugal, everything would remain within the country; but since they are foreign, they are far too expensive.'[24] The Morgado de Matheus compared the ostentatious ways of the new rich in São Paulo with those of the court in Lisbon, and took great delight in ridiculing the pretentiousness of the wives of the minor civil servants and *nouveau riche* businessmen:

> The ladies say that in this Court they cannot afford the price of shoes; they get 60$000 pin money, and shoes cost them 1$600, and they are walking on carpets; in this country, women do not earn a penny, yet their shoes cost them 4$800, and on top of this they are made of the best silk and are for street wear. In Portugal, many noblemen wear fine cloth, and in the provinces honest folk wear linen; here, the whites wear the best velvet, and none of them wears anything but holland cotton; all this is bought on credit, and they decide later how to pay.[25]

The emphasis on female leisure by São Paulo women rather suggests the social need to appear to have nothing to do; small civil servants, traders born in Portugal and wives of prosperous mule dealers had illusions of grandeur. Alice Canabrava reminds us of the extreme concentration of income and the way the urban area expanded to include middle-class sectors.[26]

In the city, which was still poor and restricted, the rituals of display regarding status were exacerbated: the presence of slaves of 'other people' was embarrassing, for their own customs were not in keeping with the rough urban area, with its violence and its dirt.

During the period of independence around 1822, the city was far from favourable to bourgeois habits: apart from one badly funded, public promenade,[27] the only events that brightened up social life were processions, *te deums* and civic festivals. The much discussed seclusion of the ever absent ladies was a custom determined by the still rather hazardous urban area. It was difficult to walk on the badly paved streets;[28] armed men, muleteers and their friends would take part in stampedes and shootings on horseback; garbage would pile up by the walls of the houses; the streets were full of domestic slaves, both men and women, carrying *tigres* (barrels full of human waste)[29] and fetching water from the fountain, with a great deal of shouting and sometimes breaking into rioting and knife fights.[30] It is not surprising that it was unusual to go out . . .

Travellers interpreted the absence of upper-class women as a symptom of patriarchal customs, like those of an oriental harem. The division and inequality of the slavery-based way of life made the adoption of more bourgeois customs difficult, and emphasized the need for display, ostentation, circumspection and the social distance befitting great ladies, who rarely appeared in public. A shopping trip to the stores was a custom which took a long time to take root.[31]

Going out involved an elaborate ritual of palanquins, sedan chairs, and embroidered hammocks, until coaches and painted carriages began to appear, after the 1840s. Going to the cathedral for processions or Mass was one of the rare public events which was fought over by those who wanted to be seen, and avoided with embarrassment by those who did not have the wherewithal to 'carry the canopy'.[32]

> There is a difference in the song,
> Of those who sing in the cathedral:
> Some sing loudly, sitting down,
> Others quietly, standing up . . .[33]

In 1839, Kidder further described important ladies sitting on mats on the ground, in oriental fashion, at the cathedral.[34] Saint-Hilaire, who visited the cathedral for the Maundy Thursday ceremony, recorded the extravagant care even the poorest women took to adorn themselves for the festival, with mantillas, shawls and the most colourful clothes.[35]

There was a rigid hierarchy in social life, and one of the characteristics of the rare gentlefolk of the land was that they hardly ever appeared in public: they spent their lives *intra muros*, visiting each other in elaborate rituals between equals. It was not until the middle of the century that they adopted bourgeois customs like walks and picnics.

Apart from the seclusion of their own houses, the refuge of the ruling classes lay in convents and asylums. From 1687 onwards, in São Paulo, first the convent of St Teresa was founded, then in 1773 the Luz convent. They sheltered well-endowed heiresses, and as in Rio were centres of an intense social life, with a great number of slaves and many festivities.[36] These retreats also admitted lay women, wives of important men of the area who had separated from their husbands, or rebel ladies resisting arranged marriages.

For fallen women, the choice was either a convent or domestic service as a live-in servant.

From the middle of the eighteenth century, fashionable materials demarcated social spheres which were worlds apart: there were woollen cloths, silks and velvets, trimmed with gold and silver, for the rare appearances of absent ladies, and on the other hand, 'for the common people, materials of an inferior kind: coarse cloth, fine Indian cotton, oakum, burel, baize, plain rough cloth, coarse cotton and stock mending fabrics'.[37]

The few great ladies hardly ever appeared in public, though when they did it was with a great show of dress. But still in 1865, Taunay was writing in his diary: 'I shall be able to say very little about São Paulo women, since I see so little of them.'[38] This also rather confused travellers, who did not always know the difference between absent ladies and 'the violets and pinks behind the window grille'.[39] In the middle of the century, the myth of the absent lady still figured in a student's diary: 'An interesting creature appeared yesterday on the balcony opposite the Souza family's old mansion: she is blond, white skinned, and was wearing a green organdie dress and a pink cameo.'[40]

In São Paulo, few women could afford the luxury of imitating the fashion of the court: the Brigadier's widow, Dona Gertrudes Galvão Jordão, with a house on the corner of Rua Dircita and São Bento; the Toledo sisters, of the Casa Verde, on the corner of the Travessa do Colégio . . . Even in 1865, somebody described the luxury with which the Marquesa de Santos and her daughter D. Maria Isabel de Alcântara Brasileira, the beauty, indulged themselves: 'a large velvet cloak, embroidered with gold, over a dress of steely blue, with a train.'[41]

These were unattainable standards, sure signs of status and the source of social discrimination in a milieu of impoverished white women, who could hardly afford to appear in daylight. It was what established the rather furtive fashion of the hidden poor, alongside that of ostentation, in the streets of São Paulo. Black baize cloaks concealed the victims of the absent lady myth: after angelus, they would go out into the streets, enveloped in black cloth, their faces hidden under hoods and slouch hats. The governors and magistates who had recently arrived from Portugal were puzzled by these customs, which they found difficult to understand.

In 1775, the governor Martim Lopes protested about the furtive reserve with which São Paulo women went about, covered up as if they were criminals: 'muffled up in two lengths of black baize, the way they are made in the stores, and wearing slouch hats on their heads; and in this way, with their faces completely covered, in the streets as well as in church, many of them hasten into men's houses, even in daylight.'[42]

Those prejudiced against the São Paulo colonial milieu were puzzled by this custom, and by the barely disguised practice of living together in a land where marriage was rare and not often formalized. They regarded it as debauchery and licentiousness, even though the custom was widespread and might be kept discreet and properly secret. An express warning had to be included in the instructions for Franca e Horta, the Portuguese governor in 1810, to the effect that common law marriages should not be investigated or attempts made to prosecute: 'a crime which should not be investigated or recorded on the grounds that it is expressly forbidden by the royal laws of Your Highness ... which one should never question, in compliance with the Charter of 26 September 1769, the only exception being the keeping and main-taining of a mistress which causes general, public scandal.'[43]

The presence of African slaves in the city exacerbated aristocratic values and the rituals of social hierarchy. In 1812, Marianna Angélica Fortes Sá Leme and Anna Leonisa de Abelho Fortes, for reasons we do not know, requested a certificate from the town hall, which would verify their social position: 'finally, we certify that the aforementioned ladies live a secluded life at home and are considered to be of great dis-tinction and of noble line.'[44]

In 1810, Franca e Horta was determined to make the city more civilized, forcing the adoption of more bourgeois customs, and intro-ducing, through charters, a fashion that was more agreeable to the eye than that of black baize and hoods, which were forbidden.[45] Impover-ished white women were the main victims of this accentuation of seignorial values, which were supported by the sentiments of a slavery-based society, and which the educated authorities wanted to reinforce with more Europeanized appearances.

Escolástica Siqueira, a very poor married lady 'with an absent husband', and without the name to evoke the grandeur of an ancestor from the seventeenth century, lived in the Travessa do Colégio, almost next door to the Toledo sisters, who lived with their eighteen slaves on a totally different social level;[46] Isabel Pires Camargo, a white spinster of sixty-six, lived off her business, north of the cathedral, without any slaves or household servants; Escolástica Rosa da Anunciação, south of the cathedral, a white widow of thirty, with two small children, also lived without slaves 'off her business'; Dona Gertrudes Maria da Conceição lived in Santa Ifigênia, with another widow of the same age, without assistants, surviving 'from her activities'.[47]

They were way beneath the social level of absent ladies. Living in the city without slaves, in full view of everybody, was a heavy burden which impoverished white women could barely face. The prejudices against any form of manual labour, which smacked of slave labour, made their day-to-day living very difficult. Authorities from Portugal, like the Morgado de Matheus, called attention to these prejudices in reports: 'No free person wishes to go into service for he holds it in the greatest contempt: as soon as servants from Portugal arrive here, they reject their masters.'[48] Vilhena made the same observations about the poor whites in the urban centre of Salvador,[49] and J. J. Teixeira Coelho about the impoverished whites in Minas Gerais: 'In the district of Minas Gerais, no white man or woman wishes to go into service because they all consider that they will be degraded by a job that is only fitting for slaves.'[50]

This is what Vieira Bueno was explaining in his commentary on secret poverty, how the people came out into the streets mysteriously at night, to fetch water, do the shopping, jobs that were more fitting for slaves than for white ladies. Hence the furtiveness that suggested the secrecy of a life of ill repute, explained in the words of Vilhena:

> there are also many women who, when seen at night in the streets, are slanderously labelled as dissolute, when in fact they are honest and virtuous, and are forced to make these nocturnal excursions because they have no one who can go out during the day to buy the necessary food, and anything else they need.[51]

One of the symptoms of the crisis of the colonial system in the mining towns[52] is the presence of a majority of single, mulatta freedwomen.[53] In São Paulo it was the impoverished white women who increased in number, in a process of overwhelming social decline.[54] The economy was not capable of absorbing the autonomous growth of the population, even of the whites, who in principle would be an integral part of the system of hegemony.

Some of the stereotypes and ideological values that relate to female social roles have less to do with a universal female condition than with the specific tensions within the relationships of power in a given society. This applies in the social project of the colonization of Brazil to the importance which is assumed by the social role of the white woman in general, reinforced by the official policy of the Portuguese Crown to compensate for their absence on the pioneering frontiers of the populating process. In colonial Brazil, among those values generated by a slave-based system of domination, appreciation of white women increased as the initial fulcrum in the colonization project. In each successive movement in population growth, starting from the coastal region in the sixteenth century, and particularly in the gold mining period, a whole complex of social practices and administrative arrangements evolved, which were to reinforce the role of white women as reproducers and as conveyors of property, as well as of the symbols of colonial superiority: colour, language and religion.

Life in the colony was characterized by an emphatic vigilance over every little gesture of the white women of the governing classes. In 1698 the governor D. Artur de Sá e Menezes was dismayed by the habit that São Paulo women had acquired of speaking Tupi with their native Indian servants: 'the majority of those people cannot express themselves in any other language, especially the female sex, and all the servants, and serious harm is resulting from this shortcoming.'[55] At the end of the eighteenth century the local dialect was forbidden in Macao, as was the use of the 'sarong', which gave the ladies an oriental appearance, more native than Portuguese. In the nineteenth century the wearing of a black cape over oriental dress was accepted, the 'dó' of Portuguese or Azorian origin. As has been seen, in 1810 in São Paulo, the authorities took objection to the use of black baize as a cover-up device . . .[56]

There was strict, daily control over the purity of customs, and women were increasingly brought to account. Some ladies were denounced for their behaviour as being reminiscent of Jewish customs: Heitor Antunes's old wife, after her husband died, 'never again ate at table or touched meat'; she would also 'stand behind the door, pour water on the floor, lift her skirts and sit down on the floor'. Her own daughters turned against her on her death bed: 'Watch out mother, watch what you say, for we are married to noblemen who are the principals in the land.'[57]

The role of the white woman as a leader of society was not one that was inherited or part of a tradition: it was a new function of power in the colonies, which soon assumed standardizing features and formal

conventions: no yielding to pagan customs,[58] no entertaining relationships with men of a different colour, and an alertness to Jewish rituals,
due to the presence of the Inquisition.

> And likewise, she, the accuser, witnessed that she had often seen the said
> Clara Fernandes preparing food, and that she did not cook her meat in a pan,
> but in a clay pot, saying that it was tastier that way, and that she mixed cereal
> with the meat, crushing it and adding seasoning, but without any cabbage,
> and the accuser and the women prisoners that were there said that this was
> the Jewish way of doing things.
>
> And likewise, the accuser had often seen Clara Fernandes, on Sundays
> and holy days, having her containers and floors scrubbed and cleaned with
> sand, as well as her pans, lamps and the rest of her dishes, and that this
> happened as often before Mass as after it.[59]

The effective absence of white women in the newly conquered lands
led to the improvisation of the status of social leadership. These were
heroic times for the making of ladies, even if they had come from the
most humble origins in Portugal, for there was a need for white women
in the colony to play the part of great ladies, to follow the example of
such pioneering women as Brites Coelho. Good, Christian women,
who were pious and virtuous, 'praying to Our Lady, making pilgrimages and practising devotion, fasting on the day before that of Our
Lady, and doing the charitable works of those who fear God'.[60]

Nóbrega's classic text appealing to the Crown authorities to send to
the colonies orphan girls and women, 'even if they had gone astray',[61] is
from this period, as is also the passage from Frei Vicente do Salvador
about the transformation of a Portuguese woman who had no dowry
from low social standing into a great powerful lady of the Pernambuco
colony.

> And so it happened that the man married a woman who also came from
> Portugal, not because of any dowry that came with her, but because there
> was no other woman there, and they knew how to make money in such a way
> that within two years they had made three thousand cruzados, and so they
> left for their land in the company of the Captain Major of Rio Grande, João
> Rodrigues Colaço, and his wife D. Beatriz de Menezes, all sharing the same
> table, and he strolling side by side with the Captain, and his wife sitting down
> on the same bench as the noblewoman; this was how I saw them in Pernam-
> buco, where they went to take the boat for them all to embark. And they paid
> her all this honour because in those times there were not yet any white
> women in Rio Grande, and it so happened that the Captain's wife gave birth,
> and so they took the woman on as a godmother, and treated her accordingly,

and the husband as godfather; and so the Bishop's divine judgement that he would return home rich and honoured came true in every way.[62]

At the beginning of the settlement in Minas Gerais,[63] the same shortage of white women was registered, resulting in a terrible imbalance between the sexes in the population, there being nearly 1,800 men to every 100 women. This improved the social value of the Portuguese woman, together with a whole policy of integration of white women in the process of colonization: 'Brazil will not become depopulated because of the shortage of women,' wrote D. Lourenço de Almeida in 1722, taking measures to prevent a drop in the reproductive strength of the colony: he forbade convents, and made it difficult for women to return to Portugal.[64]

From the beginning, the Crown had had an almost official policy for the settlement of women, with the purpose of filling a vital gap in the process of colonization. It brought in female orphans, the King's wards,[65] guaranteeing them dowries both in land and slaves, in line with the privileges of the colonizers, and in public offices, concerning magistracy and the administration of the Crown: to encourage marriage, they facilitated the rights of succession of bureaucratic and administrative offices, which gave rise to the policy of linking dowries with jobs, and the favouring of married men rather than bachelors for public posts.[66]

White women had a role, *sui generis*, of social leadership in the process of colonization: they were the founders of chapels,[67] trustees, businesswomen, administrators of estates and leaders of local politics. As heads of families, they saw themselves as leaders of family groups and local networks of power relations. Some became famous as political leaders, like Maria da Cruz,[68] Joaquina do Pompeu,[69] Josefa Carneiro Leão and Bárbara de Alencar. The latter took part in the revolution of 1817 in Ceará, and oral tradition has it that when she was taken prisoner 'an insolent man asked her why she had taken part in the war, and if it wasn't, perhaps, so that she could be queen; scandalized, she replied that this was not so, for what she wanted was to be king.'[70] Old-fashioned usages and outdated fashions which had crystallized into rules and conventions in the home country took on a new impetus in the context of the colony. This was especially so where it concerned the reinforcement of the privileges of women of the ruling classes through rights of succession: their dowries were protected by law, and in principle their husbands were unable to dispose of any properties belonging to the couple without the wife's permission. The wife could bear witness, initiate legal action, occasionally against her husband, and seek divorce, which was now allowed by the church; they could also be held responsible for any debts incurred by the husband, and this made them very good at being traders and businesswomen.[71]

The social history of the women of the ruling classes is far from being a history of seclusion and passivity, a fact clearly demonstrated by Antonio Candido de Mello e Souza, in his essay on the Brazilian family, where there is a long line of active women entrepreneurs, women who educated their children, were social organizers and trainers of slaves, efficient administrators of their lands and properties.[72]

Because of the demographic phenomena of the settlement in the territories, which meant an absence of men, there was a clear division in the spheres of activity of the sexes in the colony; in addition, there was a certain necessary, inevitable flexibility on the part of the women in assuming masculine roles whenever it was needed.

As well as this, domestic chores assumed enormous proportions, and had a complexity that would surprise anyone who has not given close study to the business of survival in the homes of colonial Brazil. Home crafts required competent leaders and administrators and involved the training of slaves and the execution of slow, arduous tasks, which meant day after day of incessant work, essential for the survival of the group.[73]

As heads of family groups, the women had the role of keeping the group together; they had to ensure harmony in the face of the many destructive forces which continually threatened the perpetuation of the privileges of the family groups at the centre of colonial enterprise. The stereotype of white women leaders as hospitable, generous matriarchs, devoted to their people, like Brites Coelho in Pernambuco, or Ana Monteiro in São Paulo,[74] was already growing in the memory of the people in the early centuries of the colony. Moral tales, like those by Trancozo, had been told throughout Brazil by women storytellers since the sixteenth century, passing from generation to generation until they had become part of regional folklore. They described the importance of strong women, who had decisive social roles in the survival of family groups.

A task which awaits the Brazilian historiographer is the careful reconstruction of this social role, separating it out as far as possible from the stereotypes, and linking it to the more realistic chain of women as mediators of social tensions in the process of colonization. Integrating women from the ruling classes into the social history of Brazil presupposes the study of regional affairs, while bearing in mind those ideological values which identified them with the colonization project of the Portuguese; it needs the sensitivity to pick up the peculiarities that were part of women's daily activities, which in the colonies had to be continually reinvented.

This is precisely what is difficult to extract from official sources, where ideal images and the concreteness of effective action seem to reinforce each other. It was the important ladies, of the calibre of the women from the Casa da Torre in Bahia, whom the authorities enjoyed serving: 'I am completely at the service of Senhora Leona Pereira Marinho, and I beg her not to keep me idle at her pleasure, so that in the service of obeying her, I may always rejoice ... I shall always make these same declarations, everywhere, and hope for many occasions to serve her, for which she will find me most willing.'[75]

It is true that there were occasions when the 'matriarchs' had the authorities worried, and opposed them, as was the case of Inez Monteiro in São Paulo in the middle of the seventeenth century. She provoked an outburst from the Count of Atouguia in a letter to the King dated 1655: 'it was not fair that because of the objection of just one woman, who was the obstinate member, a whole captaincy should be lost.'[76]

C. R. Boxer suggests that in the Mozambique *prazos* (rural holdings) there was a tendency for the rights of succession to fall, out of choice, on the line of women descendants, so as to avoid the eventuality of properties falling into the hands of men of mixed race; A. J. R. Russell Wood seems to discern the same practice among the inventories of rural property owners in Bahia in the seventeenth century.[77] In São Paulo, women controlled the organization of marriages, through which they manoeuvred family alliances and dealt in property and business: 'they are very shrewd, and inclined to marry their daughters to outsiders who are their superiors, rather than to local men who are their equals.'[78]

The younger daughters who did not find a suitable match would go into a convent. In her study of the convent of Desterro, in Salvador, Susan Soeiro shows that, even as nuns, they continued to observe the business policy of their families:[79] using their dowries, the convents acted as banks and gave credit to the local bosses, so perpetuating the interests of their families in the eternal struggle for local power.

Their real roles as administrators, businesswomen and property owners do not emerge very clearly from their petitions and demands, which are thick with conventional terms tied up with traditions and with respect for their husband's role as formal head of the family. When they were widowed, they made formal application in the inheritance papers for guardianship of the children and the grandchildren, claiming among their reasons that they were very capable of managing property, both in a financial and administrative sense, and of looking after the interest-bearing loans, as well as having the conventional virtues that the documents demanded of women: 'being married as a Christian

... even when widowed, honouring the memory of the husband; living with honour and modesty, doing the duties of a Christian woman, maintaining decent behaviour.'[80]

There are numerous requests from businesswomen, usually widows who had inherited from their husbands. In Sorocaba, Dona Maria Nazaré wanted to be a shareholder in the iron mine; in Santos, Dona Gertrudes was the owner of eighty slaves; Dona Angela de Siqueira, in Sorocaba, would sell two hundred bullocks, fifty foals and six mules every two years to herdsmen who transported them to Rio de Janeiro; another widow demanded that the authorities pay her for her cattle, which she kept for feeding the infantry. Many of them demanded plots of land; in 1713, the widow of Sergeant Major José Tavares de Siqueira asked for a plot of land in Curitiba,[81] claiming that she needed fields for her cattle; women farmers stood security for the transport of herds of oxen.[82]

Widows were accountable for debts contracted by their husbands, and the Exchequer usually collected them without any special consideration.[83] It was not unusual for widows to inherit large or medium-sized firms: Widow Rezende and sons, Widow Monteiro and family ...

When they got into difficulties with maintaining their lands, they would sell their farms, and move to the city and its vicinities with their children, where they would invest in working slaves, country homes with orchards and tenement houses. In São Paulo some of the women farm owners lived by selling off surpluses from their urban properties, which they did through their slaves, in the city streets.[84] In 1836, Mariana Roiz de Oliveira lived with her bailiff and his wife on a small farm in Penha (she was a white spinster of sixty-one), and she had twenty-two agricultural slaves; Caetana Toledo and her sisters, who were all in their eighties, lived with eighteen slaves and three household women servants in a house on the corner of Rua do Rosário, and they owned a property called the Casa Verde, which later became the name of a whole town district; Dona Gertrudes Galvão, the owner of a small landholding in Jaraguá, and of several properties, lived in the city with one of her sisters and her nephews, eighteen slaves, and a mulatta serving woman.[85]

The influence of all-powerful women usually came from the position of their families; social status and power were a help to strong, militant personalities, who were good at exercising local power, with all its risks and obstacles. However, it was as heads of families rather than as individuals that they became the targets of political persecutions. In Salvador in 1652 the widow of the superintendent Domingos Correa asked permission to move to Lisbon, because she was being persecuted by important people; threats were made against a widow property owner on the outskirts of the city; in São Paulo, honourable ladies were turned out of their houses, and protested directly to the Crown.[86]

Although by law they could not occupy public posts they could still exercise effective political power, or so documents emphasize; there they figure as witnesses in favour of a doctor who had been prosecuted by Franca e Horta, or involved in disputes between the authorities. In Bahia, Catarina Fogaça demanded the impeachment of a magistrate; in São Paulo, Inês Monteiro influenced the legal sentence on one of her sons, who was accused of murder, and even brought pressure to bear on the members of the Court of Appeal in Bahia.[87]

They may not have held administrative jobs personally, but as owners, proprietors and inheritors of jobs they were constantly intervening in public administration: Angela Siqueira led an armed mutiny, coming down from Santos with family members and foremen to secure the job of purveyor for her youngest son.[88] They could recommend and instal their sons and male members of their families in office, as bailiffs, treasurers and purveyors, as well as securing administrative benefits for their daughters. As widows, they received pensions from the Crown on account of their late husbands, and brought actions against the authorities.[89] In 1719, Isabel Faro was the owner of the post office in the district of São Paulo.[90]

There were frequent petitions from ladies involved in political matters. In Pernambuco, during the Mascates war, they sent angry protests to the Crown complaining of the fact that they had to remain in their homes, all alone, and face imminent danger of attack from the half-castes from Camarão or from Tumba-cumbês, while the men of their families were hidden in the bush . . .[91]

Highly regarded figures in local politics, they took part in conspiracies and spread information. On 20 October 1798 the Bishop of São Paulo, D. Matheus de Abreu Pereira, wrote to Dona Ana Leoniza de Abelho Fortes, a lady of influence in Sorocaba, asking her to make sure that what he told her would reach the ears of the governor as quickly as possible.[92]

The process of colonization valued white women, to the point of turning their image into the very fulcrum of the Portuguese social project of domination. This applied whether they were rural property owners, traders or played a part in the civil service of the Crown. They had strategic roles as procreators and as conveyors of property; within local government they appeared time and time again as heads of family alliances; as such they figured as mediators in the process of political organization between central and local powers.

The image of great ladies was stamped with the highest values in the ideology of power: purity of blood and their educating duties towards their children and even in training their slaves. They were adept at organizing home crafts, administering properties and arranging the marriages of their children. One can recall the exalted, maternal image in the lives of Frei Gaspar, Eusébio de Gusmão and Pedro Taques, and the privileged place filled in the literature of the time by the figure of the brave Josefa Carneiro Leão, or Nha Luisa, grandmother of the writer and memorialist Pedro Nava.[93]

Partly historical, partly allegorical, the stereotypes of the great ladies had an undeniable function in colonial society, in relation to conquest, interbreeding and settlement. In the heart of the formation of society, this myth of hegemony takes on a specific function in the city of São Paulo during the last century, in the midst of all the social tensions which arose from urbanization and which forced different ethnic elements to live together.

The beginnings of urbanization produced a population in which there was a predominance of poor women, whose precarious existence seemed to challenge the myth of the absent lady. Their world of struggle for a bare living was a faint echo of just those relationships of domination of the upper milieu: 88 per cent of the women who owned few slaves were white, as were about 60 per cent of the impoverished ladies who lived off 'the daily wages of their domestic servants'.

Nevertheless, in the margins of the ruling classes, they gravitated towards a world which was the exact opposite of seigneurial values. They lived alongside women neighbours who were of mixed race, dark-skinned, mulatta and freedwomen, who soon increased in number, either as domestic serving women, or as heads of mixed-race homes. Among them almost 11 per cent of the mulatta freedwomen had slaves, and 60 per cent kept domestic servants.[94] Among the heads of families who were black women on their own, just 3 per cent had slaves, which seemed to suggest a curious reversal of the colonial system. The other destitute women were the Indians, none of whom possessed slaves, and barely 1 per cent of whom lived with domestic servants.[95] The symbolic reversal of the white owner/black slave relations was numerically insignificant, but nevertheless suggestive of the fluidity created by the struggle for survival and the increase in the urban population of the city.[96]

The predominance of white, single mothers was another challenge to the myth of the absent lady: white women without a dowry did not marry or integrate into the aristocratic patterns of family organization. They usually lived in common law but legitimate (albeit unstable) marriages, which followed one another as the uncertainties of life dictated and they ended up by raising their children alone. Abandoned by absentee husbands, they moved in with other men, with whom they had illegitimate children: 'because of my human weakness, I had three children, Francisco, Benedita and Adelaide, who live with me, and I give them, in my poverty, the education that I possess.'[97]

There was an increase in poor women whom the social system was incapable of absorbing, and who only became part of the fringes of a slavery-based society. In a structural process of increasing poverty, they gradually filled the margins of the wretchedness of the beginnings of urbanization: it was an overwhelming historical tendency which threatened the myth of the absent lady with the spectre of its reversal.

FOUR

Ladies and Women Slaves at a Price

> I am turning brown,
> like a little Moorish girl,
> daughter of dark people.
>
> Rosalía de Castro,
> *Poesias* (trans.)

An increase can be discerned in the numbers of poor, white girls who tried to go about their lives hiding their poverty by concealing themselves beneath a secretive style of dressing, under large cloaks of black baize. Without dowry or marriage, some gave up their family names to live discreetly as kept women, using only their first names. Many of them were small-time owners of a few slaves:

> Joaquina Eugenia Alvim, a single woman of thirty-five, lived in Ifigênia, where she had a pottery and four slaves; Policena Joaquina, a white, married woman of twenty-four, lived all alone, north of the cathedral, with two slaves; 'the tenants below have a shoe shop'. . . . Dona Anna Freire, a white woman of sixty-three, lived with six unmarried sisters, a young, white servant girl and two slaves.[1]

The majority lived anonymously, as mistresses, single mothers, or illegitimate daughters, with names like

> Omciliana do Espírito Santo, with an absentee husband, and two single daughters of twenty-four and twenty-six, and only one slave girl; Escolástica Maria, a single mother of twenty-nine, with two children and three slave girls, north of the cathedral; Maria Madalena, a single, white girl of twenty-four, with a son of four and two slave girls, living in the north of the cathedral district.

They lived in rented houses, and could not even keep up the appearance of great ladies, barely integrating into the fringes of the ruling classes. There is a disturbing, persistent scrutiny of their lifestyle in the censuses: Policena Maria was a seamstress who lived in Ifigênia with two slave girls and grown-up children; Ana Joaquina, a single, white woman of thirty, who lived north of the cathedral, was a stallholder and had just one slave. Others had a few slaves, some rents and income. 'No decent means of survival' was the declaration made in the population census by the countrywomen of the outskirts of the town, who survived with few slaves and meagre means.[2]

Among the single women who were heads of families, an appreciable percentage, nearly 40 per cent of the total, possessed some slaves, and although they were not at all well off they were able to appear, if somewhat precariously, as the white owners of black slaves. They formed a heterogeneous, transitory group, for the revenue that they declared in the censuses was not enough to purchase new slaves.

They became slave owners through favours, donations and small shares of inheritances. In the record books there were frequent references to donations of slaves as marriage dowries;[3] in wills and lists of property of the deceased, slaves were donated as favours to poor female cousins and nieces who helped with domestic chores. It was customary to leave small sums of money, between 400$ and 40$000, to impoverished kinswomen, enough for the purchase of a few slaves, or occasionally for a house in the city.[4]

Many were older ladies, who lived off the remains of their husbands' estates, and by hiring out their slaves; with this, they kept themselves and their grown-up children and grandchildren and constituted extended households, which were completely out of keeping with the average urban home.[5] Other women, who were younger and kept as mistresses, would be given slaves as a present to mark the birth of a child, and this would guarantee a precarious but discreet form of survival.

> Manoela, thirty-one years old, a single mother of six small children, lived south of the cathedral, from her sewing and her stall, with three very young slaves; Benta Maria lived in Rua da Boa Vista, a twenty-six-year-old white woman, single mother of two very small children, with a slave of fifty; Maria Joana, thirty years old, also a single mother of two small children, had a grocery shop north of the cathedral, with an annual income of little more than 100$, and a slave girl Anna and her little daughter of ten.[6]

Those ladies with a few slaves constituted a whole hierarchy of well-off women in descending order, from aristocratic figures from established families to nameless concubines; most of them were white, many had one or two slaves, which were too expensive for the precarious situations of women rejected by destiny:

> Brandina, in the Rua da Boa Vista, was barely twenty years old; she was single and white, and lived with two dark-skinned servant girls and three slave girls who were in their early twenties; Theodora Maria Angélica, a single white girl of twenty-four, also lived alone, off her estate, with a servant girl of seventeen and a slave girl of twenty; Anna Luiza, a seamstress of twenty-nine, single, had two slave girls of twenty years of age.[7]

They fitted in as a whole with the general tendencies of urban slavery, which was largely made up of small proprietors, both in São Paulo and in the other towns and cities of colonial Brazil and of the Empire.[8]

Households with slaves were larger than normal, having on average 6.8 inhabitants per house.[9] According to statistics, women owners had 4.1 slaves per household in 1804, and 4.4 in 1836. In fact, most had fewer slaves than average, for in 1804, 60 per cent had only one or two slaves, rising to 65 per cent in 1836.[10]

The highest percentages of slaves and of poor free men and women were concentrated in the districts to the north and south of the cathedral. These too were the districts *par excellence* of women on their own.[11] It is interesting to note the peculiar phenomenon of co-existence and proximity between the wealthier houses, rented rooms and thatched huts, all mixed up and alongside each other.

In the city as a whole, the population was predominantly free, with a ratio of 70 per cent free to 30 per cent slaves; the same held in households of single women with few slaves, for the heads of these households were free, as were their dependants and their servant girls. Nevertheless, in some situations, the slaves outnumbered the rest and in the end predominated, because of their concentration within particular houses: in 1804 they constituted 53 per cent of the inhabitants of households with domestic help, and in 1836 at least 51 per cent.[12]

Because of the numerical concentrations of slaves, slavery was felt as an overwhelming presence, as much within households as in the urban area as a whole, where it both affected and defined everyday social relationships in general.

Small, local trade acted as a social link between domestic work and itinerant trade, creating its own connections and mediations between the sphere of household exploitation and the social dimensions of the street and the local market. It was not easy to distinguish the slave women working in itinerant trade from those in domestic service, since they alternated jobs, if the occasion demanded, or if the moods and whims of their mistresses so ruled.

One of the places in the city most frequented by slaves was the Misericórdia fountain, the only place where food could be bought in the whole cathedral area, and one of the most densely populated: 'And so day and night it was surrounded by people, the majority of them slaves, whose shouting could be heard from far away, when one passed by . . . In times of drought, when supplies were scarce, there was a daily ration, and very often conflict broke out, with the breaking of clay pots, which were the vessels generally used at that time for carrying water.'[13]

The stalls and little houses on Ladeira do Carmo, as well as the steps opposite the Rosário church, were also known as noisy places, where slaves gathered in groups: 'By night the stall would be lit by black wax tapers fastened to the edges of the selling trays, and the street cries for selling hot pine seeds, toasted peanuts, cooked yams and many other things would cause an uproar.'[14] They gathered in noisy, concentrated groups; the women vendors were obliged by law to proclaim what they were selling.[15] They would collect in bands by the bridges and in the flat lands alongside the river, where they washed their clothes; they were found in the familiar locations of the old São Paulo downtown area – on the Lorena bridge, next to Piques wall, at Zunega pond, in Ifigênia, on the edges of the rivers Tamanduateí, Anhangabaú and Tietê . . . or at the city rubbish dumps, near the Carmo pit, in Rua São José or the Acu bridge. Other meeting places were the small grocery shops throughout the city.[16]

In 1836 slaves represented well under half of the whole of the city's population, increasing only slightly around the middle of the century.[17] They never reached the point in São Paulo where they represented the levels of concentration and of demographic density occurring in the mining towns, where in the eighteenth century they represented 70 to 80 per cent of the urban population. In Salvador Bahia they constituted nearly 75 per cent of the urban population until the middle of the nineteenth century, and in Rio de Janeiro in 1821 about 46 per cent of the city's population.[18]

In spite of the fact that they did not exceed 30 per cent of the total population in São Paulo, they made their presence felt, for they would gather on the busiest bridges, and older people, like the Andradas, found it difficult to get used to Africans in the streets.[19]

Judging by the low annual income declared by a significant number of the small-time women owners of a few slaves, they must have faced growing difficulties in keeping their slaves. Incomes of 25$ to 50$

would seem insufficient for the outlay of 40$, which would be the approximate, annual cost of just one slave. It would be difficult to keep a female slave on only 50$ a year. These incomes, as they appeared in the censuses, were always a little imprecise, and one could not infer too much from such declarations. What is certain is that with 50$ to 100$ or even 200$ a year, they could occasionally keep one slave girl, but they would have difficulty buying one, even on credit. In 1836 the average price of a female slave would be 150$ to 300$; a male slave who had no trade and was about thirty years old would be 300$, and if he were skilled, 700$.[20]

The majority of the small-time women owners declared incomes of between 100$ and 300$, and there were plenty of indications that their living was precarious, and many of them lost the few slaves that they had. Even those who survived on the income from itinerant trade, which was one of the most lucrative sectors and where there was a greater number of wage-earning slaves, also felt the effects of a general process of impoverishment: between 1804 and 1836 the number of women owners in this sector diminished from 56 per cent to only 36 per cent.[21]

Of the women who owned between one and three slaves, 70 per cent had only women in their homes, or sometimes women and little Negro boys. The price of women slaves was always lower than that of men, who were more numerous and in greater demand, because they were also sought by the slave traders, the coffee plantation owners and the sugar mill owners. Within the slave population as a whole, it was the women slaves who were found in the households of small-time women owners, and this was also evidence of the lack of funds of women who were poorly off. Women spinners, for example, rarely possessed men slaves, and when they did, they were less-expensive, low-priced slaves.

Maria Joaquina, a spinner, lived in the Penha district with nine female slaves, two of them adult women: Benedita, who was mulatta and thirty-six years old, with a value of about 200$; and Beatriz, who was black, and thirty-five, and worth about 170$, together with six small children, ranging from one to eight years, who helped to turn the wheel for cleaning the cotton.[22]

Anna Roiz, the weaver, also lived in the Penha district, with two single daughters and seven slave women: two adults and five, tiny children; Joana, a black spinster of eighty, worth $24 (if as much as that), and Quitéria, twenty, worth about $210.[23]

There was usually an enormous disproportion in the declared incomes and the kinds of slaves kept by business people compared with women stallholders, the former being about ten times better off. In 1836, in the area north of the cathedral, a widow stallholder called Maria Joaquina lived with an unmarried daughter of thirty-one, earning 100$ a year, and with five slaves to the value of about 1,190$.

> Josefa, black, single, thirty years, 280$
> Vicencia, black, single, twenty-two years, 310$
> Benedito, mulatto, single, sixteen years, 480$
> Candida and Genoveva, five and two years, worth 100$ and 20$.[24]

South of the cathedral, two women 'lived off their activities' under the same roof: Anna Joaquina, with an income of barely 50$, had four slave girls, estimated at 340$:

> Benedita, black, single, ten years, 190$
> Francisca, black, single, eight years, 100$
> Bethina, black, four years, 30$
> Marcelina, black, one year 20$.[25]

Maria do Carmo, who shared the same house, had a small income of 50$, enough for the salary of a cook and some slaves:

> Luzia, black, married, sixty years, 40$
> José, fifty-nine years, 200$
> Francisca, mulatta, ten years, 200$
> Rosa, five years, 30$.[26]

Maria Joaquina, a single mother with two young daughters, all of them white, lived from her shop sales, north of the cathedral, on an annual income of 100$; she had four slave women, at an estimated value of 1,100$:

> Anna, black, single, forty-two years, 300$
> Benedita, mulatta, seven years, 100$
> Maria, black, single, seventeen years, 360$
> Gertrudes, black, twenty-six years, 340$.[27]

In wealthier households, there was a predominance of male wage-earning slaves, at higher value: D. Rita Maria de Almeida, south of the cathedral, had five slaves to the value of 2,370$, adding up to double those mentioned above:

> Francisco, black, fifty years, 210$
> Domingos, black, twenty-six years, 550$

José, black, twenty-four years, 550$
Francisco, black, twenty years, 530$
Felisberto, black, single, 530$.[28]

The majority of small proprietresses of slaves had jobs in the tertiary sector: a few of them owned small farms or businesses; half of them lived from hiring out the services of their slaves,[29] and the rest 'lived off their activities', which were related to local trade in one way or another, through selling odds and ends in the streets, or by acting as intermediaries in the distribution of foodstuffs. Out of a total of 941 slaves living in households of single women, nearly 318 were wage-earning slaves (34 per cent) in 1804; in the documents of 1836, the figures were 782 and 273 (35 per cent).[30]

Living off the daily earnings of one's slaves was a deep-rooted custom in the small towns of colonial Brazil, and it gradually intensified throughout the eighteenth century; it was a means of survival that was preferred by well-off widows and small civil servants in public administration, who hired out their skilled slaves at a high price, and thus alerted the interests of the tax authorities.

In 1768, the Morgado de Matheus criticized the custom of wage-earning slaves, as expensive, unreliable and inflationary: 'an official coming from Portugal soon becomes a Lord: he buys slaves, teaches them and gives them a trade, and ends up by collecting their daily wages'; these wages were too high; they raised the cost of labour and caused a chronic lack of manual labour, which made any construction enterprise or business proposition in the city very difficult.[31] According to him, buying slaves was the major investment of those with funds, and the fact that some businessmen facilitated the trade in slaves by selling on long-term credit brought about an increase of those people who lived off the daily wages of their skilled slaves. They were expensive because they were highly taxed and cost a great deal to maintain: 'all one's funds are invested in them, they eat and dress and eventually die, and the profit from their work . . . is unreliable.'[32]

At the height of the mining period, civil servants from Portugal, referring to a capitation tax on slaves, pointed to the disadvantages of having domestic women slaves instead of black women as slave vendors or gold washers, which was more lucrative: 'It is not fair that those who contribute to public wealth and use should be taxed more than those who are only concerned with the comfort of the individual.'[33]

Wage-earning slaves soon became a common sight in the towns and villages. In 1762, in Sabará, the delegate from a Lisbon firm could not manage to survive without working as a notary for the authority in charge of judicial collections, in addition to his job as a trader; even then, his salary was not enough to cover the cost of food, which was very high in the colony, and he was forced to resort to the expedient of buying two Mozambique negroes on credit, whom he hired out by the day as gold washers.[34] Even in the early years of the eighteenth century in Salvador, it was quite normal for minor civil servants in the Administrative Tribunal to cover their everyday expenses with several wage-earning slaves: 'one to cook for him, and look after the house; another to get water and firewood and all the other things he needed, and another to feed and look after his horse.'[35] Jorge Benci described the same situation amongst the Bahian women, who shared out money for domestic expenses among their wage-earning slave women, 'entrusting each one with her share: one of them must get flour or bread for the table, another meat or fish for the meal; this one must pay the house rentals, that one must get the oil for the lamp; and all of them must accept the job that falls to them and the price that is fixed.'[36] The Jesuit did not spare criticism of these ladies for surviving in this way, even maybe in the last resort prostituting their women slaves, and his recriminations were always associated with the ownership of wage-earning slave women.

Urbanization determined the social relations of work between slave women and their mistresses, weakening any sentimental or fundamental link that might have existed between them;[37] the rotation of jobs and the allocations of tasks by their mistresses, strictly observed in the house, compared with the relative freedom of selling in the streets, all contributed to this. Areas were defined which created a greater social distance between mistress and slave woman. They were tense relationships because of exploitation, and they were exacerbated by the difficulties in which the ladies themselves were living.

Wage-earning slaves worked to verbal contracts with their masters, away from the house, without any direct control or supervision. This was also true of women slaves, who were usually older and who lived alone in rented rooms by permission of their mistresses, keeping themselves and their children and grandchildren. Every week they would owe their mistress a certain stipulated amount, or, more commonly, the pay from four days, and would keep the rest for themselves.[38] It is interesting to note that a four-day week was a deep-rooted custom among African businesswomen from the west coast of Africa – from the Ivory Coast, the Gold Coast, Senegal and Dahomey.[39]

Washing clothes and streetselling were forms of work that were difficult to control; the supervision of domestic work, including that of women cooks and the black women spinners and seamstresses, was easier. In these cases, the price for hiring out could be agreed between proprietor and tenant, which was never the case when a slave was hired out by the job, or for a fee, as such.

These slaves had rented rooms in the minor alleys near the centre of São Paulo, where they gathered in slums 'of ill repute', in the Travessa da Conceição, the Beco do Inferno, Beco da Cachaça and Beco das Minas. North of the cathedral, on the first block, in the house of Ilma Maria, a white spinster of forty, 'there are a lot of tenants who do not want to give their names . . .'[40] In the Rua da Boa Vista and in the Cruz Preta, people noticed gatherings of black people, rooms being rented and meetings that constantly attracted the attention of the police. Many women owners let rooms to slaves in their own small houses, which became the principal nucleus for local trade in foodstuffs and a strategic centre for clandestine operations involving bulk buying, as well as the birthplace of the penny trade – closely watched by the police and tax authorities. It was the permanent tenants, small-time handlers of contraband, whom the town council wanted to remove in 1835.[41]

The majority of them were older women, above the average age of the slave population. Mostly they were single mothers, living with their children and grandchildren. In 1804 in the first district were registered several stallholders in charge of small stalls in the central streets of the city:

> Justa Maria do Rosário, single, black, forty years old, with four small children; Branca de Castro, single, black, fifty-six years old, with a daughter Rosa (single, thirty-two), and a granddaughter of nine, as well as a domestic maidservant of fifteen, also black. In 1836, Catarina, a native of the African West Coast, sixty-two, lived north of the cathedral, alone, selling odds and ends; south of the cathedral, also selling odds and ends, lived a mother and her daughter, both unmarried and black – Tereza, sixty years, and Francisca, twenty-five; another black woman, also Tereza, had a small shop in Rua da Boa Vista, where she lived alone at the age of forty, unmarried; Angela Maria, south of the cathedral, with her shop, was thirty-seven and a widow.[42]

They lived off their activities, from their businesses, as washerwomen, or selling from shops and trays, many of them mulattas, appearing by the score in the population records, as well-known figures in the city.

> At times, in the darkness of the night, a shape could be seen, carrying a fire above its head; from the street cry proclaiming hot pine seeds, one could tell that it was a black woman stallholder, who was carrying her pan of cooked pine seeds on a little stove, placed inside a wooden trough.[43]

Street trade and prostitution are aspects of town life which are closely related in the observations made by travellers and contemporaries, and that is even reinforced by the repeated need that the ladies felt to deny that they lived off the illicit dealings of their slave women. It is true that prostitution would take second place, and would be casual, simply used to complement the other money-making resources of the women slaves, who were washerwomen, businesswomen or vendors. It was a practice that was difficult to document, and which must have arisen from the relative freedom of movement of the wage-earning slave woman, since she frequently lived in rented rooms, possibly with a permanent companion, a slave of another owner, sometimes a freed-man. The formality of a religious ceremony, which was too expensive, made no sense in the everyday context of a slave's life, just as it made no sense for the majority of the population that was free but poor. Such a ceremony was the concern of the church and the ruling classes, and far removed from the usual practices of the population.[44]

In São Paulo, in the early decades of the nineteenth century, ladies took great care to declare that they lived 'from the honest living made from the daily wages of their slaves'. Such was the case of D. Pulcheria M. de Barros, a white widow of forty-one, who lived with her two little grandchildren to the south of the cathedral; she had an annual income of 100$, and lived off 'the honest earnings' of four wage-earning slave women and two negro boys, with an estimated value of 1,500$. Living in the same large house, with all the appearances of a kept woman, was Antonia Eufrosina, twenty-nine years old (with a sister who was also white and single, aged twenty-seven) and ten wage-earning slaves; she seemed to be in favour of her slave women reproducing, for half of her slaves were children:[45]

Caetana, black, single, fifty-nine years	40$
Luzia, black, single, twenty-four years	350$
Gertrudes, black, single, twenty-two years	350$
Theresa, black, single, nineteen years	360$
Benedito, black, single, nineteen years	500$
Firmina, five years	100$
Fortunato, three years	30$
João, eight years	100$
Maria, four years	60$
Felisberto, three years	30$

In the early process of urbanization, slavery in São Paulo did not seem to take on purely entrepreneurial features, or to be harnessed to the uses of gentlemen or for aristocratic ostentation: there were more wage-earning slaves, or slaves for hire, than there were in actual domestic service. A symptom of the general lack of funds?

In a few aristocratic homes, there was a clear differentiation in the census declaration between domestic slaves and those who were wage-earning. This was so in the case of Dona Gertrudes de Moura Lacerda (who lived in a large house with her sister), and also of the spinster sisters of the Casa Verde (Caetana, Rosa, Gertrudes and Maria Joaquina, who lived 'off their assets' in the Travessa do Colégio), who had eighteen wage-earning slaves and a few older ex-slave freedwomen as domestic servants. These were not, however, typical examples, for the latter sisters were landowners and owners of small farms, which was not the case with the majority of small women owners of a few slaves. Other businesswomen, with more than twenty slaves, such as Dona Maria Ignácia do Carmo, an inhabitant of Ifigênia, also established a clear difference between domestic slaves and those 'who belonged to the shop'. Slaves for domestic use were usually older blacks and mulattos, who were trained and integrated into the family customs.

Joana Emília is a characteristic example of a wealthier proprietress of a few slaves. She lived in the Rua da Boa Vista, with four small children, off the earnings of her ten slaves; these were an allotment of new slaves, with a good balance between men and women:[46]

Theresa, black, single, thirty years	350$
Delfina, black, single, twenty years	300$
Inocencia, black, single, fifty-one	120$
Antonia, black, single, twenty-one years	250$
Rosa, black, single, twenty years	250$
Germano, mulatta, single, nineteen years	550$
José, black, married, forty-one years	480$
Joaquim, black, single, sixty years	180$
Domingos, black, single, twenty-five	530$
Francisco, black, single, twenty-five	520$
	3,530$

She had no claim to any of the traditional names of old São Paulo stock, and was probably the kept mistress of a partner who was away, or only occasionally around. Another wealthy proprietress was Jesuína do Espírito Santo, a widow of fifty-one, who lived to the north of the cathedral, 'off her business'; although she was white and a slave owner, she had none of the characteristics of a great lady of the city either. Like Joana Emília, she possessed ten slaves, to the approximate value of 2,910$, which is a fair amount on the basis of the declarations in the 1836 census.

The cost of maintaining slaves in the city was a good deal less for women who owned farms on the outskirts of São Paulo, where the slaves could produce their own food instead of having to depend on the prices of local trade. The urban slave became more and more expensive as chronic deficiencies in supplies grew gradually worse. In the best of times, the expense of feeding and clothing slaves was not negligible.

The calculation of these expenses is, of course, unreliable, for we have to extract the figures from account books,[47] or from estimates of assets from the inventories of the period, with the assistance of official market tables, like those of Daniel Pedro Muller for 1836;[48] for obvious reasons, the prices of clandestine trade, which were probably lower, did not get documented.

In São Paulo in 1836, 100 grams of bacon would cost 20 réis; 250 grams of maize, 5 réis; 280 grams of manioc flour, 10 réis; 250 grams of beans, 15 réis.[49] A simple diet, close to the basic minimum, would cost between 50 and 100 réis a day, for one has to imagine that wage-earning slaves could not be so badly nourished as to make them inefficient. Food would work out at about 20$ per annum, probably going as high as 36$ (calculating on a basis of 100 réis per day).

During this same period, Jean-Baptiste Debret calculated that the minimum diet for slaves in Rio de Janeiro would cost between 80 and 120 réis a day.[50] J. J. Tschudi recorded the following prices in a sugar mill in Piracicaba in 1857: 100 grams of bacon were 80 réis; 250 grams of maize were 10 réis; 280 grams of manioc flour were 20 réis; and 250 grams of beans were 30 réis.[51] In Rio around 1860, Tschudi reported, they were already calculating at about $300 to $400 a day.[52]

As far as clothes were concerned, Tschudi tells us that slaves received three changes of clothing a year: for women there were three blouses and three skirts made of heavy cotton, plus a baize cloak, lined with cotton, a hat and a cap. The men would get three changes of shirt and trousers of woven cotton.[53]

We find the following prices in some inventories of the period:[54]

one cotton blouse	500 réis × 3	1$500
one calico skirt	240 réis	720 réis
one baize shawl or cloak	2$220	2$220
one cotton shirt	500 réis	1$500
one pair of cotton trousers	540 réis	2$560

The yearly outlay on clothing for women would be about 4$200 a year, and 4$060 for men. Adding together the outlay for food and clothing would give an average of 30$000 a year – as a minimum – for a man or woman slave in the 1830s, and it could easily rise to 40$ and over. A wage of about $200 a day, for four days a week, would only just cover the cost of 40$ a year!

From 1829 onwards, they would have to add to the cost of food and clothes that of fines and taxes, which were collected with relative rigour: hired slaves had to be properly registered; taxes were collected on craft work; there was a tithe on slaves occupied in labour on the small farms;[55] there were permits to be obtained for selling drinks, bread, foodstuffs and dry goods, and they doubled in 1829, then amounting to 3$200 a permit.[56]

Men slaves were hired out more easily and – with their trades of cobblers, carpenters, tailors and ironmongers – cost more; they would already possess a diploma, acquired through an examination in the presence of the authorities; they had to pay a fee to register, and a fine if they did not stick to the rules.[57] There were frequent references to them in the municipal records: Dona Angela Siqueira 'paid a sum of money for her slave, who acquired a trade diploma';[58] Dona Ann Eufrozina 'requests cobbler's tools for her slave';[59] in 1845 'the only official mason in the city was Ana Angélica's slave.'[60] There was an enormous difference between the wage for an apprentice and a master.

In 1836 the town council would pay $360 a day for a day-labourer slave; although it was difficult to establish an average, because the price varied almost indefinitely according to the degree of training, skill and the slave's disposition and temperament, the daily pay of artisan slaves ranged from $400 to $700 for skilled cobblers, with a little more for joiners, carpenters and tailors. The daily pay for strong slaves suitable for heavy transport work or itinerant selling was between $350 and $500.[61]

According to the observations of travellers, however, there was a preference for women as itinerant vendors, and this was perhaps the best-paid job for women among the black day-labourers: for a skilled cook or an able vendor, the daily pay varied from $250 to $500. In São Paulo the price was a little less than in Rio.[62] In 1847 the daily wage of a woman slave day-labourer belonging to Ferreira de Rezende was $400. However, the daily wages for more domestic jobs, which included housework and cooking, were much lower: washerwomen were paid between $100 and $200, and spinners and seamstresses usually the same, although these could reach $280 for spinners and $300 for seamstresses.[63]

Among the employers and owners of hired slaves there was a tacit agreement to respect the extra earnings of the slave, and once the slave had paid for his or her subsistence, the rest could eventually constitute savings, to go towards buying a dreamed-of enfranchisement.

In the cities and within the slave system as a whole, there would be a verbal agreement implying an indirect acknowledgement of the slave's extra earnings. In his memoirs, Ferreira de Rezende mentions the masters' endorsement of their slaves' savings, thanks to which they could drink brandy and smoke.[64] Police incidents served as a record of the importance that Sundays and feast days held for the slaves, for when the right to these holidays was denied them, they rebelled by absconding, as a way to guarantee their sacred terms of work and leisure, and then returned immediately to present themselves to their masters.[65] The Rio Branco law of 1871 (the 'law of the free womb') finally changed the slaves' right to savings into a legal reality: 'the slave who, by means of his savings, obtains the means to recompense his owner for his value, has the right to enfranchisement.'[66]

Small sums of 120 to 200 réis a week were essential for the slaves' survival, for this money formed the basis of their small clandestine trade, and constituted the initial contribution to their organizations in the community and groups of mutual help, like the religious lay brotherhoods of slaves.

A female slave who earned a daily wage of 200 réis would receive 1$400 a week, from which she would owe 800 réis to her mistress, who would get 40$000 a year from her slave. The latter, if she was single, would spend a minimum of 70 réis a day on her food, that is 490 réis a week. There would be 110 réis a week left over, and with that she could build up a savings fund for herself, little by little. This was a fairly distant prospect, and only became viable in the more exceptional cases of wage-earning slaves on a daily wage of over 400 réis.

The dream of enfranchisement would sometimes be realized by women slaves who had their keep provided, that is, bed and board, yet still had Sundays and feast days for themselves; these days, according to Rugendas and Ribeyrolles, would add up to more than a hundred a year.[67] The odd 200 réis every Sunday could amount to 10$000 a year.

Private savings meant the remote possibility of freedom, and in this sense the mistresses themselves exploited it as a form of discipline, when more direct supervision was impossible.

The custom of paying set contributions out of the income from their business, which they did regularly, was a familiar idea to the African women from Dahomey, who were used to paying back part of their earnings to collective organizations, which then gave them the credit they needed for buying in bulk.[68]

There was a special kind of tension in the relationships between wage-earning slaves and their masters, which resolved itself before it came to direct force, or violence, or even escape, without the authorities having to intervene very much. The rare interventions by the town council concerning slave wages were more concerned with interceding with the hirers, who were reluctant to pay the daily wages of the hired slaves.[69]

North American historiography of urban slavery has drawn a profile of an ephemeral institution in the cities, mostly represented by small-time owners, hardly compatible with the work of larger manufacturing institutions.[70] It tended to become uneconomical in Brazil after the abolition of the slave trade and the rise in food prices.[71]

The average price of a slave in his prime continued to rise from the middle of the eighteenth century, when it was estimated at an average of 55$, until 1836, when it was nearly ten times more – 500$; in 1870, at the height of inflation, it reached nearly 2,000$, before starting to fall in the 1880s.[72]

The crisis in urban slavery is a subject still to be fully explored. Apart from the inflation of slave prices brought about by the ban on the slave trade and by the coffee plantation boom, which competed with the city in its demand for manual labour (and this is well documented), there are other factors concerning the city that remain to be clarified. They involve the inflation of the slave's daily wage, the high prices of food-stuffs, the competition from the more lucrative sectors of domestic service and itinerant trade, and also competition for manual labour of freed men and women. The lack of more thorough studies and of specific information on urban slaves in São Paulo makes it difficult to analyse the peculiarities of slavery in the households of wealthy women owners.

The distribution of occupations in the free and slave population relating to the tertiary sector, which was privileged, merits more attention, and so do the remaining jobs in the city to do with primary produce, on small farms and urban clearings. Table 4.1 shows the concentration of slaves in households of women on their own. There were fewer slaves in the houses of seamstresses and women who dealt in home crafts; they tended to concentrate where there were more profitable and lucrative activities, and one can take their presence as a sure indication of the more prosperous sectors of the urban economy

Even before the 1850s, when the final process in the urban slavery crisis was beginning, there were already symptoms of the concentration of income and of slaves; in the city, mainly due to the prosperity of the coffee bourgeoisie, one could see a concurrent and parallel process of impoverishment, which slowly led to the disappearance of small-time women owners, and to an increase in the number of poor women without slaves. Between 1804 and 1836 there was a drop of about

Table 4.1 Number and percentage distribution of households of women on their own and of their slaves, by sector of activity, São Paulo, 1804 and 1836

Sector of activity	1804		1836	
	Households	*Slaves*	*Households*	*Slaves*
Primary	45 (6.7%)	210 (22.3%)	49 (8.3%)	123 (15.7%)
Secondary	306 (45.3%)	184 (19.6%)	195 (33.1%)	143 (18.3%)
Tertiary	302 (44.7%)	547 (58.1%)	342 (58.1%)	516 (66.0%)
Various	22 (3.3%)	0	3 (0.5%)	0
Total	675 (100%)	941 (100%)	589 (100%)	782 (100%)

Source: DAE, Maços, 1804 and 1836.

20 per cent in women owners who lived off home crafts; many seamstresses and spinners lost their slaves. The daily pay for slave women who were spinners, weavers and even seamstresses became uneconomical. Home crafts did not disappear from the city of São Paulo, but gradually began to occupy fewer slave women and a greater number of free women, some of whom had domestic servant girls.

The principal cause of stagnation was the competition from English goods, whose prices continued to fall after the period of independence. In the first half of the nineteenth century, there were only two attempts to open establishments producing textiles in the city of São Paulo; they were unsuccessful, employing a few dozen free women.[73] In the poorer homes, the slow, tiring, traditional techniques continued, spinning and weaving thick cloth for private and local consumption; they gradually decreased in importance.

In Rio de Janeiro, in the middle of the last century, the first sectors to be affected by the crisis caused by the increase in the daily wage of the slaves were precisely the workshops producing needlework, footwear and foodstuffs; after 1850, salaried freedmen began to replace the slaves.[74]

Relationships between impoverished women owners and their slave women, set against the background of urban slavery, were *sui generis*, and in households of single women they were in contrast with the city as a whole, mainly because women slaves predominated; this was at variance with the structural tendencies of the slave trade and slavery, which was on the whole predominantly masculine.[75]

Nearly 66 per cent of the slave women in households of small-time women owners were very young, between ten and fifteen years of age.

Table 4.2 Women heads of households with and without slaves in secondary sectors of activity, São Paulo, 1804 and 1836

	1804		1836	
Occupations	With slaves	Without slaves	With slaves	Without slaves
Seamstresses	105	75	40	74
Spinners	45	44	10	38
Weavers	7	3	3	4
Lacemakers	1	6	0	0
Embroiderers	1	0	0	0
China makers	0	17	2	17
Repairers	0	0	0	3
Winnowers	0	0	0	3
Quilt makers	0	0	1	0
Potters	0	1	1	1
Total	159	146	57	140
Percentage with slaves	52%		29%	

Source: DAE, Maços, 1804 and 1836.

They were cheaper and better adapted to the process of apprenticeship for domestic work and selling. These patterns of social contact between mistress and adolescent, the younger one being trained for more lucrative jobs, were often difficult and tense. The situation was reflected in advertisements: 'Who wants to buy a slave girl from Mozambique (13–14 years), already trained to cook, wash clothes and sell from a stall.'[76]

The need to make the slave women more profitable, and eventually to charge them part of their cost, made the relationships between the women slave owners and the slave women freer and less subject to vigilance and domestic control. The custom of hiring them by the day, or often by the month, or even the year, meant that they moved around from house to house. Slave women who were more highly trained, preferably between twenty and thirty years of age, were put to advantage in domestic jobs which were more difficult to control, like washing clothes or selling in the streets.

In order to define the social relationship of work between slaves and urban owners more clearly, it is important to have more frequent and more precise information concerning the actual profitability of the slaves: reliable facts about expenses, about how they affected the owners, and information about the conditions of hiring and the work regime. There are few facts available yet in the urban historiography of slavery. By reading carefully and critically what the women owners declared in the censuses, we can make a series of judgements and conjectures, but by their very nature they are hypothetical rather than definitive.

If we knew in what circumstances and with what frequency women owners delegated to slaves the cost of their own food and clothing, a hypothesis which seems plausible enough in view of the fairly precarious economic situation of those women owners who had few slaves, we would be able to document more clearly the nature of the social relations in small urban slavery. The actual lifestyle of the slaves still needs to be studied more comprehensively, looking at whether they lived on the lower ground floor, under the same roof as their owners, or whether they rented quarters in the city, or improvised shacks and huts at random. If they were married, did the woman and her partner share the same dwelling? According to a good many of the declarations of owners, we can infer that many of the slaves were married to slaves belonging to other people. Urban agglomeration facilitated different kinds of arrangements.

The percentage of slaves living in rented rooms, alone or with a family, did not show up clearly in the censuses of either 1804 or 1836. The town hall was already distributing orders in this respect in 1773;[77] Article 71 of the law of 1 October 1828 was aimed at controlling the formation of slums and forbade an excessive number of individuals in the same house.[78] One order, published in 1831, ruled that 'Nobody shall let a house or a room to slaves without the latter presenting a written permit from their masters, under threat of 4$ fine and two days in prison.'[79]

The circumstances of the slaves in the case of households headed by black or mulatta women were rarely made clear in the censuses. In 1804, Maria, who was the slave of Francisco de Barros, and who was an unmarried black woman of sixty, 'lived with the support of her master' in a little room with Isabel da Guiné, and they both kept animals for breeding, including eight horses; Angola, the slave belonging to Lieutenant Colonel M. da Silva Bueno, was an unmarried mulatta girl of thirty, and lived in the best of company, 'with the support given her by her master.'[80]

It did not seem to be unusual for slaves to live alone, at their own cost, or in rooms rented by their masters. Many of the black and mulatta women who were heads of households were washerwomen, sales clerks, owners of bars and small stores. There is a certain amount of doubt about whether they were slaves or freedwomen. In very few of the households – not more than five – were they clearly specified as free in the registers of 1836. In relation to the total number of households with slaves (including as slaves the black women stallholders and vendors), the percentage of slaves living independently in the city would be about 25 per cent in 1804 and 27 per cent in 1836.[81]

As far as female slaves in houses went, adolescents of ten to fifteen years old predominated, amounting to 30 to 35 per cent of domestic slaves. Looking at the total age pyramid of slaves living with their mistresses, ages were generally low, for half of the slaves were under thirty years of age.[82]

Numbers of slaves fall abruptly in the age group of those between twenty and twenty-five. This seems to testify to the wretched living conditions of young slaves in the middle part of their training period, and during their initiation into jobs. Compared with the strict vigilance of domestic work, the greater freedom of circulation and the relative independence made possible by a constant change of owners – whether because of resale when they had completed their initial phase of instruction, or because of location – was not necessarily a symptom of greater moderation in the institution in the urban context. On the contrary, the few facts available point to a high rate of mortality through disease, suicide and malnutrition. But this must remain an outline, a provisional view until there is more detailed study.

Taking the whole of the female slave population in the city of São Paulo in the 1836 census, the population declines from the age of thirty upwards, decreasing at about forty-five to fifty to about 22 per cent of the number of women slaves in the sixteen to twenty age band. Incidental information regarding women slaves in households of single women indicates that the decrease there is 16 per cent, which is still pronounced when compared with the free female population throughout the city, where the decrease is 8 per cent.[83]

It was commonplace to take in two or three women slaves for training, or to advertise small schools for teaching young girls domestic work. It was a hard apprenticeship, often made worse by the cultural differences in the case of black slave women who had recently arrived from Africa.[84] Incidents and cases involving maltreatment were hardly ever denounced in public, although the annals of colonial Brazil showed more than one outburst of violence in the records, mainly in the Acts of the Inquisition, involving ladies who were exasperated with the lack of discipline of their domestic maids.

From 1831 onwards, the weights and measures inspectors became responsible for investigating any ill-treatment of slaves in the city, as well as their usual collecting of taxes. Domestic slave women were always complaining of ill-treatment to the municipal judges. On the eve of abolition, the newspapers became more communicative about the suffering of domestic slave women: 'Ill-treated slave woman: Vitalina, the slave of . . . presented herself, horribly burned, with signs of recent ill-treatment, complaining that her mistress, Dona Brasilina had thrown a pot of boiling fat on to her back. The authority gave orders for the accused to be arrested.'[85]

The African women who disembarked after 1831 were arrested as clandestine cargo, and called the slaves of the nation. They remained in the custody of the government, belonging to various public administrative services; as such they were hired out to private individuals, by public auction, for lower prices than those paid for 'market' hirings.[86] In a circular of 23 September 1837 the provincial authorities were alerted to the case of two African women, who were on an estate in the colony of Santana, 'in mortal danger through the ill-treatment they have received'.[87] In August 1839 the case of Dona Ana Maria Francisca was registered in the office of the provincial department: the highest bidder for the services of an African freedwoman with two small children, she was returning her 'because she was very disobedient and badly behaved'.[88]

They often fled from the houses where they were serving, and ended up roaming the streets. On 6 October 1841 the Justice of the Peace for Santa Ifigênia announced that he had apprehended an 'African girl, a minor, wandering aimlessly around the streets.'[89] She had been bought at auction by one João Sertório, and had fled the house; the Justice was awaiting instructions as to what he should do with the young slave girl. On 2 January 1843 the death was recorded of an African woman, Quitéria, who worked in the orphanage, the Seminário das Educandas; another girl was sent immediately to replace her. The flight of the slave girl Jacinta was reported to the authorities in a letter dated 8 June 1846; she had also worked in the orphanage and she was arrested in January of 1847.[90]

There appeared to be a clear preference for daughters of Brazilian-born slave women, since they were already culturally adapted, and there were always advertisements for young, recently trained slave girls for sale: 'whoever wishes to buy a native-born slave girl of seventeen or eighteen years, who can wash, cook, starch, and do plain sewing . . .; a black girl who washes, starches, cooks and does all the housework, and a little sewing; a half-caste girl of nineteen; a slave girl who understands about cooking, washing, starching and can do some sewing . . .'[91]

In the hubbub of the streets, what predominated were the movements of the stevedores, the coming and going of slave women carrying garbage from the houses, or the characteristic sight of household slave women with clay pots on their heads, making for the few fountains in the city.[92]

It is not easy to build up a picture of the social cross-sections of urban slavery through the observations of travellers, since their descriptions were coloured with all possible shades of subjective meaning. The picturesqueness of the women vendors wearing cashmere turbans and coverings which range from jewellery to rags,[93] and of the half-naked slaves, seen in situations of wealth and comfort, appear side by side with the most wretched poverty, half-naked slave women, so poor that there was even legislation to prevent masters from allowing their slaves to beg on the streets.[94] The frequent descriptions of women vendors and washerwomen, surrounded by children, carrying newly born babies strapped to their backs with a cloth, exaggerate the situation. The birth rate, which was low even among the free population, was particularly low among women slaves, in spite of the fact that travellers often noticed the goodwill that existed between mistresses and the children of their slaves. In the households of single women, there was a general tendency for few children: an average of about 1.07 children per slave; 1.10 children per domestic servant; 1.65 per free dependent woman.[95]

Although it was less visible, and was kept quiet, violence also surfaced in the houses, sometimes amounting to scandalous crimes, which had their impact on a gossiping city; on 28 September 1841 a woman slave murdered her mistress with a dagger . . .[96]

John Luccock repeated the usual platitudes about wild, violent ladies with women slaves whom they tormented.[97] Flight was a desperate recourse, but one to which women slaves of impoverished ladies resorted with ever-increasing frequency. They appeared in newspaper announcements as having been apprehended in adjacent towns and returned to their owners:

> In July 1834, a slave girl was apprehended in Castro, fleeing from her mistress, Dona Anna Carneiro, in São Paulo; the Council of Justice sentenced her to 200 lashes, and to be returned forthwith to her mistress, who agreed to keep her in neck irons for the next four years.[98]

On 13 August 1834, Antonia and Teodora were returned to their owners in the Braz.[99] On 5 August there fled

> a black girl, by the name of Josefa, from Cabinda, about eighteen years old, small, very black skinned, widely spaced teeth, a thin nose, and with some

black markings of her country on her arms; she was wearing a sleeveless blouse made of thick material and a blue striped cotton skirt, which was rather worn, and a worn, blue woollen shawl. There will be a substantial reward for anybody who catches her and brings her back to Jogo da Bola street, no. 3.[100]

Urban slavery was always difficult because of its demographic concentration, becoming expensive and troubled in the face of the problems involved in supervising wage-earning slaves who circulated freely throughout the city.

The evident unrest in their lives was confirmed by police incidents, criminal lawsuits and press announcements. There were cases of drunkenness, street brawls and suicides. Joaquina, a forty-year-old black cook, born in Africa, committed suicide in prison on 31 May 1834; Quitéria Caetana, a black African woman of sixty, a troublemaker arrested on 6 July 1834 for brawling in the street, also committed suicide.[101] Several crimes of passion were evidence of the instability of the emotional life of the slaves, more easily affected and damaged by the slavery system, than was their community life, which no repressive measures managed to control. In 1834 the slave Elesbão murdered his lover out of jealousy;[102] in November 1830 the slave belonging to Dona Gertrudes de Moura Lacerda murdered the black girl, Maria;[103] in March 1823 the drowned body of a black woman, Catarina Lopes, was found floating in the river Tietê;[104] in the Taboão, the slave woman Gertrudes was questioned about the murder of her lover.[105] In the annals of events recorded by the authorities, petty theft was common, as were fights involving sharp weapons, and rioting at the fountains or in the streets.[106]

After 1831 there does not seem to have been an increase in the social safety of slave masters. There were cases of bailiffs being murdered while punishing slaves,[107] and cases were cited as warning examples, like that of two slaves who murdered Frei Antônio Inácio in 1858.[108] The exacerbation of tension involving slavery also manifested itself in some incidents causing scandal, when poor whites were punished as though they were slaves.[109]

Women under strain acted as catalysts amid the frustrations, and with their feelings and passions took on the tensions and conflicts of the social struggle they were involved in. Impoverished women complained of being treated by their companions as if they were slaves. In one divorce suit, a lady complained that her husband did not provide support for the house and children, 'starving them and not giving them anything to wear, and expecting A. to give him her daily wage, as if she were his slave'.[110] They accused their husbands of having mistresses, openly, at home, from among the slave women, which undermined their authority to such a point that they found themselves being mal-treated by their own slave women: 'the slave Joana threw insults at her, as she often did, and with such insolence that she even began to beat her.'[111] Finding themselves thrown into a process of increasing poverty and a downward social spiral, they had difficulty in handling the chauvinist social atmosphere in the town, feeling as if they were links that had changed direction in a long chain of beings, the victims of a system of domination which was in crisis.

The overthrow of slavery added to the structural crisis of impover-ishment of small-time women slave owners, which seemed to date from the beginning of urbanization; it was already becoming obvious in the 1830s, anticipating by half a century the final crisis in urban slavery, which caught them all in full decline.[112]

Before the middle of the last century, law suits and quarrels involving women who were in debt, or reluctant to pay their creditors, were already a common occurrence. In 1832 the council took out a law suit against Joana de Mello, who owed three months' rent at 6 Ladeira do Carmo; it had been agreed at 14$ a month, but, it was discovered, she did not have a cent to her name. In another case in point, Gertrudes Teresa had a room in the city which she had rented for her wage-earning slave, but she did not have the money to pay tax on her own house, an urban tithe which was collected from property owners.[113]

Some women owners of slaves who were unruly became deep in debt over fines and taxes collected for the feeding of imprisoned slaves. Some of them were eventually put in jail themselves. After the constitu-tion of 1824, the punishment of slaves became the responsibility of the council, and they were kept in a 'back-breaker' urban farmhouse for this purpose.[114] In 1835 the council decided to allow a temporary release of those slaves whose owners did not have the means to pay the daily amount for their maintenance. In that same year, Dona Escolás-tica Franca de Oliveira got into trouble with the town council because she did not have the money to pay the expenses of an imprisoned slave.[115] In 1843 another woman owner, Dona Maria Policena Pinto, ran up a debt of more than 80$ on account of a slave who had been put in prison months before, for a more serious crime. In the face of the insistence of the authorities, she ended up by giving up her slave and handing him over to her creditors.[116]

The tensions which insecurity and violence produced between the urban community and the slave population did not abate at all until the last quarter of the nineteenth century. The first symptoms of this crisis had already made themselves felt in the 1850s, when price inflation threatened to make urban slaves uneconomic, especially for small-time women owners who were not very well-off and were finding themselves poorer and poorer by the day. Not only did the purchase price rise, but so also did the daily wage and the hiring cost of the slave, to the point of favouring the competition from free labour. It became gradually more difficult to keep slaves, who seemed to be getting more and more undisciplined in relation to their owners and the police authorities of the city.

The inflation of prices of essential commodities was a decisive factor in the vicissitudes of urban slavery. In his memoirs, Ferreira de Rezende notes the high price of bacon, which went up from 85 réis to 800 réis, or even 1$000, and never came down to less than 400 réis a pound.[117] Municipal and provincial taxes were also a decisive factor in the growing difficulty of maintaining slaves in the city. On top of the tax surcharge there was the demand for manual labour from the plantations in the interior. In 1871 a tax of 200$ was collected on every slave who came from outside the city,[118] and the duty on every contract reached the price of 1$500; in 1880, 2$ was due for every transfer of ownership; in 1884 the annual tax on a slave was 5$, whereas two rural slaves scarcely earned 3$.[119]

The fact is that the slave population of São Paulo diminished between 1854 and 1887 from 28 per cent of the total population to less than 9 per cent.[120] Fines, taxes and the high price of food made women slaves so expensive that the vendors and stallholders were slowly replaced by freedwomen and free women. Municipal orders and taxes made the expenses of the impoverished women owners even heavier.

The names of women slaves appeared very frequently in the registers of municipal fines, the vast majority of them because they were involved in minor street trade, selling foodstuffs without a fixed price, or monopoly goods without the necessary permits, licences or taxes: Mariana . . . was selling salt without a permit; Joana sold meat without a licence.[121] Women slaves from the properties of small farmers on the outskirts of the town were distributing the goods straight from the fields where they worked, without paying the due taxes.

The accusations were continuous, and the competition that the street vendors represented for the established taverns and shops was felt the more deeply because the latter were overloaded with taxes which they had great difficulty in avoiding.[122] Accusations were made against women slaves who bought up fish in bulk on the highways, or bacon not in the small cottages of the local market.[123] Added to this, they were constantly watched by the weights and measures inspectors, who came to check their weights and to make sure that the stall was well swept and clean.[124] Other offences for which they were fined included not describing their wares properly, hiding their faces with dark cloaks or capes, throwing rubbish from their houses where it was forbidden, and hanging out clothes on the bridge railings, which was not allowed.[125]

In 1869 the slave Engrácia Maria was put in prison and fined for selling dry goods without a licence.[126] Between 1834 and 1871 there were municipal orders that made it difficult for slaves in itinerant trade to circulate freely; they were repeatedly prohibited from selling without tickets and express permissions from their owners, with the fine rising to more than 30$ in 1871. There were also orders which forbade slaves from being in the street after curfew. They needed passports and safe-conducts in order to be able to circulate, sell, buy, rent rooms ... In 1870 the authorities went as far as to impose a fine on poverty-stricken slaves who were badly dressed or in rags, and on slaves who brawled in the central streets of the city, or shouted obscenities.[127]

There was a continual increase in slaves who ran away or became involved in criminal offences, which became more and more violent and deliberate. In 1874 a slave who had been sheltered for eleven months on the outskirts of the city was thrown into prison.[128]

Within the limits and confines of the ruling classes, intermediate social figures began to emerge in the initial process of urbanization, constituting the lower echelons of society. In their period, they could be seen as a great hierarchical chain of beings, each dependent on the others for their protection and needs: impoverished ex-owners, ladies who lived off the begging of their slaves, ex-slaves who in their turn became small owners, slaves with domestic servants. These were the social figures who were sustained by small-time trade, a trade boosted and consolidated by the urban crisis of slavery-based society.[129]

FIVE

Slaves and Freedwomen Vendors

Zoio que tanto vio.
Zi boca que tanto falô.
Zi boca que tanto zi comeo e zi bebeo.
Zi corpo que tanto trabaiô.
Zi perna que tanto andô . . .

(Yo eyes dat done look so much.
Yo mouth dat done talk so much.
Yo mouth dat done eat and drink so much.
Yo body dat done work so much.
Yo legs dat done walk so much . . .)

From Antonio Egidio Martins,
São Paulo Antigo

The chain of social contacts between the slaves, the places where they met and from where they circulated information, centred around their small, clandestine trade. Regulations, decrees and laws which were issued against this trade were not always easy to put into full effect.[1] Many of these repressive measures focused in particular on the activities of slave women streetsellers, and on the important role that they played in the community life of the slaves.

Basically, the slaves' small trade was devoted to supplying their own people with essential commodities, as well as brandy and tobacco, all at more accessible prices. Apart from the clandestine element involved in the transfer of commodities away from legally organized business, the inhabitants of the city were alarmed by the contact that was established between the escaped maroon slaves and the fugitive Negro slave women – since the beginnings of slavery, they had gone into hiding on the outskirts of the city, in the valleys of Anhangabaú, Bexiga and Pinheiros, in Santo Amaro, and in the stretches of thicket which were to be found everywhere between the urbanized areas.[2]

Between house and street there was a continuous unfolding of mutual dependencies, interlaced and interwoven in such a way that one could not be distinguished from the other. Along with the incipient process of urbanization, the private and public domains became entangled in such a way that the fundamental property ties between the lady of the house and her women slaves gradually weakened with the practice of local trade. The social relations of local trade came finally to reflect the interdependence of those who joined forces on the fringes of the ruling classes: impoverished free women, slaves and freedwomen.

In itinerant trade, salaried slaves, who were hired out or who took their turn in the domestic service of their women owners, coexisted with freedmen and poor whites, country workers and peasants who gravitated towards the small cottages marketplace and to the access roads to the city's bridges. In the streets, involved in the fights over the most strategic spots, was the trade from those selling from trays for the kitchens of the rich; these in turn mingled with the poorest kind of trade, which consisted of basic foodstuffs gathered in the environs of the town – roasted pine seeds, herbs, fish, jaboticaba fruit, yams, maize, tobacco plants, herbal and ash soap . . . In street trade, not everything pertained to the sphere of the cookery books of needy ladies.

Slave stallwomen, selling tit-bits and biscuits, mingled with country-women street vendors (free women, poor whites and freedwomen of mixed race), who sold sugar cane juice, iced maize juice, female sauba ants and fish.[3] Their survival depended on different focal points for the organization and daily circulation of this clandestine trade, and slaves and freedmen, poor whites and enfranchised slaves were all a part of it.

In addition to the other forms of street trade, there was the penny trade, run mostly by slaves, which usually took place at night, after eight o'clock and dealt in brandy, tobacco, rue, chickens, knives, candles, pipes and clay statuettes.[4]

As a contemporary observer, Vieira Bueno was diligent in drawing attention to the coexistence in the streets of the city between local countrywomen selling from trays and the African sellers. In fact, the consumption of native Brazilian Indian dishes (studied by Sérgio Buarque de Holanda) still persisted, after going through a slow process of Africanization, from the end of the eighteenth century and the early decades of the nineteenth century: on the selling trays and the paniers of the street vendors there was a selection of old maize bread, maize flour cakes, different corn rolls, salted meat dishes, cooked pine seeds and yams, couscous with fish from the river Tietê, fish wrapped in leaves, maize flour pies, pieces of pumpkin purée, peanuts toasted with cumari pepper and salt, manioc flour biscuits of Portuguese origin, from the first exploring and trading expeditions by the *bandeiras* into the Indian terri-tories, and sweet cider and peanuts with mascavo sugar.[5]

The urbanizing area, covered with thickets and places for hunting and fishing, was favourable for gathering foodstuffs and for finding casual subsistence based on natural local goods, and it soon became possible for the slaves to learn native Indian techniques for acquiring delicacies from the local woods and the rivers. At the same time they also gained the necessary geographical knowledge which made it possible for them to hide, flee and take refuge.

The relative indifference of the authorities, and even of the more prosperous merchants, towards women slaves, who were of less com-mercial value, indirectly helped them to play their part within their small community.

Attached by strong and complicated personal ties linking them to their women owners, the slave women re-established their primitive bonds beyond the limits of the household, through the development of those social relationships which were an integral part of the itinerant street trade. They eventually created an intense community life, con-cealing it so resolutely that it was able to survive, finally restoring a social dimension to their existence which the slave trade had taken away.

Women slaves had a role of vital importance in this process of both cultural adaptation and solidarity: the family of single women helped to replace and renew the cult of their ancestors,[6] which in its turn launched the bases of a new social coexistence among the slaves. African cultural traditions gave women the tasks of providing food and distributing essential commodities, and the impoverished small-time women proprietors reaped the benefits of such talents and skills of their slave women.

Living traces of African customs could be seen in the practice of street trading, where, between 1830 and 1850, the majority of women who were taken on were slave women who had recently been released from slavery, and were deep in the process of cultural adaptation. It is significant that among the dialects of the west coast of Africa, there was a clear difference between the terms that indicated the act of selling and those that conveyed profiteering.[7] The reputation of black women from the African Sudan reached São Paulo, and spread to Beco das Minas, later known as Rua 11 de Agosto, which was a meeting point for slaves of Sudanese origin and where there must have been a house for Muslim worship. Travellers helped to celebrate the street-selling talents of black women from the African Sudan, as well as those from Dahomey, Nigeria, Senegal and the Congo. Though far from constituting a majority, they entered the port of Rio de Janeiro in appreciable numbers, where they were preferred as hired slave women vendors, since they adapted poorly to more domestic tasks.[8]

Documentation concerning the origins of women slaves is complicated, widely scattered and very fragmented, because of the prevalence of smuggling, which the authorities attempted to control in a conventional sense from 1831 onwards, and more severely after 1850. According to newspaper advertisements and to rare manuscript censuses in the São Paulo archive distinguishing between the origins of the slaves, there was a preponderance of slave women from Angola and Mozambique, of the Bantu group, who incidentally also dealt in street and market trading in their own places of origin, selling foodstuffs and basic commodities.[9] There were also trade practices from Dahomey and the Congo, of the Muslim slave women, mainly Yorubas, who supplemented their domestic work with streetselling and with small stalls where they worked at night.[10]

On the west coast of Africa, small trade was essentially a female business. By buying basic goods in bulk and reselling them, these women were guaranteed important social roles, and within this sphere of their own they acquired independence from men and, if not prestige, certainly the role of thrifty provider and of organizer of the circulation of foodstuffs. Apart from its economic function, this trade also had a social and religious significance, tightening the community bonds and even resembling the tribal cult of their dead ancestors.[11] For men, the principal areas of activity were linked to war and to trading in gold, livestock, slaves, monkey skins, and later, through the Europeans, to the export market. Even when African women were married and could rely on their husbands' tribal networks as well as their lands – which they had to till – they were still used to having to support themselves and their children on their own dowry, and so remained financially independent, even after marriage.[12]

Slavery by its very nature represents cultural uprooting and disruption, and it is therefore a system incompatible with traditions, undermining ethnic customs and native heritage. A regime of forced labour meant breaking with a social way of life, with the religion of one's ancestors, with the tribe, with community life and one's blood relations.[13] The African woman slave in São Paulo did not lead a daily life which was dictated by or inherited through the customs of her people, but went through a brutal process of cultural adaptation and the apprenticeship of new trades, and she had to create anew all fundamental social ties and relationships in the community.

The basis of community contact among the slaves was barter, which extended, at a second stage, to the rituals (of cooption) of religious fraternities. In the streets of the city, barter in kind alternated with trading for money, and took on a character which transcended the purely economic. It acquired all the ceremonial significance of a tribal ritual: barter implied reciprocity, and this was especially so with the barter of prestigious goods (brandy, tobacco), or commodities with magical or religious significance (herbs, cockerels). It established new social links between the buyers and the sellers, strangers to each other, people uprooted from their lands, and this small trading of theirs strengthened and perpetuated those links.

The practice of street trading by slaves and the enfranchised community, with the possible collusion of the white owners of small grocery shops, inns and food stores, elicited frequent complaints, and the law tried to repress it, not only on the assumption that there were clandestine sales going on, for these were an accepted fact, but because of the aggravating element (according to repeated complaints) of having to deal with a trade in stolen goods.[14]

Since the sixteenth century, crude subsistence trade among slaves had been an established custom of slavery in the sugar mills of the coastal regions of Pernambuco and Bahia: it arose from the custom the owners had of leaving their slaves' nourishment up to their own efforts and permitting them to keep Sundays and holy days for their own subsistence trade. At the end of the eighteenth century, during a period of famine and shortage brought about by the cyclical crises in the fortunes of sugar, slaves who had rebelled at a sugar mill in the Bahian region made demands that confirmed the existence of this local form of barter. They wanted to increase these subsistence activities and demanded a greater number of days off in order to do so, as well as canoes for the transport of their small surpluses.[15]

It is not especially useful to examine the origins of this practice among the slaves, since syncretism and improvisation were basic elements of slavery, which was constantly being replenished by the traffic in new slaves. Customs from Dahomey and of Muslim slaves in general were adopted generally and transmitted throughout the different ethnic groups of slaves. Slaves from different countries and of different languages, living together, established for themselves the practices of solidarity and of syncretism studied by Roger Bastide.[16]

The street trade run by slaves in the city of São Paulo was a melting pot of the most diverse cultural assimilations and customs. On the fringes of the coffee economy, the town housed the leftovers from the slave trade intended for the coffee plantations, and, after 1850, the community of Brazilian-born slaves of different origins, who were soon joined by the interprovincial traffic bringing slaves from Rio and mainly from the north of the country. In São Paulo, local business merged with the community life of the slaves in an active process of urban accommodation, in which the native Indian barter goods were traded side by side with African 'quitandas' (barter goods) from Bahia. The ceremonies that formed the background of the backwoodsmen, voodooism and the rites practised by the slaves from Rio, all ended up by merging in the São Paulo fetishist ceremony, described by Bastide as 'a moving encounter of all the forces of magic in the world'.[17]

It is equally difficult to unravel and distinguish the roles played by slave women vendors in the service of their owners from those directed towards the needs of the slaves themselves – as quack healers and religious leaders. We have a record of the words used by the slave women accompanying the funerals of poor women stallholders, along with song and dance, in the Rosário dos Pretos church, from 1827 onwards:

> Yo eyes dat done look so much.
> Yo mouth dat done talk so much.
> Yo mouth dat done eat and drink so much.
> Yo body dat done work so much.
> Yo legs dat done walk so much . . .[18]

The concern of the older slave women and freedwomen to ensure a funeral service for themselves and members of their families found its way into the written documentation of the ruling classes. The fear of 'being left behind' as ghosts, which was clear in their wills, was consolidated in the 'mass for the deceased'.[19] The funeral ceremonies were led by the slave women or the freedwomen themselves, acting as intermediaries between the world of the living and that of the dead; in this capacity, they washed the bodies of the dead slave women, prayed and interceded in their passage to the kingdom of the dead, thus assuring that they would not be left to wander about as 'souls in torment' for lack of the proper rituals.

Kátia Queiroz Mattoso transcribed the words of an old stallholder, an African woman from the coast of the Sudan, who died in Salvador in 1805. Damiana Vieira belonged to seven different guilds, and her will showed the power that the community links of small itinerant trade were assuming. She ordered masses to be said for her dead husband, for her daughter, who had also died, and even for 'the souls of those people with whom I did business, buying and selling'[20] – more likely to be slaves and freedmen than people from the world of gentlefolk or landowners.

The obsession with funerals is characteristic of the wills and testaments of ex-slaves; it would appear that they saw an opportunity of begging for a fitting funeral in their will: 'and I appeal to National Justice to give this document full validity, bearing in mind the state of my wretchedness.'[21] In 1791, Josefa de Souza Ribeiro expressed the same anxiety in her will:

> For the love of God, and out of charity, do me this favour, because I have been too poor to allow for this occasion, and have not had enough money to pay for a funeral, or to make provision for my soul, and for this I ask again, and I beg you to have my body placed in a sepulchre, and for a few prayers to be said for the salvation of my soul, as you consider fit.[22]

The petitions that appear in wills are for funerals and masses, for half a chapel or two chapels, all dictated in a hurry before dying.[23] Those older slave women and freedwomen who had standing in the community could be sure of offerings and rituals, and could also rely on the religious organization of the brotherhoods of mulatto and black people, which guaranteed them a place beneath the church floor.[24]

The training and expertise of the wage-earning women vendors, which guaranteed a living for their mistresses, also developed in a pattern peculiar to the slave women themselves. Unmarried grandmothers and mothers supported their families, living in rented rooms all over the city, mainly in the area of the cathedral; as slaves, they enjoyed the confidence of their mistresses, who frequently ended up by giving them their freedom; and then they also enjoyed prestige and influence among other slaves, becoming leaders of their social and religious community. During their daily routine of work and leisure, they alternated between the strategic spots for doing itinerant trade, and 'special places' for the magical and religious intensity of their improvised cults. They acquired a reputation as quacks and sorceresses; Maria D'Aruanda and Mother Conga became well known in the city. The authorities looked on them with suspicion, and they were persecuted as 'slave rousers'.[25]

The practice of any kind of community ritual by the slaves was initially only controlled through the (necessary) tolerance of their masters. In the towns and cities, however, it started to take on features which evoked repressive legislation. But the authorities never managed to get the better of this secret, clandestine element, which was a vital part of the life of the slaves.

Since the early presence of African slaves in São Paulo, clandestine trade had been associated with the banditry that existed in the city, and as such was repressed on the grounds that it was a way of trading in stolen goods. In 1720 orders were implemented from the start against the misappropriation and the falsification of gold, and the sale of mercury dichloride (a corrosive agent of gold) and of camphor was forbidden among the blacks.[26] As time passed, repression was limited to the stealing of cattle and the sale of leather by the slaves.[27] Banditry involved others besides escaped slaves: the documents speak of vagrants of mixed race, bastards and mulattos living in the Pari and the brushwood around the city.[28]

In 1783 an attack was organized on a hiding place for maroon slaves, at the farm belonging to the deceased Catarina Correia.[29] From this period onwards, there are constant references in municipal documents to the salaries and the appointments of official slave-catchers, who were responsible for repressing and keeping watch over the slave refuges in the urban area. In 1831, the council ordered the closing of a passage between Anhangabaú creek and the Bexiga 'on whose banks thieves and escaped slaves had sheltered'.[30] The residents were told to cut down the sedge, which grew very high in the city squares, so that they could not serve as hiding places for slaves who were escaping by night.[31] The council repeatedly produced orders forbidding slaves from going around armed with sticks or sharp weapons;[32] only wood-cutters were allowed to carry a hatchet and scythe.[33]

The order of 17 November 1832, one of many, forbade the game of *capoeira*: 'Concealed in the sleeve of their jacket, or in their trouser leg, they carry a small stick, in which is hidden a kind of dagger.'[34] The authorities took precautions against any kind of get-together, such as at the fountains, where brawls and rioting might start, or near the Rosário church, in the Largo da Misericórdia,[35] where the women used to meet at night. In February 1832 they forbade houses or rooms to be let in the Rua da Cruz Preta 'to slaves and vagrants, who gathered on Sundays and Saints' Days with mischief in mind, causing a scandal by their debauched meetings and their drum-playing ceremonies'.[36] They made it difficult for the slaves to have any kind of festival, including religious ones, like those in honour of São Francisco, of the Rosário and of São Benedito, which were organized by the brotherhoods; they now required formal petitions and special permits.[37] They forbade meetings from taking place, or any of the traditional festivals, like Carnival or the Scorning of Judas.[38]

A careful watch was kept on the lodges and the gambling houses, like 'the one in the aforementioned area of the river Anhangabaú'.[39] From 1742 on, the council periodically confirmed the right of the slave-catchers to shoot to kill.[40] In 1835 they tried to throw some slaves out of some rented rooms in the market of small cottages officially reserved by the municipal authorities for their commerce, accusing them of dealing in contraband food.[41]

The clandestine trade of the slaves was always a favourite target for the authorities, who associated it with the repeated assaults against farmers on the roads and on the estates around the city, and even with the burglaries of the storehouses; the sporadic, petty thefts of food-stuffs and, most often, of breeding animals (cattle, pigs and hens) were attributed to the assaults of fugitive slaves who came from their hiding places (quilombos) in the vicinity.[42] Legislation also kept the spread of clandestine shops, lodges and bars for the slaves under careful supervision. Legal action was constantly being taken against the setting up of taverns and bars without licences;[43] taxes were regularly increased on the consumption of locally made brandy.[44] In 1808, Pedro de Godoy Leite was arrested, fined and definitively barred from 'running a public shop in this city' by the Justice of the Peace, because 'the culprit must be considered the cause of those disturbances, by turning his house and shop into a gambling house, and allowing in all kinds of undesirable people, like negroes and black slave women; he allowed continual revelry, especially at night, which greatly disturbed the neighbourhood, and he refused to desist, however many warnings he received.'[45]

In 1809, the authorities made a new attack on

> the evil habit of grog shops, which stay open at nights till after hours, selling drinks to anyone who wants to buy them, ending up in quarrelling and injuries, and sometimes resulting in death; there are also black women stall-holders selling in the streets after hours; similarly there are black grass-cutters, selling grass for the horses in the same way ... We order that from the moment of this publication forthwith, as soon as it strikes nine o'clock at night, all the aforementioned drinking houses must close, and all black women and men selling odds and ends should go home.[46]

There was an increase in repressive orders and laws against the slave women who sold from trays in the first decades of the gold boom. After 1728 they were seen as dangerous elements in Minas, given the freedom with which they circulated through the mining areas, going in and out of the camps, possibly smuggling gold, and carrying food and information to the black women slaves in hiding.[47] In 1719, referring to a general threat of a slave uprising, the Count of Assumar cited the slave women and the black freedwomen as occasional connecting links in a conspiracy.[48] In São Paulo, the authorities tried to limit the movements of the black women vendors, conscious of the danger that lay in the contacts among the slaves, especially escaped slaves: one measure after another was taken to forbid them from leaving the city 'beyond the bridges',[49] and their shops were closed after six, seven or nine o'clock.[50] These orders concerning closing hours were aimed at preventing the nightly gatherings of slaves in the clandestine storehouses and the grog shops, but proved ineffective and impossible to put into practice.[51]

The women were often accused of being accomplices in the attacks by slaves against the town's small cottages market, as well as in the misappropriation of farm produce and foodstuffs on their way along the main access roads into the city: 'the negroes persist in their insolence, on account of which provisions of flour, beans, bacon and poultry are in short supply, as well as many other things that are needed in the city: and recently they have invaded some of the houses on the outskirts of the city, whose tenants, not having the power to defend themselves, were robbed and ruined; there is the possibility that this kind of liberty will lead to even further outrage, possibly against the wives and children of wretched country workers, who, because they are poor, cannot withstand the violence of so many negroes together, all armed.'[52] According to the accusations, black slaves armed with stolen weapons not only carried out these attacks but misappropriated foodstuffs from the city market in order to hand them over immediately to the black women stallholders so they could sell them piecemeal and under cover.

It would probably have been in the interests of the merchant retailers to exaggerate the insecurity in the city and the scale of activity of clandestine trade at times when they found themselves in difficulties and under pressure. There were moments of acute crisis of provisions in the city, in particular in 1803, and again, years later, in 1828. On these occasions the authorities called on the help of the slave-catchers to guarantee the safe entry of foodstuffs into the city:

> in view of the extraordinary shortage of all foods in general which are needed to supply this city, it has been deemed necessary to place slave-catchers at the entrances to the city, to ensure that such foods can get through to the places they are destined for, for public trading; the aforementioned slave-catchers are to be under the direction of the weights and measures inspectors, each slave-catcher earning 160 réis a day, because they work for the welfare of the public.[53]

At the same time, the municipal authorities were taking measures against black women who were selling in the streets, by increasing fines and putting up both the taxes on the permits to sell and the specific weights and measures taxes on selling from stalls and trays. The women were obliged to proclaim aloud what they were selling, and were confined to certain fixed points in the city.[54] From 1831 onwards, the laws became more frequent and more severe. In 1836 they raised the tax on goods that circulated on the selling trays by a prohibitive 2$,[55] and in 1847 they tried to organize itinerant trade by limiting it to markets.[56]

Another symptom of the crisis concerning urban slaves was doubtless the increase in enfranchisement, especially among women – domestic and wage-earning slave women and street vendors. Those very coins which in the burial rituals of the slaves symbolically bought their passage to the hereafter put an end to the relationship between wage-earning slave women and their needy mistresses. Their daily wages and savings, hoarded by dint of hard work on Sundays and saints' days, those coins of survival and of leisure . . . all put together eventually bought them their enfranchisement, and so they moved out of slavery and into freedom. These were the coins of this shadowy economy at the start of urbanization, which encouraged the unofficial power of women slaves, welding the shifting links in the great chain of beings made up of impoverished owners, slave women, women hired out (left to economize their own savings), freedwomen and domestic maidservants.

The increase in mulatta women who were former slaves was viewed with suspicion, not only because of the prominent part they played in small urban trade, but also because they were the most likely links and means of contact with husbands and sons who were slaves, some of them on the run. Municipal orders were specifically directed against these women in the attempt to repress itinerant trade, and they repeatedly insisted on including all and every itinerant woman vendor, whether slaves or freedwomen.[57]

Black freedwomen never predominated in the population of São Paulo in the way they did in the small mining towns of Minas Gerais, especially in the period of decline at the beginning of the nineteenth century. There was, however, a significant presence of freedmen and women, mainly women, in the city of São Paulo in the middle of the last century.[58] In households of single women, the percentage of mulatta and coloured women had increased moderately between 1804 and 1836: mulatta women were more often heads of households, and black women were kept as domestic servants.[59]

Small-time women slave owners, faced with the rising costs of maintenance, resorted to the promise of enfranchisement as a means of disciplining their wage-earning slaves: by fixing their release at a price below the value of the slave women, they stimulated incentives and encouraged work paid by the job.

What is still needed is a more systematic history of the processes of enfranchisement in the city of São Paulo: glimpses into the documentation which is accessible would seem to confirm systematic research carried out in Salvador, Bahia, Campos, Rio de Janeiro and the mining cities.[60] The enfranchisement of women rather than men also predominated in São Paulo, mainly of vendors, but also of those in domestic service, concubines and prostitutes. Many of the enfranchisements were conditional and retained the former slave women in domestic service as maids in the households of impoverished women owners. However, black domestic maidservants and mulatta freedwomen were still linked by family or community ties to husbands and sons who were slaves, and they tried to liberate them in their turn and help them in their fight for freedom.[61]

Many of them were married to slaves, although they might not live under the same roof. In 1776 there was a reference in the council documents to Rita, a freedwoman, married to Sebastião, a slave belonging to Antonio Vaz de Oliveira;[62] in 1804, in Freguesia do Ó, Anna Joaquina 'was a domestic servant of Ignácio ... and married to the slave Agostinho, belonging to Captain Gabriel'.[63] The town hall periodically gave permission to mulatta freedwomen, like Anna da Costa, to build their own houses.[64] In 1835 the mulatta freedwoman Desidéria Rosa, who was married to João, a slave, lived in a little room in Ladeira do Carmo market, from which she begged them not to evict her.[65]

Freedwomen figured frequently in the police offensives which were made against the nocturnal meeting places for freed slaves:

A mulatta freedwoman was found in the postcoach which had come from the night revels that took place in the lands and brushwood belonging to Manuel Francisco de Britto ... and she proved to be a vagrant, an idler and a trouble-maker among slaves, and was given a term of eight days to try to find an honest occupation and was punished with an [exorbitant] fine of 15$, and the lodge where the revels took place was pulled down.[66]

Repression increased after 1834, when there were added rumours of conspiracy and revolt in different places in the interior; action was taken mainly against the grog shops and gambling houses belonging to whites or freedmen, and where slaves were allowed access: 'they set up gambling and drumming ceremonies in their houses, and allowed slaves to attend even during the hours for buying and selling in the shop.'[67]

Freedwomen were always being arrested and forced to promise a 'term of good behaviour' and to pay very heavy fines: 'Ignacia Alves de Siqueira and her three daughters, Francisca, Anna and Maria ... because they caused a scandal among the people, allowing gambling, drum ceremonies in their house and admitting slaves.'[68]

Written sources allow only the odd glimpse of the links of solidarity that bonded the slaves and the freedwomen. It is as difficult to find out about the way the slaves organized their lives as it is to find out about the freedmen, though travellers occasionally made a few sagacious remarks. Debret was quick to discern the importance of the work of the slave women vendors as arbiters in the religious fraternities of the slaves, and the way their activities increased and eventually included the collection of funds for mutual help, and especially for funerals.[69] Ribeyrolles caught sight of the strange manifestations of reverence and respect for companions in slavery which they showed to one another, signs of the importance which they assumed as magical figures, with superiority and power – something which was misunderstood by observers from the ruling classes.[70] Debret suggested this in his descriptions of household slave women, who showed their rank by the way they dressed; he discerns a certain hierarchy in the order in which they filed down the street, one after the other, as if there were hints of mystery and darkness at the limits of the authority of their mistresses, and also in their ambiguous meanderings, which were difficult to follow, but where a world of resistance and intense interaction among slave women came into view.

Women stallholders who were well off, slave women and freed-women vendors all took part in local trade, and brought to this penny trade all the intrigue of social intervention, which was a microcosm of the great chain of human beings in the social hierarchy of slavery. The preponderant presence of women was a peculiarity of the poorer sectors of the urban population, increasing as one descended in rank.

A considerable part of the militancy of Luís Gama, the black aboli-tionist who practised law, was closely connected to the chain of hier-archical links which made up the network of clandestine trade. He filed numerous lawsuits demanding the release from slavery of prostituted slave women, pointing out the legal precedents that existed from the previous century: in 1754, in the middle of the period of the Portuguese minister Pombal, a law forced any owner who prostituted his slave girl to resell her for one-third of her value.[71] Luís Gama took up the cause of the freedwomen stallholders when they were forbidden from selling in the central streets of the city. He himself wrote the petition they sent to the authorities in 1873 complaining about the competition from the immigrant Portuguese women, and asserting the historical rights they had acquired by practising itinerant trade in the city streets.[72] The militant side of abolition in 1888 brought a more systematic political character of organized protest to the crisis of slavery, which was now well advanced. As such, it superimposed itself on the structural movement of impoverishment which connected small urban trade with the crisis of impoverished women owners, the increase in enfranchisements, the insurrection among urban slaves, and the specific tensions relating to the spheres of poorer women, both free white and freed mulattas, in their struggle for survival.

SIX

The Local Community

> Alone I wove my linen,
> Alone I sowed my kitchen garden,
> And alone, I go to the hills for firewood,
> And alone, I watch it burn in the hearth,
> Not at the fountain, nor in the field,
> Thus will I pass away, with my burden.
> He will not come to help me up
> Nor to lay me down on the ground . . .
> The pot is boiling . . . my broth
> Alone I will sup.
>
> Rosalía de Castro, *Poesias* (trans.)

A suggestive aspect of the coexistence between free women and slave women in São Paulo lay in the tensions arising from economic decline and the encounter in the lower echelons of society of impoverished white women, ladies who were no longer ladies, ex-slave women still living in the shadow of domestic service, domestic serving women and mulatta women who had left the houses of their mistresses to set up their own households.

The majority of them, nearly 60 per cent of single women in the city of São Paulo in 1836, had no slaves. They were part of the process of the growth in the town and increased in number along with the poverty of the urban milieu, living an existence of mutual help within the neighbourhood and constituting both the supply and demand for the penny trade, of which they were the main agents. In spite of everything, slavery had an effect everywhere, and the proportion of mulatta and black women among the free female population gradually increased as a result.

In the more central districts of São Paulo in 1836, among the women who had no slaves, the percentages of white and non-white women almost balanced out: there were 172 whites, 136 mulattas and 28 blacks. The greatest concentration of non-white women, whether slaves or freedwomen, lay north of the cathedral. South of the cathedral square was a district of extreme social contrasts, where, under the protection of the wealthiest mansions belonging to traders and land-owners, opportunities arose for free women, mainly white, to take on service work: sewing at home either on commission or on a daily hiring basis, selling odds and ends, teaching little girls. Ifigênia and Penha were the poorest districts, where the greatest number of seamstresses and spinners lived: there were smallholdings, bits of cultivated land and stalls, mainly belonging to white women.

There was strong prejudice against jobs that were considered more degrading. Disposing of rubbish, fetching water from the fountain, the work of washerwomen, cooks, shop assistants and itinerant sales-women were all jobs usually taken on by black or mulatta freedwomen; many of the women spinners were mulatta; poor white women preferred to be stallholders, seamstresses or farmworkers, living off their work and their businesses.[1]

In the more central households there was fierce competition between free and slave women; freedwomen vied with rented slave women for daily pay, fought for opportunities for minor service work, itinerant trade and even domestic service. The strong contrasts in status and indications of social difference were deeply rooted in the relationships of these people, living side by side, day after day, and they took on their own special characteristics according to the demographic density of households of single women. Different districts were characterized by different degrees of necessary famili-arity, of proximity and social space. There was the 'secretive poverty' alongside the slave women at the fountains and in the roads at night-time; there were the big houses belonging to white women, with their ground floors let to shoe shops or carpenters' stores usually run by dark-skinned people. North of the cathedral, 'Dona Policena Joaquina de Oliveira, a twenty-four-year-old married white woman, lived with her little son and a couple of slaves, and had a tenant carpenter on her ground floor. In the same district, Maria Clara de Souza, a forty-one-year-old white widow, lived in a big house with her unmarried daughters, of twenty-four, seventeen and fifteen, all white, plus seven very young slaves and a "downstairs tenant" with a cobbler's shop, run by a mulatto freedman of twenty-nine.'[2] Worth remembering here is the story of Oswaldo Elias Xidieh about the

Table 6.1 Households headed by white, mulatta and black women in districts of São Paulo, 1836

Districts	Whites	Mulatta	Black	Households of single women	Total households per district
North of cathedral	78 (55.3%)	53 (37.6%)	10 (7.1%)	141	340
South of cathedral	108 (63.5%)	44 (25.9%)	18 (10.6%)	170	570
Ifigênia	75 (57.7%)	48 (36.9%)	7 (5.4%)	130	442
Penha	47 (61.0%)	24 (31.2%)	6 (7.8%)	77	208
N.S. of Ó	31 (66%)	15 (31.9%)	1 (2.1%)	47	183
Total	339	184	42	565	1,743

Source: DAE, Maços, 1836.

honest, devout woman stallholder who lived next to the dark-skinned cobbler, who was 'the devil' himself.[3]

Ethnic tensions sometimes arose within households themselves, where white domestic servants lived side by side with mulatta servants, often separated by large age differences, which were an appropriate social barrier between them, proving both convenient and necessary.

Among women heads of households, the majority continued to be made up of white women, in spite of the rapid increase in mulatta freed-women who established themselves as heads of families. Among domestic women servants, mulatta women predominated. Table 6.2 once again shows data for the central districts of São Paulo. Freed mulatta women tended to establish themselves at their own expense, whereas black women continued to be confined as maids in domestic service; among the latter, the number of those who established themselves as heads of households tended to diminish, and those in domestic service in the houses of third parties tended to increase.[4]

Table 6.2 Female-headed households, domestic servants and ethnic origin, São Paulo, 1804 and 1836

	Heads of households		Domestic servants	
	1804	*1836*	*1804*	*1836*
White	346	333	79	56
Mulatta	132	187	124	75
Black	52	36	32	33
Total	530	556	235	164

Mulatta and black women who established themselves at their own expense were typical of a society in transition, for although their situation might be unusual, they in their turn eventually owned women slaves and servants. Indian women rarely figured as heads of households in the censuses of the districts that we investigated; they were probably numerous in Pinheiros or in Santo Amaro. They hardly figured even as domestic servants, although until the end of the eighteenth century, according to tradition, they constituted almost all the domestic service in *paulista* houses; perhaps they were counted as mulatta women?[5]

Freedwomen very often stayed on in the same houses, continuing as domestic servants, on conditional release from slavery. In the end, they received small sums of money as inheritances, and some of them ended up buying small houses, where they established themselves as heads of households, in a long, painful cycle, which never freed them from the status of being very poor women, imprisoned in the structural unemployment which kept them in the city.

In the houses of single women, the domestic arrangements had some peculiarities which suggested the way they survived, and revealed the acute social tension which surrounded poverty in the midst of a slave-owning society. The majority were matrilocal homes, a high proportion of them being extended households; the prevalence of such arrangements was well above the average in the city, where they were rare and atypical of the population as a whole. In these households of single women, the dependent adults were usually daughters; they had their own form of family organization, which had ties from the group to the neighbourhood through the authority of the oldest woman head, a grandmother or a mother; from this base they improvised an intermittent and uncertain livelihood as profiteers and agents in small trade. With the instability of common law marriages, which followed one after another, it was their way of maintaining, albeit precariously, a minimum of security and continuity of the family group. It also maintained a certain code of values, pertaining, for example, to relationships 'with coloured people', which they needed to observe as an integral and essential part of their organization for survival.

For daughters of 'secretive poverty', the protection of the ruling classes was not always possible. Although they found themselves in need of the mutual help of the community, they had strong prejudices concerning the daily coexistence with slaves of other owners or with black freedwomen: friction often arose at the fountains and washing places in the city. More often than not, impoverished white women tried to place their daughters in a more protected environment, in the Santa Theresa or the Luz female retreats, or occasionally as domestic maids in houses belonging to relatives or godmothers who were more comfortably off.[6] Their everyday way of life was opposed to the seclusion that was characteristic of the ruling classes; the women normally did their sewing in the doorways of their houses, and cooked in the open air, chatting as they squatted or sat about on mats. Geared to the values of a hierarchical, slave-owning society, poor white women attempted to uphold their social ranking in the neighbourhood community, keeping a friendly distance and safeguarding a system of respect for blood and family ties: 'birds of a feather flock together.'[7] The repertory of popular sayings and proverbs was heavy with prejudice against men with thick lips, the curly hair of black men,[8] the boldness of mulattos. In the stories told of an evening, the pretty young girl, 'as white as milk', who was carried off by a dark-skinned black man, must die and turn into a star, rather than consummate the relationship.[9] Marriage to a black man or a mulatto was frowned on:

> The tigress had a daughter
> Who was fair of face;
> So as not to mix with the other race,
> She made her marry her first cousin.[10]

In the melting pot of change and transformation in which their way of life established itself, especially in the more central districts, it was imperative to have an organization for survival which would support the family group in the face of the process of cultural development to which it was exposed. Against the backcloth of the values of traditional 'rustic' culture, it had to cope with the strong influx of the African presence, and what was left of the remaining *mestizos*. The rather intermittent and casual contact with muleteers who were on the move gave these districts and their neighbourhoods a complex character, heavy with racial tension. There was an increase in freedwomen, mulatta women and ex-slaves. Because of the lack of roots and lack of continuity of inherited values, the matrilocal organization of family and neighbourhood groups hardly produced what, in other milieux, constituted a community; in the households of poverty-stricken women, with their concentration of females, what protected them in the midst of racial tensions and the continual disruptions to which they were exposed in the circumstances of their lives was the leadership of mothers, of the older women.

Some of the popular stories collected in São Paulo and the surrounding areas comment on the situation of poor white women who had to frequent the fountains and public watering places which were the epicentres of the slaves' social life. In a story of African origin, the 'humming bird' – a magic, irresistible force which also appears in Bahian collections of folk tales – drew household slave women, their mistresses and ladies to the drumming ceremony at the fountain, and the father's whip was needed to restore appropriate order.[11] In rustic versions of the Portuguese story 'A Moura Torta' ('The Cross-Eyed Moorish Girl'), there is a comment on the power of fate that brings the poor white girl and the black slave girl together, side by side, at the public fountain; in the end, despite the hazards of fate, the destiny of the white girl, temporarily in decline, was suitably restored; the social phenomenon of impoverishment reclothed itself in an aura of 'bewitchment'.[12]

The story told of how, by chance, one day by the city fountain, a white girl met a slave girl with her clay pot. The white girl was naked (impoverished), waiting for her boyfriend, who had gone to find some clothes. Both of them were reflected in the water at the same time, and the slave girl, very excited, mistook herself for the white girl, dropped her pot and went excitedly home. There she was scolded and sent back to the fountain, this time with an iron pot. And so, time after time, in a repeated coming and going, she finally managed to usurp the place (and the boyfriend) of the white girl. When they did look at each other, and not their reflections in the water, as they stood side by side at the fountain, the custom of *cafuné* became the pretext for them to make friends with each other. The black girl, in a subservient and deceitful manner, made the offer to the white girl to 'de-louse her hair', where-upon she stuck a magic pin in it. Could this be a veiled reference to the rivalry for daily work between white girls and slave girls in the city? The story, which is in general prejudiced against the clever, wicked, black girl, tells how she eventually married the white girl's boyfriend and became the lady of a wealthy house; this anomalous situation, which was necessarily fleeting, lasted but a brief time, and the white girl returned to her place in the sun . . .[13]

In the stories that were told, there were often scenes in which a young white girl fell sick because of the evil eye or bewitchment, and she was changed from a princess or a rich heiress into a black ragamuffin; she was worn out by the degrading jobs that belonged to slave girls – look-ing after the hens, the ducks, washing clothes. Invariably her destiny or status was rightfully restored in the end.[14]

In the São Paulo versions of the story about the girl on her way to market to sell eggs, her thoughts filled with illusions of grandeur, it is not clear if the target was the pretensions to greatness of impoverished white girls, or those of freedwomen who were going up in the world: 'Dona Orgulina' reminds us of Gil Vicente's Mofina Mendes or of Maria Parda (Maria 'Mulatta') from 'Auto das Regateiras' ('The hucksters' trade'), though in the present story she was even more desti-tute as she made her way to the fountain to fetch water, which was the lowly task of a slave girl. Each of her wishes came true, one by one: to have somewhere to live, furniture in her house, some nice clothes, 'a baize cloak', 'a hat for going out for walks', some hens on the ground floor to give her eggs, a cow to give her milk. The refrain told of her coming and going to the fountain with her pitcher, until her dream of getting married came true. Then her presumptuous dream of status surfaced, to be 'lady of a two-storey house', a poison which corrupted the illusions of poor women; Dona Orgulina started to put on airs and

'Beautiful women without a dowry' From *Landseer*, ed. Cândido Guinle de
P. Machado (São Paulo: Lanzara, 1972), p. 129.

'Itinerant trade and neighbourhood links' G. Theremin, 'O aqueduto' (1832), in *Saudades do Rio de Janeiro* (Berlin: L. Sachse, 1842).

'Forbidden drum-playing ceremonies in the streets' Abraham Louis Buvelot, 'A carioca' (Gustave Moreau), in *Saudades de Rio de Janeiro* (1842)

'When they broke many water pitchers' From J. M. Rugendas, *Voyage pittoresque au Brésil* (Paris: Engelmann, 1835), part 4, plate 14.

'It was not political events that shaped their history' From J. B. Debret, *Voyage pittoresque et historique* (Paris: Didot, 1835), vol. 2, plate 12 (detail).

'Poor white women, mostly single mothers' From J. M. Rugendas, *Voyage pittoresque au Brésil* (1835), part 2, plate 18 (detail).

'Near the tray-sellers and the trivet stoves'   From J. B. Debret, *Voyage pittoresque et historique* (1835), vol. 2, plate 26 (detail).

'A woman stallholder shows her punishment for attempted escape'   From J. B. Debret, *Voyage pittoresque et historique* (1835), vol. 2, plate 42.

'Women stallholders attend a forbidden *capoeira*'   From J. M. Rugendas, *Voyage pittoresque au Brésil* (1835), vol. 3, plate 16.

'The funeral of a black woman stallholder was a very festive occasion'   From
J. B. Debret, *Voyage pittoresque et historique* (1835), vol. 3, plate 7 (detail).

'The slave woman and the standards
of a great lady'   From J. B. Debret,
Voyage pittoresque et historique (1835),
vol. 3, plate 7 (detail).

'The poorest women concealed
themselves under black baize
cloaks'   From J. B. Debret, *Voyage
pittoresque et historique* (1835), vol. 2,
plate 30.

'Poverty, with no decent means of survival'   Thomas Ender, Watercolour 236, in
O mundo de Thomas Ender, ed. Gilberto Ferrez (Rio: Fundação J. M. Salles, 1971), p. 278.

'Working links between generations'   From J. B. Debret, *Voyage pittoresque et
historique* (1835), vol. 2, plate 34.

'Impoverished white women with their black wage-earning slaves' From *Cento e quarenta aquarelas de J. B. Debret*, ed. Ian de Almeida Prado (Paris, 1955) (Collection Castro Maya), plate 13.

'Schools for teaching slave girls to make lace' From Charles Ribeirolles, *Brasil Pitoresco* (Rio: Victor Frond, 1859–61), plate 68.

'Between them, sellers and buyers constituted their own clientele' From *Cento e quarenta aquarelas de J. B. Debret*, ed. Ian de Almeida Prado (1955), plate 38.

graces . . . and lost everything, reverting to her original poverty. Among poor women, the rule of the community was the sharing of poverty, which allowed colour prejudices, but ruled out unreasonable pride.[15]

The censuses, with their impression of regularity, give little indication of the movements and the dynamism of life situations and cycles, as they became entangled with each other, were built up and then broken down, in a flux which was in keeping with the passing of time, and which was more extreme in the city, where the means of livelihood were precarious. The female population of the city, although tending to be sedentary, moved from the outskirts to the central districts of the city; they lived in temporary partnerships, successively, with poor men, mulcteers, their apprentices or qualified artisans, who gravitated towards the pioneering areas of the province.

The commercialization of domestic services, minor itinerant trade and prostitution, occurring intermittently and irregularly in the more central districts, called for forms of reinforced family leadership which would guarantee the survival of the group in the midst of disintegrating forces in the everyday life of the urban poor. It was precisely those households headed by older women, both nuclear and extended, which benefited from the leadership (both economic and moral) of maternal authority and from the coordination between kinsfolk and the neighbourhood – in a process of constant change and adaptation to each other – that made the preservation of traditional values possible in the face of the disorder to which the poor found themselves exposed.

The average size of household among women who had no slaves was not very indicative of their internal organization, which varied a great deal. The lowest averages of 3.8 and 2.8 inhabitants per house, recorded in the registers of 1804 and 1836, were a result of the high number of households consisting of only one person, especially north and south of the cathedral square, forcing the statistical average down.[16] However, over 60 per cent of the female-headed households were nuclear or extended, often under the authoritative leadership of older women between the ages of forty and sixty, who predominated strongly in the group of single women. The greater the number in the family group, the more assured were they of its necessary income to survive. Table 6.3 shows the shares of different kinds of family organization in districts of São Paulo in 1836.

Older women, mothers of families, rarely figured as domestic servants, or as dependent on their children. In their overwhelming majority, they were the heads and providers of their families, and very few declared that they lived off 'the help of their children',[17] although almost all of them counted on the family contribution of grown-up

Table 6.3 Family organization in female-headed households

	Number	Per cent
Solitary	156	26.4
Nuclear	234	39.7
with small children	(86)	
with adult children	(148)	
Extended	160	27.1
Sorority	40	6.8
Total	590	100

children (mainly daughters, who worked with them and lived under the same roof). Among extended households, some homes stand out for their unusual concentration of females, including two generations of single mothers: grandmothers, daughters and grandchildren.

This maternal leadership was one way for single mothers to secure the recognition of their illegitimate children in the neighbourhood, where they became reintegrated.

> Maria Gertrudes, a seamstress, lived south of the cathedral with her daughters Anna Joaquina, Florinda, Joana das Dores and Joana Benedita, as well as two little grandchildren of one to seven years of age;
>
> Francisca, a black freedwomen of fifty-nine, lived in the Rua da Boa Vista with her daughters Dionizia, twenty-eight, Benedita, fourteen, and three little grandchildren of one to seven years of age;
>
> Maria Joaquina, a mulatta woman of forty-two, lived in the same street, where she lived from her business, with her daughter Joaquina, nineteen, and a little granddaughter of a few months.[18]

As well as figuring in the registers of the population, they often appeared in stories, where emphasis was laid on the respect owed to older people: such was the cautionary tale of the tin plate, or of the over-patient mother with sly, lazy daughters.[19]

This kind of household has been widely discussed in more recent studies on family sociology,[20] and quoted as 'abnormal', a symptom of social collapse and the disintegration of the family. In fact, in the city of São Paulo it was one form of organization for survival, mainly for washerwomen, women vendors, seamstresses and spinners; it happened as much among poor white women as among black freedwomen.

The domestic pattern for single women was the nuclear household, headed by the mother, with grown-up children. In the absence of slaves and domestic servants, they used their own grown-up daughters, and occasionally their grandchildren, as helpers in the home; they also counted on the salaries of their sons, who were carpenters, cobblers, soldiers, tailors. This was what guaranteed their daily livelihood.

In households without any domestic help, there was a predominance of adult dependants, mainly daughters (who usually did the same work as their mother). Dependants constituted 45 to 48 per cent of the inhabitants of those homes which had, among dependants and domestic servants, a concentratedly female population of single women.[21] Among dependants, most of them female, 20 per cent were children from one to ten years of age (194); 35 per cent were adolescents between ten and twenty years (327); 40 per cent were grown-up children (362); 5 per cent were 'others', such as relatives, kinsfolk, outsiders (70).[22]

Out of all the households of single women, slightly fewer than 30 per cent consisted of solitary women, living in hovels or in rented rooms in the more central streets of the city: São Bento, Ladeira de São Francisco, Rua da Boa Vista, São José. Among these were prostitutes, girls of easy virtue, who had abandoned their families and cut themselves off from their neighbourhood. The most needy and wretched could include solitary older women who had to fend for themselves, possibly with young domestic servant girls living with them or occasionally small grandchildren:

> In Ifigênia, Escolástica Maria de Jesus, an Indian china worker, lived with her little grandson of four; an elderly spinner with two little grandchildren and a mulatta domestic girl of nine. North of the cathedral, Maria Borges, a forty-six-year-old white spinster, lived 'off her job as a servant', with thirteen-year-old Virgília; Maria das Dores, a forty-year-old white spinster, a stall-holder, lived with Maria Firmina, nine years old, possibly a granddaughter or a domestic servant.[23]

They stood out because of their poverty, having no help coming in from the salaries of their grown-up sons, which were usually higher than their own.[24]

The leadership of a family, where the control was over households with grown-up children and grandchildren, included the management of rent and the salaries of the children. 'Antonia Pires de Araújo, a white widow of fifty, a seamstress, lived south of the cathedral with her daughter Gertrudes, a single mother of thirty-nine, who was a seamstress, plus two granddaughters and three grown-up sons, each one with a trade: José Antonio, thirty-two years old, single and a locksmith; Amaro, twenty-two, single and a cobbler; and Manoel, twenty years old.' According to police records, she was in difficulties in July of 1838 because of a crime committed by her son Amaro.[25]

> Joaquina Escolástica lived off the proceeds of her shop in Ifigênia, with several grown-up children: João Bernadino de Souza who dealt in cattle and earned 300$ per annum, Anna Ignácia, nineteen years, Maria Isabel, seventeen, and Zacarias, a carpenter of sixteen, as well as a domestic maid Maria Magdalena, forty-four, who was white and single. Umbelina Joaquina, a seamstress, lived south of the cathedral; she was mulatta, single, fifty years old, and earned 100$; she lived with her twenty-year-old son Jacinto, who in his turn earned 150$. Juliana de Almeida, a mulatta widow of fifty, lived in Ifigênia 'from her spinning', with a daily paid domestic servant who earned 50$. Anna Joaquina, a seventy-year-old mulatta widow, who was a spinner, lived with a domestic servant, a carter who had an annual income of 76$800.[26]

As well as their other concerns, they confronted the authorities over the violent enlistments directed at their sons and husbands, who were periodically removed by force from their homes and land. In spite of decrees that exempted them from serving in the army if they were married and employed in farming or in a city job, it only needed the odd protest about vagrancy or drunkenness for them to be taken away to the River Plate, Santa Catarina or Sacramento fronts, or to be forcibly recruited for military service in the national fleet. Luís Antonio de Souza, for instance, 'aged eighteen, single, white, excellent for the service of the army, who, in spite of being an only son, is an out-and-out vagrant, a roamer of the streets, of no use to his mother . . .'[27]

The women did not, however, always agree with the point of view held by the authorities, and reacted with petitions and demands by the hundred:

> Maria Magdalena protests that her son, who is in prison, is her only son, and the one who maintains the household . . . Maria Antonia da Silva tells of her husband, who was accused of vagrancy, and enlisted for the front, where escaped or unruly slaves were sent; he managed, however, to escape from prison, they were married officially in church, and she is requesting his release.[28]

There were instances of violence, when many women were taken prisoner, accused of hiding their sons or husbands, or of sheltering deserters in their homes.[29] The official documentation is thick with the complaints and repeated requests of third parties who interceded on their behalf, for they would often be able to find a person of influence who could protect them, as a result of the tangle of personal relationships created by the paternalism of slavery.

In 1810, a judge protested about the influence of an insistent mother:

> It does not surprise me that the supplicant, a poor, uncultivated woman, blinded by maternal love, should try every means of securing the release of her son. What does confuse me and concern me is that the supplicant should find those three reverend priests who, abandoning their high principles and their obligations as loyal subjects and good men, should resolve to produce such false testimony.[30]

Women would often resort to the authorities as a means of strengthening their own influence when they did not manage to get their own way within their own families, or among relatives or neighbours, mainly to alter the balance of family quarrels. This was the sphere of the universal anecdote revolving around the figure of the disagreeable mother-in-law. The picture was of an overbearing woman, who decided the marriages of her children, mainly daughters, and who continually intervened in neighbourhood affairs, resorting whenever necessary to petitions, claims, quarrels, lawsuits and demands. One such woman asked the authorities to recruit her son-in-law to serve in the army, because he was maltreating her daughter: 'Since she is poor, she cannot take on the legal responsibilities of divorce, and fearing for the life of her daughter, she asks for her son-in-law to be enlisted.'[31] Numerous documents show them interfering in one way or another in the marriages of their daughters. In an official letter dated 16 November 1821, Antonio Manuel, an inhabitant of the district of the town of Santos, asked the Vicar General to help him to get back his wife and children, who had abandoned him; in Freguesia de Nazaré another abandoned husband denounced his mother-in-law because his wife had left him 'through the persuasion of her mother'.[32]

They also resorted to the authorities when their younger daughters were seduced and abandoned:

> Rosa Maria from Juqueri parish maintains that about two years ago a young man by the name of Antonio Joaquim came to her house, and in spite of the fact that the supplicant did not know his origins, he proposed marriage to her daughter Maria Joaquina; there was a delay in the marriage, and he had relations with the daughter of the supplicant, which resulted in a son, and the supplicant wanted the marriage to take place, but he did not, and left for the house of Gertrudes Something-or-Other, about half a league away from the supplicant.

The request, directed to the commandant of the district, was to the effect that the outsider should be enlisted and sent away from the district.[33]

In the all-too-frequent cases of strangers or cousins who broke their promises of marriage to adolescent girls, the complaints became a neighbourhood ritual, as if it were necessary to make the rape official, and to give immediate recognition to a rite of passage that pertained to the young and to the ways and traditions of everyday life.

Maria Umbelina da Silva appealed to the brigadier commander (who in his turn asked the president of the province) to denounce the national guardsman of the Second Legion who had led her daughter astray.[34] This led to petitions, quarrels and lawsuits in which there were cited cases of rape, indecent assault and seduction ... the infamy of uncles, friends, neighbours and cousins in 'the name of friendship, neighbourliness and compaternity'.[35]

Among the 276 women heads of families who lived with grown-up children, 84 lived from their jobs and from small itinerant trade, 76 were spinners and chinamakers, 45 seamstresses, 34 farmworkers and countrywomen, 27 washerwomen.[36] It was difficult to separate clearly the occupations involving home crafts from their commercialization, which they negotiated on their own account within the neighbourhood itself. Nothing was sold in the shops or in the small cottages of the local market. Women spinners, chinamakers and weavers depended heavily on the mutual help of the neighbourhood, and would engage in night-work, often in other houses, in exchange for small favours of food; they would help each other on the occasions of festivals, funerals and baptisms.[37] Extremely poor, they increasingly turned in on themselves, protecting an area of their own autonomy. A neighbour had some leftovers of beans, beeswax, flour and soap in her house; So and So had killed a pig; a third person needed two pieces of cloth, some local brandy and ceramic pots or pans for her son's 'new house'. The transactions were settled over friendly chats, gossip and conversation. Out of this grew a natural suspicion of outsiders, whether men or women, and the need to belong to the district, to the neighbourhood.[38] It made them strengthen their precautions against adulterous women or women living as mistresses, against the rape or seduction of young girls, against men who abandoned their wives – the kind of trouble which stirred up hatred and quarrelling among the family groups of their community, itself the basis of the small trade which was their livelihood.

They had indisputable superiority in questions of neighbourhood business, where they got their own way, just as they did with the authorities, who, in general in these areas, limited themselves to endorsing the agreements of the neighbourhood. Authoritative old women often headed protests against 'women who went around as concubines', 'unruly women', 'vagrants':[39] 'Two years ago two men appeared in the parish of Pontal, accompanied by two women, who had behaved scandalously.'[40] Another woman suggested 'having Esmeria Maria de Itaquaquecetuba arrested, for being "disorderly", and disturbing the neighbourhood'.[41] At times, in gestures that claimed to be more exemplary than motivated by personal revenge, they meted out justice with their own hands. This was the case of two or three ladies who cut off the hair of two of their neighbours, a mother and daughter, who were both accused of living in concubinage. The judge kept the angry ladies in prison for a month, pardoning them 'because of the wretchedness in which they lived'.[42]

Neighbourhood quarrels and rows were a way of life for these women who negotiated for the service of domestic servant girls and interceded in commercial transactions. They acted in the name of everyday practice, appearing in brawls and personal quarrels as mediators, counsellors and conciliators for 'terms of respectability'.[43]

As heads of households and single women, they always declared a principal occupation and occasionally an annual income: spinners, seamstresses, washerwomen and vendors lived off their work . . . but they alternated different occupations, for they lived by improvising ways of combining service jobs with small trade in leftovers from domestic production, to which were added small plots of land which they tilled and where, whenever possible, they had a few domestic breeding animals. The days and years went by for seamstresses and spinners in doing piecework at home and in daywork for washerwomen, cooks and vendors, and chores for home consumption – looking after animals, making soap, bacon, flour.

In effect, they counted on the work of everyone – children, adults, dependants and domestic servants. Child labour and collective family income (of the domestic group as a whole, to ensure a daily subsistence for each member of the family) is an age-old aspect of poverty, and one which was already present in the São Paulo districts in the early decades of the last century. It was this that made leadership indispensable, to organize the alternating between the jobs which were necessary for survival in the milieu of the poor. As organizers and distributors of tasks, the heads of households who were older women were outstanding; they negotiated small transactions, as well as piecework and salaried jobs for their daughters and grandchildren.

Table 6.4 Age bands and occupations of female heads of households in districts of São Paulo, 1836

Ages	Washerwomen	Seamstresses	Small trade	Artisans	Farming	Total	%
15 to 20	7	8	6	4	0	25	7.4
21 to 25	6	17	6	2	1	32	9.4
26 to 30	9	14	12	7	2	44	12.9
31 to 35	7	7	8	4	2	28	8.2
36 to 40	8	11	16	6	6	47	13.8
41 to 45	8	7	11	7	4	37	10.9
46 to 50	4	8	6	13	4	35	10.3
51 to 55	3	3	6	2	7	21	6.2
56 to 60	5	5	4	13	5	32	9.4
61 to 65	3	3	5	5	1	17	5.0
66 to 70	2	3	4	11	2	22	6.5
Total	62	86	84	74	34	340	100

Source: DAE, Maços, 1836.

The authority of these women who were heads of extensive, matri-local households made itself felt in the acceptance and the protection given to the illegitimate grandchildren of common law relationships, many of whom were brought up by their grandmothers. It was they, too, who decided what should happen to the children after birth, in cases when they should be given away to strangers or abandoned as found-lings. As well as this, they were responsible for organizing child labour, and allocating children between the ages of seven and twelve through-out the neighbourhood, to help with domestic or business chores.

Generally speaking, in households of women on their own there was a lack of children, who appeared in only 36 per cent of homes, this being a much lower number than the average in the city, which was about 50 per cent.[44] The lack of children, apart from reflecting a structural tendency of the city,[45] presented a characteristic element: an extreme imbalance between the sexes, so extreme that it is suggestive of the tradition of keeping little girls and rejecting little boys, or handing them over to a third party to be brought up (see table 6.5). Among grandchildren living alone with their grandmother, there was a pre-dominance of males.

Table 6.5 Dependants in female-headed households, São Paulo, 1836

Age bands	Children		Grandchildren	
	Male	*Female*	*Male*	*Female*
0 to 5 years	49	69	28	23
6 to 10 years	26	49	14	30
11 to 15 years	56	61	9	9
Total	131	179	51	62

Source: DAE, Maços, 1836.

The custom of abandoning sons, or handing them over to others to be brought up, related to the very high number of illegitimate children, mainly of adolescent daughters between twelve and sixteen years, and was widespread over the city as a whole. Maria Luisa Marcílio calculated that the number of illegitimate children in the cathedral districts between 1741 and 1845 was about 39 per cent.[46] There is no reason to suppose that it was lower in households of single women. In 589 of these households, taken as a sample from the four districts mentioned, there were illegitimate children in about 230 houses, that is

39 per cent. In these 230 households, 86 were nuclear families of a mother and her small children, 69 were extended, including grand-mothers bringing up grandchildren, 56 were nuclear of grandmothers alone with grandchildren, and 19 had children of relatives or domestic servants.[47]

In São Paulo the phenomenon was more openly discussed in the records of governors and magistrates in the second half of the eighteenth century. A strategic place for abandoning many children was directly in front of the house of Bishop D. Matheus de Abreu Pereira, at 20 Rua do Carmo, right on the corner with Ladeira, a spot which was often frequented by washerwomen, vendors and stall-holders, since it was very near to the small cottages market: 'as soon as he heard one of them crying . . . he would hasten to send his servant to get the child, and from the window he would baptise that very baby, fearing that pigs or other animals that wandered about there might eat it.'[48]

The instability of common law marriages and the high number of unmarried mothers in all age bands and from all levels of people in the houses were both features of urban São Paulo society, which was very unequal, taken to an extreme of hierarchy, with a high level of concentration of wealth. Matrilocal organization was also a defence mechanism, giving greater stability to family groups in the face of the temporary nature of relationships between men and women.

Laima Mesgravis, who made a careful study of the subject of illegitimate children, found that there was a particular tendency to reject poor, white babies. Not until 1825 was a foundling hospital installed in the *chácara dos ingleses* (English farmstead), from where the children were sent to nursemaids in the Santa Casa, and later to the orphanages of Glória and Santana.[49]

Apart from the abandonment of babies, there was the custom of handing them over to a third party to bring up. The practice was well documented in wealthier houses where there were many slaves and domestic servants. Around 10 per cent of households of single women were made up of elderly women with grandchildren or orphaned babies in their houses.[50] There was a mixture of contrasting social extremes in the urban milieu, which made the placing of less favoured children possible.

Their work as intermediaries and negotiators of small trade trans-actions within the neighbourhood, based on the exchange of mutual favours, made it easier for women on their own to carry out this job of redistributing children, which by nature depended on social contact. Literature confirms what the censuses suggest: in *A Enjeitada* ('The

Abandoned Girl'), by the nineteenth-century *paulista* novelist Bernardo Guimarães, Rosa's daughter was brought up by Nhá Tuca, an elderly stallholder, who lived on the road to Penha; Alfredo Mesquita showed in *Sílvia Pelica* how the custom of taking a poor infant into the home was deeply rooted in the upper echelons of São Paulo society.[51]

The authority of the older women, as heads of the family group, included the power to decide the future of their grandchildren. Occasionally they were cited in legal proceedings, accused of infanticide. Generally the judges alleged lack of proof, and they were not convicted. Anna Theresa, a countrywoman in Guarulhos, was accused of murdering two newborn babies belonging to her daughter, 'one of them still in the womb, by using poisonous herbs which she gave her to drink, and the other, as soon as it was born, by wringing the baby's neck in front of her'. She had even threatened to kill any children her daughter might have in the future. From the evidence the judge decided that the daughter was an 'idiot', and concluded in his verdict that 'the grandmother had not killed her grandson.'[52]

There was a demand for small children in the houses of poor, older women, many of whom brought up grandchildren or abandoned children. Others organized work for minors, placing them with third parties to work, for instance, in grocery stores.[53] As a result of the constant demand in the poor neighbourhoods and also in the city in general, numerous requests were made to the Santana orphanage. In 1836, Gertrudes Maria asked the seminary for an orphan boy, so that she could teach him to read and employ him in a job. On 18 August 1846, Anna Theresa de Jesus asked them to give back her son so she could employ him. Little girls between seven and twelve years of age were destined for houses where they worked as maids and were instructed in domestic chores. In 1836 there was a report in the census about a little girl of twelve, Joaquina, 'put to work' in the house of Maria Cândida, a forty-year-old white widow living in the third block to the north of the cathedral.[54]

Family and community relationships were essential conditions for the organization of the services and activities of local trade. The primary links, mothers and daughters, acquired an extraordinary power, for it was the condition of being accepted by the group, and the connection for making orders, deals and carrying out jobs, that made survival possible. An underlying tension could be seen between the matrilocal organization of homes headed by mothers of families and the cyclical movements which affected the majority of dependent daughters, granddaughters, maids, adolescents, all young people in

their twenties: biological and social life rhythms meant that they had to
make and unmake life situations, adjusting to different homes, which
kept changing as the years passed, and through it all they were never
able to lose their status as poor girls who were socially disqualified.
These young people were caught up in the hard struggle for survival,
forced to improvise in a haphazard fashion, without any prospects of
permanent or secure standing. As very young dependants they would
leave their maternal home to live in temporary sexual unions as concubines; abandoned, they retreated to solitary households of single
women, north of the cathedral; at times they resorted to seeking the
protection of wealthier houses, working as young maids for elderly
ladies. They frequently went back to live with their mothers, taking
their illegitimate children with them, coming under the protection of
their grandmothers and helping once more with the family income and
its daily struggle for a precarious livelihood: 'What God gives to us, we
eat, what we lack, Saint Anne will provide.'[55]

The choice of marriages for the children was within the power and
jurisdiction of their elders: 'In answer to the request of Zeferina Maria
de Jesus, by which she declares that it is to her liking that her daughter
Francisca de Paula, fifteen years of age, should marry João Nepo-
muceno, I find no impediment other than the disproportion of their
ages.'[56]

The older women were often accused of being witches, sorceresses
and, above all, procuresses. Their active role in perpetuating their
mores had nothing to do with the values of the ruling classes: they tried
to protect the family group from disintegration, accepting single
mothers and illegitimate girls and recognizing sexual liaisons. Theirs
was the practice of traditional common law usages, continually reinvented and adapted to the process of incipient urbanization, to the
changing districts, to poverty, to the needs of neighbourhood trade and
home crafts. They figured constantly in documents, lawsuits, petitions
and requests, always in confrontations, asserting their own values of
everyday lore in the face of the bourgeois authorities, of governors,
justices of the peace, judges, magistrates – in general, enlightened
people, reformers and Europeans convinced of the necessity for civil-
izing and transforming 'backward' customs.[57] Those authorities criticized them as 'peasant women', who lacked a convenient and
appropriate family organization, on the model of the local elite. As for
the local influence of the women of the district, they respected them
with the tolerance that befitted men of substance and power, with
reservations and a condescending tone, bearing in mind the 'lack of
intelligence that corresponded with their state' and the 'uncivilized

ways that went with the wretchedness in which they lived'; in the official documents they always appeared to be condescendingly 'attentive to the state of their poverty'.[58]

São Paulo sources make reference to many clandestine marriages like those in stories of scholarly tradition, of Amadis de Gaula for example, marriages which were systematically forbidden in Portugal, principally during the reign of D. Maria I. In September 1824 an enquiry was made into the 'celebration of secret marriages', which contravened the orders of the Council of Trent; on 2 January 1840 the vicars of Lorena and Taubaté were denounced for celebrating marriages without the legal authorization. 'Arranged' marriages were also quite common, like that of one individual who wrote to the president of the province in a report dated 7 April 1835, saying that he had fulfilled his duty: he had 'married Joaquina Olinda dos Santos, Your Excellency's maid, and brought her to the Seminário da Glória'.[59]

Temporary concubinages would founder after a lapse of time and leave the young girls on their own, occasionally with small children. Domestic maidservants were drawn into this labyrinth of fleeting forces, and in their turn once more set in motion the cycle of dispossessed women, endlessly unfolding. First they were dependants, then alone, later maidservants and in a final turn they sometimes returned as dependants to the matrilocal refuge.

These were cycles and spirals, shaped like the *ouroborus*, the serpent eating its own tail, reminiscent of the repetitive routine of accumulating and growing, and in their turn also evoking fertility rites of that eternal reflowering and beginning again. In the setting up and breaking down of homes and life situations, the rigid division between the spheres of activity of the sexes turned into provisional structures of integration and of vagabondage. It is a story of precarious survival, at the mercy of the social tensions brought about by the system of slavery, which would re-establish itself, break down, and then set itself up yet again.

In the case of the censuses, which only reflect sudden cuts in time, one has to see further than the static document, which gives the erroneous impression of a point at the same time fixed and moving: households and age groups suggest the variability of life situations and life cycles succeeding each other in a continuous movement which keeps on recomposing itself and starting afresh. Lone young girls, in their households of single women, have strayed away from other households, where they appeared as dependants or maidservants. Even the freedwoman who sets herself up as head of a household appears in the previous census as a slave belonging to an elderly widow stallholder.

In the first half of the last century in São Paulo, life situations changed at a pace which was accelerated by the instability of marriages and common law relationships: 'My husband kept me with him for about six years, and then abandoned me.'[60] Popular songs for the guitar referred to herdsmen companions who 'live in a far off land': 'I am going away, I am going away, next Monday . . .'[61] Cycles and phases and the changing of the generations, ways of searching, disillusion, a new beginning:

> The pleasures that I had
> Have all been taken away:
> Even the roots were pulled up
> And put out to dry
> So as not to be avenged:
> Even the seed
> Is to be burned.[62]

São Paulo versions of popular stories tell of the vicissitudes and incidents in the life cycles of poor women. The daily life of São Paulo women was projected into universal situations: with the intention of fulfilling her destiny, to marry Joãozinho, Mariazinha had to overcome a whole series of trials and achievements, rescuing him from Hell, being forgotten by him, learning the job of seamstress.[63] Usually the trials and tribulations began after marriage, when the bridegroom was enlisted, or was bewitched, or he abandoned his wife.[64] Then there began a long pilgrimage through life, which can be matched, in a parallel fashion, with a critical reading of life cycles in the censuses – since the princess must wear iron soles on her shoes, forge a bronze staff with her own hands, and go out into the world through the phases of a journey, gradually growing older as she proceeds.[65] At the mercy of the needs of the moment, she may turn into an old beggarwoman, a black ragamuffin, a granny who looks after ducks.[66] Seven years of bewitchment follow, rhythmically linking the phases marking the change in generations: feminine characters were obliged to leave for foreign lands, in search of their kind,[67] and then descend again into Hell, where they survived by doing domestic work.[68] Lost among the wild animals in the scrubland, our heroines had to learn the trades of hired women slaves, of sewing, stallholding and that of black women selling from trays; they dressed like men[69] and struggled hard to survive.

The view of marriage as a necessary evil, difficult to avoid and presenting the dark, depressing prospect of a life of poverty and hard work – 'It is better not to get married'[70] – is reflected in popular sayings and in the tradition of the popular theatre of Gil Vicente: the farce of Inez

Pereira is echoed in documents and in civil and divorce proceedings.[71] The words of Branca Anes the Brave were familiar.[72] The São Paulo and Minas version of some popular stories featured Bluebeard husbands maltreating and exploiting their wives and leaving them forsaken: 'In the early morning he would call his wife to look after the pigs.'[73] The poor woman's fate was to work and support her husband, and be subjected to sound beatings, not because she was at fault, but at the whim or fancy of her companion: 'The sea is married to the sand, / It beats upon it whenever it wishes.'[74]

Being abandoned for another, younger woman was another feature of the popular picture of marriage as a destiny, and appears in the story of Count Alarcos, and in the vengeance of Juliana against D. Jorge.[75]

Another representation of life without dreams was that of domestic work as a bewitchment and a necessity. 'Seven years of labour', which had to be carried out as a magical task or by supernatural force: Mariazinha escaped from Hell, fleeing away on horseback, her arms of war of the most domestic kind possible – soap, pins, cinders.[76] Similarly, in the African popular story, the women fought against a great, wild woman, and the arms with which they faced this threatening monster were those of everyday use: spoons, forks, pans, wielded in a continual and obstinate struggle for fertility and survival.[77]

The petitions and demands that were made reproduced the life paradigms and the situations represented by popular stories: voluntary abductions, clandestine marriages, one liaison after another, defencelessness, maltreatment and abandonment. Daughters who ran away from home were threatened by their mothers that they would 'turn into stone'. Captivated by the fantasy world of popular imagery, they would dream of a prince who would carry them off far away from the chronic deprivation in which they always lived. There was the myth of Cinderella, the dreams and fantasies of status regained, compensating for the humiliation of being reduced to the degrading jobs of a slave woman, day in day out. Girls who were dependants of poor mothers, and young servant girls living in the houses of third parties, would often run away, staging 'voluntary abductions', of the kind which filled the evening tellings of stories: stories about White Flower, Melusine, Magalone, Green Coconut and Pumpkin, the Tomb of the Lovely Flower, and 'The Shoemaker who married a Princess'.[78] Rebellious young girls spent their time being shunted between their mothers and the Seminário da Glória, like the 'student Martinha', who was sent back to her mother on 14 May 1846 'for being very rebellious'.[79] On 19 December 1840 orders were given for the young Francisca Maria 'to be caught', as she had escaped from her asylum.[80] In spite of prejudice against unequal unions in the slavery milieu, in these stories it was by abduction that prosperous muleteers came to marry 'princesses'.

Poor girls wanted to be like Cinderella and be royal. 'Near the palace there were some washerwomen who were poor, so poor that one of them, disheartened, said to her mother: "Mother, I would like to be a princess, if just for a day, and get married, if only to the Frog Prince."[81] In the female-headed households of the city there was no scarcity of young concubines between sixteen and twenty-five years of age, who were kept and maintained, along with two or three wage-earning slaves, and sometimes also domestic maids.

The fantasy of status in colonial Brazil laid special emphasis on silk and velvet dresses, with gold or silver lace, as a symbol of ostentation and opulence among the powerful, and this became the dream of slave festivals and masquerades. 'If she were mine, I should always keep her dressed in silk' were the words of a priest seducer, recorded in the Acts of the Inquisition.[82] Alvarenga Peixoto, in a letter to a friend, ordered a pretty skirt for his slave girl Bárbara.[83] In the gold-mining towns, traders made up special stocks for black women who were kept by prosperous miners:

> 6 lengths of ribbon of half-hand length, cut on the bias in the old-fashioned manner, which they call labyrinths, which black women use to wear on their skirts . . . assorted colours of flame, red and blue and the colour of gold and yellows . . . 4 pieces of assorted gold and silver lace and small-point, that should not be too costly . . . 6 dozen ladies' silk stockings, red and blue and gold coloured . . . 100 pairs of shoes for the aforementioned, trimmed with beads of various colours, in large sizes, some with polished heels and others with English style heels, which are lower and thicker.[84]

Domestic maids, freedwomen and slave women were given names from popular imagery, such as Eufrosina or Florinda, which recalled the heroine of *Dom Duardos*, who ran away from her father's house to go and live in England:

> I am going to foreign lands
> For fortune guides me there:
> If my father should look for me
> For he loved me dearly,
> Tell him that Love is carrying me away
> In spite of myself.[85]

According to São Paulo documents, young girls would run away with their lovers to Santos, Moji Mirim and Taubaté,[86] and the authorities occasionally tried to return them to their mothers' homes, or to

bring them to the local hospital, if they were orphans of eleven or
twelve years of age.

> Tell me my daughter, my beautiful daughter,
> Why did you linger at the cold fountain?[87]

In inventories and popular stories, in the Acts of the Inquisition, in
female imagery in general, among traces of the scholarly culture of the
fifteenth and sixteenth centuries, and in more recent stories, there is a
long series of abductions and escapes, ways of defying the values associated with the social disqualification of poor girls, who had no dowry,
in the poor, slave-owning milieu.

In the oral tradition, the picture of domestic work presented by the
stories was a fairly shadowy one. It described work beyond their
strength, which could only be achieved by magic; Mariazinha survived
in Hell by her domestic accomplishments.[88] It is difficult to document
the working conditions in the home, the degrading jobs of a slave
woman, the cohabitation of white, domestic maids with freedwomen
and slave women. There was ill-treatment, the terrible condition of
their living quarters, ill-health . . . all leading to ever-changing relationships and a continual rotation of domestic maids, who moved from one
place to another. The 1804 census indicated a continual movement of
domestic maids leaving and entering household employment: 'Because
the maid Felizarda has left, and Bernarda has replaced her (household
67) . . . because the maid Gertrudes got married and is no longer here
(household 396) . . . Data does not compare since a maid is missing and
there appear two new slaves (household 250) . . . two more maids have
started work (household 25).'[89]

The censuses revealed a continual movement of dependants placed
by their mothers as domestic maids in the houses of third parties in
return for bed and board. Some of them ended up establishing themselves as heads of households, endowed with small inheritances or
dowries; others, who were domestic maids of widowers or bachelors,
ended up as their sexual partners (even though their mothers might file
law suits to have them sent back – 'she has not the slightest desire to
return to the company of her mother').[90]

There were a fair number of petitions and complaints made by
mothers about the ill-treatment their daughters had received, and
protests about the abysmal wage they earned, which provided some
documentary evidence on the life of domestic maidservants. It was a
kind of informal slavery, which began to disappear as it came to be
replaced by domestic slave women. In 1804, of the households of

single women, more than 45 per cent had domestic maids, and in 1836, barely 18 per cent, these chiefly the poorer homes: women stallholders sent their maids out to sell in the streets; poorer seamstresses and spinners kept young girls to help with the family income, in a process which has been defined by Alzira Lobo de Arruda Campos as 'the symbiosis of poverty'.[91]

Table 6.6 Age bands in São Paulo households, 1836

Ages	Women heads	Dependants of female sex	Maids in households of single women	Maids in households of bachelors
0 to 5	—	75	17	—
6 to 10	—	87	12	—
11 to 15	1	82	22	—
16 to 20	28	99	27	13
21 to 25	51	64	13	15
26 to 30	58	62	25	22
31 to 35	44	35	8	9
36 to 40	81	37	19	9
41 to 45	64	14	7	8
46 to 50	71	21	3	15
51 to 55	40	13	4	6
56 to 60	60	6	6	12
61 to 65	33	7	7	9
66 to 70	11	1	11	—
71 plus	32	6	—	—
Total	574	609	181	118

Source: DAE, Maços, 1836.

The age bands of domestic maids and dependants reveal some of this movement between poor households, especially the departure of young girls between fifteen and twenty-five years of age, and also the age pattern of girls in the houses of widowers and bachelors.[92] Young maids between seven and twelve clustered in households of single women, and these households also seemed to represent a refuge from the general destitution for ladies in their late sixties.[93]

There was permanent tension among dependent daughters, maids belonging to domineering ladies, and the heads of matrilocal households, who were looking for permanence in the family group, which was the guarantee of their survival.

Femmes fatales, adventuresses, women who had been thrown out and characters from scholarly imagery, like the dancer Maria Peres[94] or Isomberta, who set off alone in a boat to sail in search of her love, were not endorsed by everyday custom and even less so the heroines of collections of courtly poetry and song, adulteresses like Isolda or Dona Ausenda. The values held in the districts of poor women tolerated successive relationships, but not ones that alternated; prostitution, even as an additional means of survival, was disapproved of and condemned.

Nevertheless, there were Magdalenes and prodigal daughters appearing, in name and person, with a persistence worthy of mention.

The most hopeless and precarious situations were those of lone women who could not count on the support of a family group, making their livelihood very difficult, for they were isolated in the city without the support of the neighbourhood network. A few, not more than 6 per cent, increasing to 9 per cent among the poorest who had no slaves,[95] shared rooms with sisters or women strangers. There were some seamstresses who lived together in the Ladeira de São Francisco; others kept their 'old clothes' with women friends.[96] The 'sorority' type of household was characteristic of the more central areas, to the north of the cathedral, where there were lone young women of sixteen to twenty years of age, the majority of them freedwomen of mixed blood, taking turns over jobs in small itinerant trade or various services, work as seamstresses on a daily hiring basis, and prostitution. They were not as numerous in the city as travellers and contemporary observers implied. In the censuses, the young women constituted 36 per cent of households of lone women in the central districts,[97] the others being more likely to be very poor ladies of fifty or over.

With the difficult job of improvising their own survival on a day-by-day basis, they would turn to prostitution as an alternative means of earning money: customs established by slavery and by the settlement of the frontiers opened up paths as far as the Padre Belchior creek.[98] Their clientele, which was intermittent but secure, was formed by apprentices and herdsmen on the move, minor civil servants and shop clerks. The brothels and gambling joints seemed to be concentrated in the smaller streets north of the cathedral, like Boa Vista, São José and Cruz Preta.[99] The records show the presence of black freedwomen in shops where they held celebrations, with drum-beating ceremonies, dances and meetings, until late into the night.[100] Police documents revealed the connivance of orderlies and women clerks who, 'instead of doing their duty of patrolling the block', were reported for spending the night 'in revelry, at Ana Angélica's house'.[101] Prostitution was perhaps less commercialized in São Paulo than in Santos, where huge numbers of very young seamstresses attracted the attention of historians.[102]

The activities of São Paulo women on the streets made an impression on the French traveller Auguste de Saint-Hilaire, who seems to have exaggerated aspects of them. It is significant that he should comment on the lack of cosmopolitanism, and on the aggressive behaviour of the French prostitutes: the São Paulo women were reserved and secretive, and behaved with caution and disdain.[103] Who knows whether he did not confuse them somewhat with the nightlong movements in the cathedral square, when domestic maids, slave women and poor girls took advantage of the night to go out into the streets to meet husbands, companions and slaves from other properties, or to do jobs that those living in 'secretive poverty' preferred to carry out in the discretion of the night?

In documents and in police reports, there were numerous references to seamstresses of ill-repute and to prostitutes. It was a furtive world, where violent passions prevailed and there was a high incidence of crime; jealous muleteers would use sharp weapons when fighting their rivals.[104]

In one of the many police incidents, a seamstress who was a witness recounted that she was in her room, trying to go to sleep at two in the afternoon, when her girlfriend, with whom she shared the room, half opened the window from the street and threw a knife inside. They were strange, unsettled habits which forced this seamstress to take advantage in this way of the hours of daylight.[105] There were specific references to dark-skinned freedwomen in some rooms in the Rua da Boa Vista. 'Catharina, thirty years of age, lived in the same house as Mariana, who was forty-one, and Francisca das Chagas, all of them black and "freed". In an adjoining room Isabel, who was twenty and white, lived together with Maria do Carmo, also twenty and white, and they "lived off their work".'[106]

Separated from their matrilocal households, the women led the precarious existence of 'fallen women'; wretchedness and hunger forced many of them back to their maternal home, in search of a refuge and the support of the community.

> Barbara Fortunata, a single, mulatta girl of eighteen, lived from her activities in the Rua da Boa Vista, to the north of the cathedral, with two small children; Alexandra Rosa, a single, white woman of twenty-eight, lived in Ifigênia with two small children and a young maid of twelve, who was also white; Anna Dionisia, a white woman of twenty-three, lived alone in Travessa do Colégio, with an older domestic maid.[107]

The larger households, which could count on a family income from the adult members, offered better conditions for survival than solitary households; as well as this, they could depend on the mutual help of the neighbourhood, which was more difficult for loose-living women, or strangers who were 'down and out'. It is true that the authorities never interfered in their lives, unless scandals had been reported by the neighbours. In these cases, the women could be arrested and banished from the city if they did not promise 'a period of honest living', when they usually agreed to return to their mother's house.[108] The case of 'fallen women' was not elaborated very much in stories, except as an example of something to be avoided. However, the subject of the suffering of abandoned girls who had been thrown out of their homes and were wandering about alone in the world was a fairly common one and often quoted in the stories told of an evening.

These stories interwove several independent themes with each other. There was that of the strong woman who was capable of artifice and cunning and of improvising stratagems and contrivances for dealing with unexpected situations, and who was continually faced with adversity for which she was unprepared, and in the face of which established and inherited values were of little use. In such cases, emphasis was laid on qualities such as courage, intelligence, wit and cleverness – on their boldness and inventiveness in assuming informal roles. The wisdom of women who were capable of facing new experiences was clearly visible in the lives of glorious saints such as Catherine of Siena or Joan of Arc, or in the cycle (universal in folklore) of clever young girls or warrior maidens, like Mariazinha, the daughter of the fisherman, and Dona Lobismina (the Lady Werewolf).[109]

Another theme in the popular imagery of poor women was that of the repentant Magdalene, who expiated her sins and returned to the maternal hearth. This had connections with the legendary women hermits, like Maria Egipcíaca, or Zózima, who expiated the evils of their youth in the desert so that one day they could return to the community of their people, purified and redeemed.[110]

Women who were abandoned in lonely woods, in threatening forests, in the midst of wild animals, would survive on roots; at the height of the dangers to which they were exposed they found protection in symbols of their own femininity, in heavy-topped trees and hidden grottoes.

> Being alone, in a wood
> Dark and sad, in gloomy shadows
> All covered over . . .[111]

These were the images that were repeated in the tragedies of Inez de Castro, in the Spanish ballads of cape and sword, in Bernardim Ribeiro, in the eighteenth-century book of Margarida da Silva Horta, and also in the São Paulo versions of the stories of Hansel and Grethel and of Snow White.[112] In Vieira's sermons, Our Lady was represented by the image of a leafy tree planted in the middle of a street, far from the walled gardens, because as a woman of the people her place was in the street and in public areas, where she survived with a strength that offered a refuge to the defenceless.[113]

The commonest theme and the one that was most widespread in popular and scholarly stories was that of the pure young girl who, faithful to the values of her people, has been wronged and slandered, and has to go through a thousand trials, until her innocence is recognized, and she is rightfully restored to her own family. Such was the figure of the woman victim, eternally faithful to her absent husband, in stories about oppressed women who survived adversity without betraying the values of their people, without even being aware of themselves as individuals, save in a partial or fragmented fashion. Scenes of endless adversities combined in the stories of women victims, like Inez de Castro, Griselda, Genevieve of Brabant and Boccaccio's Porcina. Taken from the scholarly literature of the fifteenth and sixteenth centuries, revived in Trancozo's stories and reappearing in the São Paulo versions of storytellers,[114] they have been perpetuated in popular imagery and still survive in popular literature.[115]

The women wandered through the world in search of their absent husbands and loved ones; victims of destiny, they acquired the power of epic heroines and of good fairies, becoming women who were capable of improvising their own survival.

SEVEN

The Magic of Survival

– Qual é o seu nome, boa samaritana?
– Eu me chamo Tereza de Jesus; e você?
– Eu sou Jesus de Tereza, disse Nosso Senhor.

(– What is your name, good samaritan?
– I am called Tereza de Jesus; and you?
– I am Jesus of Tereza, said Our Lord.)

From Oswaldo Elias Xidieh,
Narrativas Pias Populares

In the middle of the nineteenth century, travellers and observers found the cost of living in São Paulo, as far as house rental and food prices were concerned, relatively moderate and easy. Their point of view was different from that of the local town women who were living on the bread line, who existed on those margins of survival which are extremely difficult to reconstruct from written sources: served by a small clandestine trade, urban wretchedness remained a silent element in documents, full of its own subtle nuances and elusive shades of meaning.

The prices of essential commodities are difficult to recover because of the lack of concrete information; the parameters and points of reference are the same as those that guided the estimates on the expense of urban slaves in chapter 4. Some of the records on the outlay of institutions like the orphanage of the Seminário da Glória and on the cost of orphan children revealed prices which were appreciably lower than those indicated in the official tables of Daniel Pedro Muller; the effect of itinerant trade would probably be to distribute them even more cheaply.

Salaries of 40$ a year would be within the margin for subsistence; spinners and countrywomen or seamstresses earning 19$ or 25$ would not have enough to live on without help from relations and neighbours. Free, female manual labour could not count on many opportunities for earning money in the city. Few jobs were salaried, because not many of the textile factories employed girls; shops and established businesses did not usually take on women as clerks or assistants, and wealthier houses tended to keep domestic slaves rather than maids.[1] On the whole these women lived outside institutions, spreading themselves in equal numbers between jobs in itinerant trade and domestic crafts. Those in the retail trade survived the best, with just the competition of slave wages, because domestic crafts constituted a poorer sector, difficult to commercialize, and going through a slow shrinking process because of the competition from English manu-factured goods, which were imported more and more cheaply.

Brazil's entry into the free trade sphere of the British Empire was reflected in the daily life of the poorer women in the city of São Paulo. Even in 1768 the Morgado de Matheus was commenting on the gradual replacement of home-spun thick cloth by English velveteens and baizes, and on the discarding of rough Itu coverings for Castela blankets.[2] In the neighbourhood of Vila Rica, John Mawe described the poor women of the population, dressed in English prints: 'Some of them throw woollen mantillas over their shoulders, which are trimmed with gold lace or Manchester velvet.'[3]

In São Paulo, spinners, weavers and seamstresses went on making a living from producing thick cloths and clothes, ceramic work, tiles and pottery. The registers of the population between 1804 and 1836 indicate a clear process of impoverishment of this sector, for the number of small-time women slave owners went down by 16 per cent during this period. It is possible that these symptoms had something to do with the growing fear about the municipal tax, as embroideresses, lacemakers and net weavers stopped declaring their occupations. In 1822, there were still 94 of them who declared that they made a living from making lace.[4] By 1836 it was as if they had ceased to exist in the city. In spite of the omission of the census, in a letter to relatives in Rio de Janeiro in 1838 the romantic poet Alvares de Azevedo referred to the famous *crivos* of the *paulista* embroideresses, which were fashion-able in Rio.[5]

As well as these jobs for more skilled hands, there were small, home-based workshops scattered throughout the city, like the candles and wax establishment belonging to Manuela do Nascimento, near the Piques bridge, and the one belonging to Ana Joaquina da Cruz, in Rua

São Bento. There was a soap 'factory' in Rua da Boa Morte, and in Rua do Rosário and Ladeira de São Francisco hats were made. It was as if there was a revival of the crafts that had occupied women and their Indian servants in São Paulo in the seventeenth century. There was a great deal of small-time home-based production in mattresses, candies, confectionery, liqueurs and brandy.[6] Activities with low profit margins suffered least from the competition of female slave labour. A certain tendency emerged, taken overall, among the women who declared their occupations in the population registers, for poor, free women without slaves to abandon home-craft industry (−8.5 per cent) in favour of jobs in service and small-time trade (+11 per cent).

Table 7.1 Female-headed households without slaves by economic sector in São Paulo

	1804		1836	
Primary	32	11.2%	34	8.5%
Secondary	147	51.2%	171	42.7%
Tertiary	108	37.6%	195	48.7%
Total	287		400	

Source: DAE, Maços, 1804 and 1836.

The lowest incomes were those of women who made their living from the home-craft industry, mainly spinners, weavers and seamstresses, whose declared incomes varied between 20$ and 60$ a year. It is no easy task to work out their workload and what they earned per day from their declarations of annual income, for one needs to bear in mind the continuing presence of occupations using obsolete techniques, which brought in little, and also the fact that they had to alternate jobs with an effective earning capacity with activities that were hard, time-consuming and a vital part of domestic subsistence. There would not be more than four days of gainful employment in a week, making about 208 effective days per annum, and one has to add the same amount of time in subsistence work, such as dealing with animals and the making of flour, bacon, lard and soap, all activities that played a vital part in the maintenance of the domestic group.

In the area of unskilled services and domestic chores, one day followed another in a continual, exhausting routine, punctuated by a slow, intermittent rhythm of demands and specific commissions. It was a life of continual work, which did not observe Sundays or holidays –

which, according to travellers, were frequent and even excessive (over a hundred a year).[7] Small local trade only got going at weekends, on procession days and days of civic festivities, when the inhabitants from the surrounding areas came to town, and a local fair took place at Campo da Luz, called 'Pilate's market'.[8]

There are plenty of references in written documents to that continuation of work which did not respect Sundays and saints' days; since the sixteenth century, washerwomen and women stallholders had been denounced in the Acts of the Inquisition for working with their black slave women, openly, on forbidden days.[9] They also figured in exemplary tales, as in the pious stories collected by Oswaldo Elias Xidieh, where there are several episodes in which Jesus surprises washerwomen at the stream and spinners working in their homes, ignoring the days of the Lord.[10]

A daily wage of between 130 and 250 réis had very little purchasing power. Itinerant women vendors and washerwomen would earn a little more, between 280 and 350 réis; women stallholders and ladies who 'lived from their businesses' declared a higher annual income, over 150$ (400 to 600 réis a day), although they too depended on the irregular fluctuations of demand in an extremely limited market.[11]

From 1850 onwards, inflation rose much higher than the prices we indicate, which are from information collected from documents of around 1835.

One hundred and thirty réis would buy very little:

1 quart measure manioc flour (730g)	$030	
beans (1.13 litres)	$060	
½ arratel bacon (230g)	$040	$130
1 pound bacon (453g)	$100	
1 quart measure cornflour	$040	
1 quart measure corn (730g)	$030	$300
1 quart measure salt (1.13 litres)	$060	
½ measure local sugar cane brandy	$110	
¼ measure peanut oil	$120	$590

A daily wage of 250 réis would barely provide for enough food for one day, since it was difficult to add the consumption of salt and table oil to the basic diet. The daily wage of artisans, carpenters, tailors and soldiers, which was about $600, did not buy much food:

2 quart measures beans (2.26 litres)	$120
2 quart measures cornflour (1.58 kg)	$080
2 arratels bacon (920g)	$160
1 quart measure salt (1.13 litres)	$060
2 quart measures rice (2.26 litres)	$120
½ measure local sugar cane brandy	$110

A popular dish called *sustança*, thick stews, flour with fat, 'mixtures' of flour and beans, along with a great deal of effort in the domestic preparation of food, which was based on primitive, colonial techniques, helped to keep hunger at bay. There was little salt and little sugar, excepting the honey collected in the native Indian manner. They had access to produce from residential plots, including cabbage, chicory, sowthistle, and others; to papayas, caster beans, lemons, green spices, seasonings, coriander, garlic, wax plant;[12] to soft fruits, water melons, balm mint, pennyroyal, anise and elder. They were spared total poverty by having relatively ready access to native produce, which was made easier by the fact that the city was thinly urbanized and uninhabited lands were spread throughout the whole town.

In spite of local prejudice against manioc flour and maize flour (boiled in water) among local countrywomen producers, the very poor crop workers, the women who supplied cornflour (a little more numerous) and the ladies who owned manioc plantations, and whose flour was a little cheaper, managed to make a living: 'Maize flour is too coarse to be sifted: food for dogs.'[13] There were hand pestles in nearly all the houses, to crush the corn; a few small places had water driven engines, but the rest prepared flour from corn in the traditional, domestic manner: 'the grain was pounded, after being left to soak for a few days to make it softer. The mixture that resulted was then roasted in a large copper pan, then passed through a wide meshed sieve, a coarse kind of sieve, called *sururuca*.'[14]

In 1836, three women made a living from making coarse sieves: 'One of these women, south of the cathedral, was called Escolástica Francisca; she was a white, single mother, living with two small children. In Penha, there were two more young women, both white, single mothers: Luzia Maria, who was twenty years old and had two children, and Florinda Maria, "a native of Rio de Janeiro", twenty-two years old, with a baby of a few months and a six-year-old son.'

A good deal of thick *canjica* was still consumed, a dish of grated green corn, coconut milk and cinnamon: 'the rich eat it because they like it, and the poor out of necessity, since all it needs is to be well cooked';[15] fine *canjica* is 'better than rice'.[16] There were corn loaves and *paçocas* (corn puddings), which, in the religious tales told by the women storytellers, miraculously multiplied.[17]

The frequent references in the inventories to copper ovens, millstones and hand presses, are explained by the fact that the processing of manioc flour continued to be a domestic job, ingeniously adapted from a native Indian technique and using old-fashioned millstones which had been brought from Portugal since the seventeenth century, and were originally used for making wheat flour.[18]

1 pestle	$320
1 wheel and press	12$000
1 copper oven	16$000
1 local manioc wheel	6$400
1 copper oven for roasting flour	13$600
1 wheel, a press with tools for making manioc flour	10$000
1 copper oven, 15 pounds in weight, each pound at 8,000 cruzeiros	12$000
1 copper pot, 12 pounds in weight, each pound at 6,000 cruzeiros and 40 réis	7$680
1 small copper pot, 3 pounds in weight, each pound valued at 4,000 cruzeiros and 80 réis	1$400
1 copper oven in good condition	14$000
1 copper pot in good condition	3$200
1 manioc wheel and press	8$000
1 pot, six and a half pounds in weight, each pound valued at $400 and all for	2$600
1 manioc press and wheel	8$000
1 copper oven, 20 pounds in weight, now old	6$400
1 bowl, also of copper, of 6 pounds, each pound valued at $480	2$880
1 copper pot, 20 pounds in weight	10$000
1 old press	5$000
1 copper pot, 40 pounds in weight, each pound valued at $720	10$080
1 wooden wheel for grating manioc	6$400
1 copper oven for drying flour	16$000
1 copper pot	9$000
1 press wheel	6$400
1 pestle	$240
1 cask	$320

Copper ovens and pots, left over from better times, were still expensive, in spite of passing from generation to generation. Very rarely, the opportunity arose for acquiring occasional party items: a chicken, between $500 and $900;[19] a cheese for $200;[20] a pig for 3$800; a red heifer cow for 8$000.[21]

The preparation of bacon was hard work, though worthwhile, once it was hanging in the chimney: 'They take all the fat off the animal with its hide; they leave the lean meat for eating . . . the fat is rolled up and pressed inside baskets, with a little salt scattered on the top and around the roll.'[22]

As far as utensils and equipment were concerned, there was a predominance of simple improvised articles like clay pots and bamboo baskets, which were also reminiscent of native Indian techniques: 'Their links with the environment are much closer than one can possibly imagine.'[23] In 1836, there were seventeen Indian and *mestizo* women who were making pottery and living in Ifigênia, several of them 'natives of Pinheiros':

Anna Candida, a twenty-eight-year-old spinster, with a little daughter of three and an old domestic maid of seventy-seven, an Indian woman, called Anna do Pilar . . .

Ludovina, single, twenty-four years old, living alone.

Maria Estrela da Paixão, a sixty-year-old widow, lived in Penha with her unmarried daughter and five little grandchildren.

They made china and clay pots in the way described by the sixteenth-century French chronicler Jean de Léry and found by the traveller John Mawe at the beginning of the nineteenth century, in Pinheiros, Santo Amaro, Barueri, Itaquaquecetuba and São Sebastião: pots, pipes, pitchers and casks, just like the clay pots from São Luís de Paraitinga, Iguape and Paranaguá.[24]

Amid the very poor cottages, which were painted yellow and pink on the outside,[25] and were black with grime on the inside, there was an increase in the native Indian methods of domestic building and design. Contemporary observers described dark, unprepossessing places, mud and thatch huts put up in the streets without any sort of alignment; the houses were wattle and daub, 'with a dividing wall', without proper flooring, just trodden earth, like the one Saint-Hilaire visited in Penha.[26] In the cold months, they would light a fire in the house. Otherwise, the oven was set up elsewhere, in one case next to the 'tiled washing shed'. Carlos Lemos recalled the origin of the kitchen in the indigenous Indian huts, and the non-existence, in the primitive sheds, of any room set aside for food. The stove, or stone trivet, was improvised with forked branches and stones arranged on the floor; there would be a few clay pots and vessels. This was the same kind of stove that itinerant women vendors carried about with them, and set up wherever they wanted it. Debret described one, near the maize sellers: 'Close by them a few smoke-covered stones constitute the improvised stove of a simple kitchen, for which the only vessel needed is a cauldron, not much bigger than the palm of one's hand.'[27]

John Mawe also wrote an account, which emphasized the darkness of the smoke in the poorer kitchens:

> a filthy room with a muddy, pot-holed floor, full of puddles of water, where here and there were small stoves made up of three round stones, and where clay pots for cooking the meal were set; as the main source of fuel is green wood, the place is always full of smoke, and since there is no chimney, this smoke finds its way out through the doors and other openings, leaving everything black and covered in grime.[28]

Saint-Hilaire made reference to the simple, makeshift furniture, pieces generally made at home by members of the family themselves: 'a shelf for pots and pans, a couple of benches, and pestles intended for pounding maize to make flour.'[29] In the inventories there are lists of home-made objects which are simple and provisional, mixed up with objects which have been inherited one way and another, from grandmothers and godmothers from times past, objects like tin plates, 'an Indian musket', an old hammock, a tablecloth, a wire basin, an old stool, 'three little oriental cups', and large native sieves.[30] Inventories of possessions of the period show the following:[31]

1 old bed, woven from embira	$800
1 ordinary bed	$480
1 bed, woven from lianas	$320
1 ordinary bed	$240
1 large box, with lock	$560
1 old bench	$160
6 tin plates	1$440
14 stone-dust plates	1$120
1 soup dish	$200
1 large teapot	$640
2 small saucers	$080
2 dozen old used iron forks	$960
$\frac{1}{2}$ dozen small cups and saucers	$360
15 used iron spoons	$640
1 large porringer	1$600
1 ordinary porringer	1$000

1 smaller, imperfect porringer	$240
1 round porringer with an imperfection	$320
1 small, very old cupboard, with compartments	$960
1 small box, with lock	$960
1 locally made folding bed, woven from lianas	$200
2 old tin plates	$480
1 cast-iron pot	$960
1 coffee pot, without lid	$200
6 clay jugs	$360
1 yellow mug	$160
1 iron for starching	2$000
6 stone-dust plates	1$000
1 old handmade folding wooden bed	$640
1 small box	$480
16 candle moulds, each valued at $100	1$600
1 oratory with a saint's image	1$200
1 old wooden box	$960
4 folding wooden beds	$640
1 old sideboard, with drawer	$640
3 old tin plates	$480
1 long bench	$320
1 old folding bed with carved or decorated wooden headboard	$480
1 old folding bed with wooden rustic headboard	$240
1 large old table	$480
1 small old table, with drawer	$800
1 old side-table, without drawer	$240
1 oratory, with doors	1$800
1 box made of local wood, with a small hidden partition within the drawer, without key	1$280
1 box of local wood, woven from lianas	$320
1 large box, without a lock	1$280
1 bench of local wood	$120
3 ordinary benches	$200
1 axe-carved box of local wood	$320
1 bench of local wood	$160
1 bed of local wood	$320
1 large trough	1$600

1 bench	$320
1 good, small box with lock and key	1$000
1 folding bed woven with embira fibre	$640
1 folding bed woven with lianas	$480
1 folding bed woven with lianas	$320
1 tub for carrying water	$480
1 pestle	$320
1 large tin plate	$800
1 small tin plate	$320

Many of the craftwork objects were still made in the Indian manner, like mats for sitting on the floor, folding beds woven from straw and lianas, troughs made from fig tree roots, leather vessels, wooden spoons, furniture roughly carved with an axe, clay gourds, drinking cups, bottle gourds, glazed clay jars, vessels made from a hollow calabash, horn or coconut for drinking water, bamboo baskets for keeping food, straw baskets, fruit baskets, sieves made from vegetable fibres, tucum sacks, wicker fish baskets, cane mats, cane drying mats for holding soap, screwtree sticks or forks, Indian knives for scraping manioc.[32]

The lowest daily wage was that of the spinners, about 4 or 5 vintéms a day, roughly 100 réis a month, which was below the necessary minimum. Ana Leme, a white fifty-year-old widow, on her own, lived in Ifigênia, and declared that she lived on her wage of 20$ per annum; Maria de Jesus Nascimento, sixty-seven years old, lived in much the same way. Those who had grown-up daughters and a few children living with them did better, for the work they did, which was tiring and difficult, depended on the collaboration of many people, especially the children, who did jobs delegated to them by their grandmothers. The census showed most of them living in Penha (thirty-five of them), in Ifigênia (twenty-six), and in Nossa Senhora do Ó (ten).[33] 'In the parish of Ó, Ursula Maria de Jesus, a white, eighty-year-old married lady, lived with four grown-up daughters, who were white and unmarried (Ursula, thirty-six, Anna, thirty-four, Francisca, thirty-two, and Maria, thirty).'

Many of the women also counted on their grandchildren: 'Gertrudes Maria, a white fifty-year-old widow, lived in Penha with her unmarried daughters, young girls of twenty or so, Maria, Anna and Josefa, and two little grandchildren, Marina, eight years of age, and João, of four.'

Older women, when they were on their own, usually got help from granddaughters or from adolescent maidservants:

Filomena Maria, in Penha, mulatta, single, forty-seven years old, with Brandina, mulatta, twelve years old; Francisca Javier, in N. S. do Ó, forty-one years old, single, mulatta, with Maria, also mulatta, fifteen years old; Francisca Maria de Jesus, south of the cathedral, a widow, mulatta, seventy years old, lived with Margarida da Silva, also mulatta, eighteen years old, 'a live-in washerwoman'.

Many women who had grown-up sons at home lived on their wage of 20$, plus the family income brought in by their sons, who were artisans, servants hired by the day, or carters.

In Ifigênia in 1836, Anna Joaquina lived off her spinning; she was forty-two years old, single, mulatta, and lived with a domestic servant Antonio, mulatto, thirty-two years old, who was a carter, with an annual income of 76$800, and his wife Claudiana, mulatta, twenty-one years old; Escolástica Maria lived with her brother, a carter, who in his turn earned 50$ per annum, and also a young nephew.

In his book *Caminhos e Fronteiras*, the historian Sérgio Buarque de Holanda described the primitive, antiquated method of spinning, which persisted even into the nineteenth century. Rather than machines for cleaning the cotton, the eastern 'churkas' or the cotton gins, widespread amongst São Paulo Indians in the middle of the seventeenth century, they preferred the process of manual carding which was a foreign technique readapted by the Indians and in turn copied by white women, because they claimed that the long-fibred cotton they planted at home was not suited to more modern methods. Purely manual techniques were characterized by a 'persistent adherence to tedious, tiring processes'; the work was arduous and poor, and held in low esteem.[34]

Four arrobas of unprepared cotton would be needed to render one arroba of cotton for spinning. The average price of raw cotton in 1836, according to Daniel Pedro Muller, varied between 1$600 and 1$280. A minimum of 5$120 (four arrobas of cotton) would therefore be needed to make a start on any piece of work. Spinners, who were very poor, generally received their raw material from intermediaries, and they then spun it on commission. In his memoirs, Vieira Bueno described the primitive methods of cleaning the tree cotton, which was the kind planted in farms and houses in the outskirts of the city: 'it was a small, wooden, hand cotton cleaner, which any clumsy carpenter could make. It was so small and manageable that it was usually the children who worked it.'[35]

According to inventories in Penha in 1840, such devices only cost

$500. A cotton gin wheel was about 5$000 in an inventory from Ifigênia in 1836, and a spinning wheel about 2$000.[36] Perhaps it was for this very reason that they went on using the manual hoop for defibring the cotton, instead of machines:

> Instead of a carding machine to defibre the cleaned cotton, they used a tightly stretched thread, in a small hoop, which was made from a wooden stick especially for this purpose; the operation consisted in plucking the thread with the thumb and forefinger, on a certain amount of cotton, placed on the floor, enough to form a batting . . .
> There were few houses where the spinning was done on a wheel (the 'spinning wheel'), the hand spindle being much more popular . . .
> In all this kind of work they made full use of the service of minors who, if they were slaves, carried out tasks in a way rivalling any others in the dexterity with which they twisted the long 'bundles', making the spindle spin on the floor for a long time.[37]

In 1836 barely fifteen out of seventy-two spinners possessed slaves.[38] Spinning 'with someone else's thread' was a practice which was documented in São Paulo stories; in the story of the Frog Prince, the young woman accepted the work instruments as magic offerings.[39]

Spinning was not a solo job, but rather one done in groups, and in this way, the spinner women (like the weavers) could resort to the practice of neighbourhood help, or the 'night rousing of the neighbours' – an evening task which was improvised by women in the community, who would come along with their small children to spin. It was the only means of clothing their family and themselves, for they barely had enough food to live on.

> Twenty-three women
> Were in our mutual help group (*mutirão*).
> Midst these women
> There was a great heap of cotton.
> The wheel on which I spin
> Spins a lot of cotton,
> Ay, Ay, my little dark girl, you are
> The mistress of the group.[40]

From September to November, the neighbours would work in their mutual help groups: 'and in this way they go from house to house, as they complete their jobs: the work consists in preparing and spinning the cotton and making clearings for planting. This is how the poor are employed . . . and spend their nights happily with music and merry-making.'[41]

The home-based industry of native cotton material was a colonial custom which was in crisis in the third decade of the nineteenth century; though it was kept going because of poverty, it soon began to be uneconomic. Women weavers were becoming extinct. Among those who appeared in the registers of 1836, only one had six slaves. She was Anna Roiz, who lived in Penha, a white widow of seventy, with two spinster daughters. The rest were very poor: 'Joana, black, eighty years old, lived in Ifigênia, with Quitéria, who was twenty, and Porandina, ten, plus four little black urchins.'

In Ifigênia there lived 'Marianna do Espirito Santo, thirty-four years old, a white widow, with four small children; Luiza Maria dos Santos, a single mother, fifty-nine years old and mulatta, with Maria Jesuina, also mulatta, and twenty-eight years old'. They had the use of some old looms which they had inherited, and which they would no longer have been able to afford, since they cost between 12$ and 16$. There was a time when a loom was worth, at the most, the same as ten arrobas of raw cotton.[42] Domestic work such as this depended on the raw material being provided by a third party, and it was more like a mutual help activity within the community. It also provided an opportunity for bartering, and this was a common practice in mutual help work, when the women of the neighbourhood would get together for a whole collective commission. D'Alincourt pointed out that among the poor women of Jundiaí it was rare to find a house without a small loom.[43]

> Now we are going away,
> With much satisfaction.
> At our head goes the mistress
> Of our lovely mutual help group.[44]

In 1800, according to the records of Governor Antonio M. de Castro, home industry provided enough to clothe all the slaves among the black and mulatto people of the administrative area, as well as two-thirds of the other inhabitants.[45] Around 1820, as recalled by Vieira Bueno, both the poor and the well-off still usually wore cotton, harvested, spun and woven at home: 'the cloth is woven on the loom of some neighbourhood weaver. Even well-off people wore cloth at home which was called three yards, because it was made of a finer thread, and a pound of it would render three yards of woven material.'[46] According to the kind of thread (thick, medium or fine), only 'one pound of thread would render respectively two, two-and-a-half or three yards of cloth.'

There were not many weavers who were able to weave without the raw material being provided by a third party; the traditional payment was a commission of one in every ten lengths of cloth.[47] The times described by the historian Sérgio Buarque de Holanda, namely the last quarter of the seventeenth century, were long since gone. In those days, São Paulo magnates owned extensive plantations of cotton and provided manual work for hundreds of natives; the cloth then represented the local currency. By 1836, very poor women would just manage to feed their families by exchanging cloths left over from domestic consumption for other merchandise; in this way they managed to pay their small debts.

It was a degrading job, seen as fit for slaves, and the Indians in their time regarded it as a punishment.[48] In addition, it was traditionally badly paid: 'Women weavers who used somebody else's loom for their weaving earned scarcely 5 réis; this was less than bakerwomen, washerwomen, oven women and market women, whereas the owners of looms, as far as salary was concerned, were comparable with coarse cloth (burel) weavers, that is, they would get 8 réis for a day's work.'[49] In 1836 they would not be earning more than 180 to 200 réis a day. Vieira Bueno made reference to the continued use of cloth of an old maritime brand, three-and-a-half spans in length, which was still in use in his time. Under 'sundry dispatches' in the state archives there are lists of cloth prices – these in the accounts from the seminary for orphaned children, São Luís do Coração de Jesus, of 17 August 1834:[50]

1 yard broad cotton cloth	$320
1 yard narrow cotton cloth	$200
1 yard blue-striped cloth for making matresses	$560
$\frac{3}{4}$ yard cloth for making trousers and jackets	$170
$\frac{3}{4}$ yard broad cloth	$200
$\frac{3}{4}$ yard close-woven cloth	$180
$\frac{3}{4}$ yard blue cotton cloth	$192
1 yard madrepore	$200

Among the occupations connected with home crafts, the most common was that of seamstress. These numbered 180 in 1804 and 114 in 1836; within their numbers, the percentage of ladies with few slaves diminished from 58 per cent to only 35 per cent.[51] The poorest of them helped to make cloth, yarn and woven fabrics at home, and received salaries comparable to those of spinners. The majority were young women of little over twenty, the daughters of seamstresses. Some houses were like real domestic workshops:

> Gertrudes Maria das Dores, a thirty-seven-year-old white, single mother, lived south of the cathedral with her seamstress daughters Anna Rosa,

Florinda, Ignacia; Anna Francisca, a sixty-three-year-old white, single mother, also south of the cathedral, worked with her daughters Joaquina Maria (twenty-seven), Rosa Maria (thirty-one) and two small grand-daughters.

Women spinners were also very often made up of two generations of single mothers – mother and daughter working together, as if in a family workshop. Unlike the seamstresses, who were mostly white women, spinner women were usually mulatta: 'Antonia da Luz lived in Ifigênia with her sisters and nephews and nieces; she was forty-two years old and single, Beatriz was thirty-seven, Anna thirty-six, Gertrudes thirty-five, Maria forty, and another Gertrudes thirty-eight, all of them mulatta.'

Among seamstresses, as well as the dependent girls of twenty-odd years, there were girls on their own, living in the more central districts, where they hired themselves out to work by the day in the house of a third party. Because the job of seamstress was associated with single girls, it was identified with prostitution in the city. Both spinning and sewing were humble occupations and were associated with domestic slavery.

The older ladies in the central districts had marked differences in salary. Some earned salaries between 570 and 300 réis for four days' work, and some of these 'dressmakers' had one or two slave women; the poorest earned 25$ to 30$ a year, about 130 réis a day, but might still hold on to domestic maids, who lived in.

The majority of the poorer seamstresses worked on commission, and it is not easy to disentangle the prices charged for their piecework. In 1804 one seamstress made twenty-eight shirts for the orphan children, charging 170 réis for making each shirt; they would ask 270 réis for a mattress (200 réis for the labour, and 70 réis for the material).[52] In an inventory of 1842, 'a cotton cloth mattress' was valued at 480 réis, 'and an old shirt at 400 réis'.[53]

The range of clothes worn was probably as unequal and varied as *paulista* society itself. On the whole there was a predominance of casual clothes, which were simple and cheap, made by a seamstress, who did not make very much money. 'Casual dress was a calico skirt and a blouse with open-work embroidery on the front',[54] which provided work for seamstresses and embroideresses.

Because of small debts and uncompleted business, the inventories of the period show plenty of information and prices concerning pieces of clothing which hardly differed from the more basic clothing of the slaves. 'Among the lower classes the men wore trousers and jacket of any thick kind of cotton material, the women, a skirt of calico or striped linen and a calico shawl for the street.'[55]

There was clearly an enormous disproportion among prices for more luxurious or imported clothes, as for example, with mantillas:[56]

1 ordinary mantilla	6$400
2 shawls	1$000
1 woman's riding habit, made of blue cloth	5$000
1 black, French silk dress	6$000
1 black drugget skirt	1$600
1 calico skirt of Portuguese cloth	$160
1 local calico skirt	$240
1 white house dress	$640
1 white embroidered dress	1$760

The market for the work of seamstresses extended to the demand from wealthier people, for when they were at home they too wore clothes made from local cloth, often handwoven and embroidered. As well as this, the seamstresses made kerchiefs, tablecloths and face towels, which were woven by hand, fringed, open-worked and embroidered. An inventory gives:[57]

2 kerchiefs of American cotton	$400
2 old cotton towels	1$000
2 bedspreads and 4 kerchiefs of old cotton	6$000
1 old quilt	$640
1 old kerchief	$320
2 hand towels	$640

Striped cotton mattresses with half an arroba of wool, or horsehair, were also pieces of work for poor seamstresses, as were open-work, fringed hoods, tablecloths with blossom designs, serge cloaks, a sort of common lace, gentleman's serge, large tablecloths of fine, lace-edged cotton and cotton towels with lace-work, open-work and fringed edgings.[58] The bedspreads described by Vieira Bueno were among the more elegant products: 'They made their rolls of material to sell to the more well-to-do and wealthier housewives, along with their hammocks, fleecy bedspreads, some of them very showy, with figures and designs in bright colours, interwoven with woollen threads pulled from baize remnants.'[59]

The most expensive cloth was English baize or cashmere, which was used to make cloaks which the better-off and wealthier ladies wore over their dresses when they went out, and which men used as capes or cloaks. These garments passed from hand to hand, remnants of better times, and figured in the memoirs of Ferreira de Rezende, who observed that they were worn in the need to disguise the poverty of the clothes worn underneath.[60]

There were still people breeding domestic sheep for wool, although less as the techniques for spinning wool became more antiquated: the practice had dwindled since the end of the seventeenth century, when the manufacture of felt hats flourished in São Paulo. Interweaving woollen yarn with cotton textile was an ancient custom dating from the time of the Indian apprentices to the Jesuits; this was the method they used at the end of the seventeenth century to make felts, hats, hammocks and bedspreads.[61]

'In 1836, in Penha, Gertrudes, a white unmarried woman of twenty-five years of age, lived from making bedspreads, with her sister Rosa Jacinta, one slave and a married couple who were domestic servants.'

Countrywomen wore 'a yard of blue baize' over their cotton dresses. The price of the baize varied a great deal according to where it came from and what it was used for; the men also wore woollen capes at times, in bright colours or plaids. In an inventory of 1833 a heavy, baize green cloak was valued at 4$, and in 1834 an elegant, red cloak of heavy baize, trimmed with black velveteen, at 9$.[62] There were plenty of capes for poorer women, made from thick cotton, or calico shawls, which were much cheaper, always in bright colours.

Many of the ladies who 'lived off their yarn' or from their sewing, and who earned very low wages, between $100 and $250, could not survive without alternating these jobs with keeping small pieces of land and animals for breeding. These often figured in the municipal orders – chickens, hens and pigs, which the ladies simply left to roam in the streets near their houses. 'Joaquina Maria lived in Ifigênia from her sewing; she had four children, and reared two calves (4$ each) and two cows at approximately 15$ each', which certainly constituted an important part of her survival in financial terms. 'Joaquina Antonia, a spinner, sixty-six years old, single and white, lived in Penha with a domestic servant; she kept thirteen cows and a bull calf.'

Poor countrywomen and countrywomen without slaves were few in number in the registers compared with seamstresses and spinners. Since they were mostly white women who were socially down-and-out, they were all neighbours and of similar social status, sharing jobs and household expenses. Of the twenty-seven countrywomen who figured in the registers of 1836, nine were extremely poor and wretched, probably leaseholders. These single women with small children did not have anyone to help them in their work on their small crops, and declared in the census that they had 'no decent means of survival'. Some of them lived in Ifigênia, earning between 19$200 and 28$ a year. In general, they barely produced 15 to 30 alqueires of manioc flour.

Antonia Joaquina, a mulatta widow of forty-four, lived with her daughter, an unmarried mother, and two little grandchildren, on an income of 19$200 per annum; in Ifigênia Gertrudes Maria, a white widow of forty-five, lived with two other elderly ladies, and only produced 20 alqueires of manioc flour; Anna Joaquina, in Ifigênia, forty-four years old, married, with her husband away, had a 'badly behaved' son (according to the neighbours) called Antonio Benedito, fourteen years old, and a 'very small manioc field'.[63]

Joaquina Maria de Andrade, a white married woman of twenty-eight, with her husband away, lived on a farm in Ifigênia with six small children. The 40$ which she got from her fields did not give her decent means of survival.

From these twenty-seven countrywomen, about sixteen scratched a bare living from their fields, and eleven declared that they reared a few animals. The latter were better off, for they earned more with the returns from their scanty herds of animals! They had incomes of between 50$ and 100$. They sold half of what they produced, and consumed the rest. Those who could count on the labour of adult children were better off.

Maria Dionizia, a thirty-nine-year-old single, white woman, lived south of the cathedral with two grown-up daughters, also single mothers, and her grandchildren; she relied on her cornfields, and the flour she made at home (12$50), three oxen (45$) and two colts (14$); in Penha, Maria Joana, a white widow of forty, lived with grown-up children and grandchildren; in Ifigênia, Virginia Maria, a thirty-eight-year-old, mulatta widow, lived with her daughter and four small grandchildren, and would make 16$ from the sale of 20 alqueires of corn, 13$76 from 8 alqueires of beans, 6$400 from 5 alqueires of flour. She used all her fields, and sold breeding animals, probably on a sale or return basis: twenty oxen (300$), fourteen sheep (28$) and eleven colts at 7$ each.

Apart from the hierarchy of poverty dictated by colour, there was also a hierarchy of jobs, in which the work of washerwomen and vendors seemed to be the most despised, the kind of occupations fitting for slaves. Washerwomen's wages were about the same as the average of the poorest seamstresses, spinners and vendors. Most of these women were of mixed blood,[64] and likely to be older, with grown-up daughters, or just with granddaughters or adolescent domestic maids. In 1836 they earned between 40$ and 50$ per annum; based on about four fixed days of work a week, this would come out at a daily wage of $190 to $240, which was very little. From an inventory of the time, an iron cost 2$000.[65]

In the middle of the last century, the expense of washing clothes was listed separately in the outgoings of a student: about 640 réis per dozen items of clothing, that is 50 réis per item, washed and ironed, perhaps even perfumed with rue.[66]

In 1834, in the outlay of a children's orphanage, 2$520 was spent on washing 3.9 dozen items of clothing in the month of October, and 2$226 for 3.4 dozen items in August of 1835. This would work out at barely 28$ a year.

> North of the cathedral lived Cecilia Maria, a forty-four-year-old, single, mulatta woman, with one daughter; she received 40$ per annum. Rosa Pereira, twenty-four years old, single, mulatta, lived in Ifigénia and earned barely 20$ per annum. Ana Maria, a black spinster of sixty, living on her own in the south of the cathedral district, received 40$.

Among these, Rosa Pereira was unusual in that she was a daughter with a dependent mother.

Washing was never sent out from the wealthier houses, since they had domestic slaves, so the washerwomen lived off a poorer clientele, living in households that were not very well off, and with no domestic help. Their services were most in demand in the central districts, from institutions, seminaries, student lodgings, hotels, muleteers' messes and houses that were not very well off. It was considered to be a job for slave women and freedwomen, but certain popular songs attempted to remove the blemish from this work of slave women by equating them with the figure of Our Lady, who 'did the washing, and St Joseph would hang it out to dry', a somewhat unrealistic distribution of domestic work in the slavery-influenced chauvinist values of the poorer classes.[67]

Debret described the job as characteristic of wage-earning slave women, whom he depicted calling on their clients for their bundles of clothes, and going to local farmsteads and creeks to do their washing.[68] The freedwomen would beat their washing in the ponds near the town's public fountains. The French traveller Auguste de Saint-Hilaire described the way in which the washerwomen milled around in the Carmo flatlands,[69] and Vieira Bueno recalled them working on the edges of the Tamanduateí, near the hills of Porto, of Carmo and of Fonseca, and especially in Ifigénia, in a pool which was then called Zunega, and later the Paissandu Square.[70] There are numerous descriptions of travellers eyeing the half-naked washerwomen in the streams, with water up to their waists.[71]

During the process of urbanization in the city, there was a permanent state of tension between the washerwomen and public health regulations: one municipal order followed another, repeatedly forbidding washing in the public fountains, or the hanging out of clothes on the bridge posts.[72]

Soap was another item of the home-craft industry, using herbs or leaves from the aloe and the timboúva tree: 'they also used horse manure and lemon juice, the latter to set the colours on printed cotton.' The homemade kind was a dark colour, and unsuitable for more delicate clothes.[73] As well as washing and ironing, the washerwomen also fitted in sewing, for many of them did mending at the same time, and then returned the clothes scented with jasmine, sweet acacia or other natural herbs. 'She lives from her sewing and selling', or 'she lives by washing and sewing' – these were jobs which were often combined:

> Luzia, a thirty-year-old, single, white seamstress, lived south of the cathedral with Gertrudes, a forty-eight-year-old washerwoman, single, mulatta, and her son who was a soldier. Also in the same house lived Maria, a mulatta washerwoman, a tailor called Luis, thirty years old and mulatto, who earned 6$ a month, and Braziliana, twenty-nine years old, single, mulatta and a seamstress.[74]

The itinerant saleswomen were mainly mulatta slavewomen and freedwomen, with daily wages that ranged from $200 to $400 in the most privileged cases. Held in the lowest possible esteem, it was a humble, hard job. The women who were described by travellers were, on the whole, the black women who sold from trays, or the penny saleswomen selling aluá, boiled corn, bananas, coffee, green maize and paçocas. But there were poor, white countrywomen as well down on their luck, who also appeared on the streets, among the slave women.[75]

In his memoirs, Ferreira de Rezende described a woman stallholder from Freguesia do Ó, who passed every day in front of his house, selling vegetables and eggs, and sometimes a basket of fresh fish, 'for next to nothing'.[76] In Nossa Senhora do Ó, a rural district with small sugar mills and cane plantations, most of them were farmworkers with slaves. In the registers of 1836, ten women vendors were recorded, six of them free, among them one white: Josefa Maria lived with some sisters, who were white and single mothers, with small children. South of the cathedral, Bernardina Luiza, a thirty-nine-year-old, white woman who had come down in the world, declared herself a 'huckster'; she was single and constantly on the move. In Ifigênia, Francisca Maria de Jesus, a vendor, was a mulatta widow of forty-five, with two small children and an income of barely 40$ a year.

Many of the ladies from the central districts of the city, mostly white, made a living from small local trade, with considerable differences in living standards and in domestic arrangements. The older women predominated, some of them single women, with slave girls and domestic servants, several of them bringing up their grandchildren. In smaller numbers around them were young girls, also single and living in the centre, mostly mulatta, constituting the free workforce whom small-time women employers sometimes contracted to complement the help from children and grandchildren.

Some of the women owned shops, stores and small sales establishments: they had to keep weights and measures, and were formally obliged to declare their business accounts to the tax office.

South of the cathedral, Quitéria de Camargo, a white widow of forty, lived from her grocery shop with her children of eighteen, seventeen and ten, and three other minors . . . In Ifigênia, Dona Joaquina Escolástica, a white widow of fifty-one, lived from her shop sales, with a son who was a trader in livestock (he earned 300$ per annum). North of the cathedral, a mulatta lady, who was a widow and a single mother, called Efigênia Maria, had a grocery store, and lived with her grown-up children (Francisca, Anna and José).[77]

Other ladies lived off their activities as businesswomen and acted as intermediaries in small commercial transactions; they tried not to declare their incomes, and clearly practised clandestine trade.

Anna Francisca, a white, single mother of forty, lived in the north of the cathedral district, in Rua da Boa Vista, with her grown-up children (Ignácia, twenty-eight, Escolástica Maria, eighteen, and Francisco da Silva, twenty-three) . . . South of the cathedral, Custódia Maria da Silva, a white widow of fifty, lived off her activities, with her grown-up children (Rita Maria da Silva, thirty, also a widow, Felisberto Antonio, thirty, and José Antonio, thirty) . . . Gertrudes Thereza, a white, single mother of thirty, lived in Freguesia do Ó with her small daughters; a Portuguese lady, a widow of fifty, lived off her activities in Ifigênia, with her grown-up daughters and two little granddaughters.[78]

The majority of women who lived off their activities in São Paulo were intermediaries in small business deals involving household surpluses such as soap, flour, candles and bacon. They were poor, and their many transactions were piecemeal and not very lucrative: for example surpluses of flour in exchange for a quart measure of salt, brandy or tobacco. Sometimes they bought up large quantities of maize, beans and bacon from the country farmers to deliver to a dealer who had more resources. The ones who owned slaves sometimes ended up with savings, from income of more than 1$ a month. As ever, to live off their activities, those women with no servants depended a lot on cooperation throughout the neighbourhood, a whole network of personal contacts, and the help of members of the family group; the incomes they declared varied between 60$ and 100$ per annum, based on four days of well-paid work a week, though their activities did not follow a regular pattern.

Through these women, consumption and trade almost merged in the incipient economy of the town, which was still almost a part of the backwoods. They were still influenced by magic and by a belief in miracles, and this is how they appear in the popular stories. The smallest household surpluses yielded a return, which was maximized through the contrivance of these astute women, who would go from door to door, making lists of the neighbourhood's needs, and whose small businesses held an aura of witchcraft: 'quarts of maize flour which would produce several alqueires ...'[79] When they had plots of land, they avoided declaring them to the registrar, so as to evade the enquiries of the tithe collectors, who acted with a violence that was exacting and despotic: 'Nothing to declare' is the prevailing phrase in the official surveys of many of the small-time countrywomen. They also got round the fixed prices of foodstuffs by claiming to 'plant food to eat themselves', but in fact keeping the produce that they laboured over to sell for public consumption: they transported the sparse harvests from their lands in carts, in tiny quantities. They got past the inspectors on the bridges by claiming that they were transporting merchandise from the land to their houses in the town, where it was to be used for their own consumption.[80]

The small rural properties and orchards of the country estates competed for sites for the small street trade in São Paulo. The produce from the poor country workers did not mix well with the products from the forbidden orchards on the wealthier country estates. Fruits, a precious resource for the street stalls, with sweets, marmalades and guava jams, were sold by slaves who belonged to the wealthy women stallholders and the mistresses of nearby estates. Curiously segregated from each other on the streets, the itinerant trade of poor country workers and that of the rent-paying women stallholders are also separated from each other in stories of oral tradition, and even in scholarly literature, where forbidden orchards take on a mythical aura. The idea of a promised land in the new world[81] seemed to grow out of the fertility rites of a rediscovered paradise: precarious land tenures, tinged with sacrifice, were compared to forbidden areas, ranging from the king's garden where the wicked princess went to gather honeycombs in secret, dressed like a little black boy,[82] to the rich orchards of the stories of Minas Gerais and of the memories of the contemporary Brazilian writer, Pedro Nava, coloured with the sap of the fruits of Nha Luiza, his grandmother.[83] In the urban area, the orchards of the larger estates were carefully delimited, contrasting with the allotments of recently cleared land, which were dangerously open to access and only temporarily possessed. One kind supplied the stalls and provided sweetmeats for their lady owners; the others supplied the small penny trade.

Access to the fields and food became more difficult when the thickets and uncultivated lands were reduced within the urban area and for 'seven leagues around'.[84]

In the popular stories of old São Paulo, the much-desired access to the fields and vegetable gardens was sometimes given fantastical, macabre connotations. This occurred in a folk tale collected in Piracicaba, which was an area devoted to sugar growing. It told of a lush, fertile bean field, yielding a harvest of more than ten bags, which had sprung up from the wounds on the back of a broken-down old nag. Months earlier, a couple of old country workers had turned away an old horse, throwing an old bean bag over the sores on his back 'to stop the flies from breeding in the sun'. This tale seems to be reminiscent of the overwork suffered by old slaves, or by freedmen who kept on clearing lands for their masters; or perhaps it was a simple reminiscence of the general difficulties of poor people in the country in finding lands on which to plant their subsistence corn. One fine day the hungry farmworkers saw the same horse coming back with a field of beans flourishing on its back: 'Good Heavens, a walking field, have you ever seen the like?'[85]

In the stories told of an evening, hunger always appeared in the background of their daily struggle for survival: 'And the Prince was seized with a desperate desire to grind flour,' considered to be food for slaves.[86] They were able to eat only by a miracle, by doing impossible, superhuman domestic chores, or as a result of magical providence: cloths and magic pots produced banquets from nothing, unexpectedly, without them asking, or responding to sheer desperation.

The role of leadership by women who were heads of households, as providers for the family group in the hard daily struggle, had an aura of sorcery, for it was they who manipulated the telluric forces of fire, water, fat and salt.[87] They also had their role as macho women, which was recorded in satirical verse:

A *paulista* woman from Taubaté,
A wild horse,
And a woman who pees standing up,
Good Lord, deliver us . . . [88]

Among the images of young, toiling women, full of life and over-coming the most difficult obstacles, there were figures of warrior maidens: dressed as soldiers, they behaved like witches, riding down a staircase on horseback, with magical hand movements, as if they were cutting the winds with a knife through the air.[89]

As women, they assumed the roles of men, warriors and providers for the home, and as such they were obliged to maintain their male companions: 'living at the expense of a woman's work' was a refrain engraved on the minds of the poor, and expressed in Joãozinho's cry for help whenever the situation got difficult: 'Help me, Maria-zinha!'[90]

Other images were superimposed, in which young, enterprising, inventive women would meet up and join forces with old, authoritative, despotic women; the wild animals which represented the instincts would burst from the head of an old witch, like the wild dogs which saved Joãozinho and Mariazinha, called iron-tearer, thunder and wind-breaker.[91]

In São Paulo versions of popular stories, the everyday chores of the poor took on an air of sorcery. Surviving under the harsh conditions of daily life was an exhausting job, and was achieved through magical contacts and supernatural interventions. Metaphors of hunger and images of the struggle to survive are embodied in the figures of old, domineering women: their foul forms could be seen fishing in rivers of empty waters;[92] as ghosts on lonely paths, they were seen bending over bundles of firewood, which they put together and then undid, in a com-pelling, deadly spell. There were little old women who drew water from the well with a worn-out rope.[93] The tasks were thankless and miser-able, done by women struggling with the impossible, and against the wretchedness that always lurked. In the images of the leadership of old women, there was an implicit suggestion that they 'were in league with the Devil', and that they were struggling within the thresholds of magic and the supernatural, as if there were a basic, intrinsic affinity between them and death: at their command, the Devil would go to fetch water from the well with an open-work basket.[94]

They appeared in stories as mean and tightfisted, although there was no alternative for those who were on the brink of nothing. One old woman stallholder refused Jesus hospitality; another threw a poor old man out of her house; a third took in an unsuspecting traveller, with the intention of robbing him.[95]

Pedro Malasartes (Peter the Mischief-maker) appears in folk tales, and once he managed to get a little wax and a few pennies out of a lady, with great difficulty. Much cunning, and perhaps a shred of faith, was needed to get anything in the way Malasartes did, securing from a good little woman all the ingredients he needed for a tasty 'river pebble' soup – fat, vegetables and flour.[96]

Wretched and needy, such women would rather throw the remainders of their cooking to the pigs than offer them to poor beggars. The story showed the importance of breeding domestic animals as an essential part of feeding the family group; it commented on the wretchedness which led to the breakdown of social links, instead of generating charity and mutual help. One niggardly old woman got her just desserts after she had died, being condemned to appear as a ghost at midnight among the pigs in the pigsty.[97] One popular figure, representing poor old parsimonious women, was St Peter's mother, who figured in a series of legends in the stories of old São Paulo: 'They say she was very mean. She never gave alms to anyone, and had a very bad temper: one day she went to wash some onion leaves in a stream, and she dropped a little leaf, which sailed downstream to where a poor washerwoman was soaping clothes. It was her way to Heaven, the only good deed in her life.'[98]

Everyday life stretched these women almost to the limit. They were the heads and providers of the family group, and had to cope with hunger and everyday needs, and at the same time they had to behave sociably in the neighbourhood, since custom demanded it, and this, in fact, was the main secret of their survival.

Home crafts formed part of the penny trade, together with a series of natural products which were collected for subsistence and which indicated the margins of survival, wretchedness and incipient commercialization. The new and partial urbanization, with its relative abundance of vacant plots of land, and almost free access to the thickets, river banks and flatlands by the water 'for common use', allowed survival and mitigated the wretchedness in the city precincts. Natural products from the surrounding hinterland were in full use in the households of poor white women or freedwomen. Native Indian methods were enriched by the new African resources.

The methods of preparation of Indian dishes which were described by the historian Sérgio Buarque de Holanda were still being used in the city of São Paulo in the middle of the last century, maintained both by the availability of natural products and by the social milieu.

All the land between the river Tamanduatehy and the Tabatinguera road belonging to the estate of Assis Lorena, the governor's daughter, was covered in thicket . . . From the Carmo bridge downstream, all the left bank of the Tamanduatehy was also jungle. To the west, the whole area of land, later called Morro do Chá, which is accessible today by the viaduct . . . was covered in thicket . . .[99]

A few forbidden orchards where no trespassing was allowed, many forests, lianas, fruits, fish, palm cabbage . . . all these things guaranteed the poorest women not only survival, but community life as well, in a flexible social network promoted by slavery. Side by side, free and slave women developed personal ties, which combined a violence and a kind of tolerance in the sense of contained outbursts. They lived a community life both distant and close, their poverty separating them, yet also binding them in the forced community life of the growing town. Their methods depended on the precariousness of an incipient capitalism, the feebleness of the organization of the administration and the police force, under the distant, controlling eye of the more powerful, and the impossibility in practice of enforcing orders, enclosures and municipal fines.

It was this that allowed the use and abuse of the timbo, a fishing net made of a poisonous bark, in the frequent plundering of fish.[100] Francisca da Silva, a mulatta woman of forty-five, with five grown-up children, lived from her spinning and fishing.[101] There was an abundance of certain kinds of fish in the Tietê and the Tamanduateí, where the odd woman would make a living, helped by the fishing skills of her children and grandchildren. Sometimes epidemics were caused in the city because women vendors put rotten fish into circulation.[102] They also harvested shellfish and fresh water crabs, which the chronicler Jacob Penteado was still enjoying in 1910, and fell back on insects from the bamboos.[103] In September and October they caught flying ants, the female sauba ants, which they sold on the street stalls, to be eaten roasted.[104]

Some of the women dealt in palm cabbage picked on the outskirts of the city, trading along with slaves. Several municipal orders dealt with the trade in cabbage, and that in other delicacies from the interior circulated on the trays: baked yams, roast potatoes, hot pine seeds, ibás (a fruit of African origin), catfish or river shrimp couscous, native Brazilian jaboticaba fruits, guavas, guabiroba fruits, Brazilian cherries, Surinam cherries, cambuci fruit (fruit from a tree of the myrtle family), pineapples, wild bees 'soaked in tree honey'.[105]

On top of this diversity of resources from the city, there were magic arts and African fetishism. The authorities, mainly the ecclesiastic ones, tried to put a stop to the healing arts of the sorceresses: 'They believed in the infallible virtues of certain concoctions, like the antidote which grows in the uterus of ruminant animals.'[106] When they wanted to let blood, instead of a lancet they used birds' beaks, myrtle stings or the teeth of a monkey or a rabbit.[107]

The secrets of quack medicine were engrained in the everyday life of the poor women of São Paulo, part of that armoury of survival skills that took up all their energies. In 1816 the vicars-general opened another investigation into 'anyone who practises sorcery or any who are witches and practise similar things; if there is anyone who uses Diabolical Relics and is in league with the Devil . . .'[108] The women used to collect 'amulets' and household medicine from the Tietê and its tributaries, and hold 'witchcraft sessions against bad air currents, stupor, the evil eye, poisoning and animal bites'. Their cures were anhuma (a kind of wild turkey), cow and opossum dung mixed with such things as tobacco, local pepper and sour lemon juice. Some of the sorceresses became famous, like Ana do Largo da Forca and Donana Curandeira: 'Breezes that are alive, breezes that are dead, stupor breezes, paralysis breezes, excommunicated breezes . . .' Even at the end of the century there were stalls and drug stores selling 'a disordered collection of dried leaves, roots, bark and fruits', which would cure pestilence, malaria and fever.[109]

Until the middle of the century there were still easy means of access to the produce from subsistence harvesting, but at the same time lands and brushwood were slowly being incorporated into the process of urbanization: 'where the public goes to take out gravel'.[110] Country houses that were not properly enclosed, with walls of mud, figure in the memoirs of Vieira Bueno, and Bernardo Guimarães, the nineteenth-century writer born in São Paulo, also described them on the outskirts of Freguezia do Ó: 'ownerless estates, surrounded by old, ruined walls, abandoned to the ants and the pigs'.[111]

In 1845 the inhabitants of Ó protested, and demanded that municipal measures be taken against individuals who were damaging the paths 'repeatedly hunting native pigs and catching bees'. In the middle of the century they were still hunting partridge and kid goats in the Anhangabaú valley and the Santo Amaro district.[112]

The increasing value of lands in the more central areas of the city marked the beginning of the banishment of poor women to the remoter districts. The inventories made reference to humble shacks, in a poor state of repair, which passed out of the women's hands for ever; they recorded meagre inheritances, small hovels bequeathed by domestic servants and poor freedwomen, like the one at 1 Rua de Sta. Ifigênia, or the one in Rua da Constituição.[113] At 10 Rua dos Bambus, the cottage of a former slave woman created a huge problem in the law courts: her nephew and niece, the sole heirs, were unable to take possession, because 'slaves cannot inherit'.[114] This was the road described by the nineteenth-century chronicler Ferreira de Rezende as totally covered in thicket, the houses in a row, 'all on one side'. At the same time the Rua dos Timbiras was still marshy and full of sedge.[115]

In the last century, from the 1830s, tens of dozens of requests began to come forward from the outskirts of the city: in 1834 someone called Margarida asked the town hall to concede her a plot of land behind the estate belonging to Dona Gertrudes; on 24 July 1843, Anna Rodrigues requested a plot 'on this side of the São Bernardo thicket, because of the state of poverty in which she lived, so that she might build a house with a yard'.[116] Requests for the legalization of property also began to arrive in quick succession after 1850.

In 1857 the town hall began a series of measures aimed at forcing owners to enclose their lands with 'plastered walls, which should be whitewashed and covered with tiles', adding to several new urbanizing regulations.[117] The roads were widened, new buildings were erected, and after the 1870s the bourgeois influence gave a new feature to the central districts – iron railings. Towards the end of the century the prosperity of the bourgeoisie created by the coffee boom, and changes in the city intensified by foreign immigration, set the seal on the increasing tendency to enclose lands and to complete the occupation of particular areas.

At the same time, bourgeois prejudice was growing against the itinerant trade of mixed-race and black women. With inflation, demand grew for the strategic sites for the stalls, which were subjected to new taxes and more drastic municipal measures. In the centre of the city of São Paulo, the final throes of slavery threw the small trade of poor women into confusion. In 1873, Paula de Jordão, Antonia Maria das Dores, Maria da Conceição and Anna Maria da Silva sent a petition to the town hall on behalf of freedwomen stallholders, with Luís Gama, lawyer and former slave, as intermediary. They protested that they had been forbidden to sell opposite the small cottages market and the governor's palace, where they had been used to setting up their stalls; as the municipal orders banished them from the streets, and as they did not have the resources to rent rooms and passageways inside the houses, in the way the Portuguese women were doing, they were deprived for ever of their livelihoods.[118] In 1876 local women stallholders were once again sending a document to the authorities, also protesting about their expulsion from streets where they had always sold, to 'keep them from poverty'.[119] They received a provisional permit to sell in the square, opposite the new market. Before long *baits* (small fish) were being sold amidst the green corn puddings and the cooked pine nuts.

From 1877 onwards, the colonial centres in the surrounding districts of Santana, São Caetano, São Bernardo and Ipiranga instituted a total change in the local subsistence production that fed the city, and at the same time reorganized the whole system of supplies. The railroads utterly transformed the local system of access for local trade provisions. The districts of Penha and Ó were no longer the points of access for the muleteers and dealers in provisions in the region; Piques, where the mules were quartered, was superseded by the train station.[120]

As urbanization gathered pace, itinerant trade soon withdrew from the streets of the centre and moved out to the new limits of urban poverty. Immigrant Portuguese and Italian women rented rooms and drinks stores in the city, or came into the centre with carts laden with grapes, milk, butter, firewood and coal;[121] their presence brought about a reshaping of the urban arena for survival and a great transformation in the provisions trade.

Any breaks in the structural continuity of poverty and unemployment were not real, but only apparent, for very few freedwomen or women in poverty were absorbed into the new industries that appeared in the city.[122] As for the rest, new districts of poor women emerged at the limits of the outer urban areas, in the districts of Brás, Belenzinho, Bom Retiro and Cambuci ... and their struggle for survival began again, almost beyond the reach of the legal authorities, and hidden from history.

Notes

ABBREVIATIONS USED IN THE NOTES AND BIBLIOGRAPHY

ABN	*Anais da Biblioteca Nacional do Rio de Janeiro*
ACM	Arquivo da Cúria Metropolitana de São Paulo
APJ	Arquivo do Poder Judiciário
APM	Arquivo da Prefeitura Municipal de São Paulo
Atas	*Actas da Câmara Municipal de São Paulo*
DAE	Departamento do Arquivo do Estado de São Paulo
DH	*Documentos Históricos da Biblioteca Nacional do Rio de Janeiro*
DI	*Documentos Interessantes para a história e costumes de São Paulo*
HAHR	*Hispanic American Historical Review*
IeT	*Inventários e Testamentos do Arquivo do Estado de São Paulo*
JLAS	*Journal of Latin American Studies*
JSH	*Journal of Social History*
Maços	Maços de População, no Arquivo do Estado
RAMSP	*Revista do Arquivo Municipal de São Paulo*
RAPM	*Revista do Arquivo Público Mineiro*
Registro	*Registro da Câmara Municipal de São Paulo*
RIHGB	*Revista do Instituto Histórico e Geográfico Brasileiro*
RIHGSP	*Revista do Instituto Histórico e Geográfico de São Paulo*

INTRODUCTION

1   Machado de Assis, *Esaú e Jacob*, in *Obra Completa*, Rio de Janeiro: Aguilar, 1959, vol. 1, p. 936. Joaquim Maria Machado de Assis (1839–1908) is a widely read Brazilian writer.

2 E. P. Thompson, *The Making of the English Working Class*, New York: Pantheon, 1956, p. 13.
3 Emmanuel Le Roy Ladurie, *Montaillou*, Paris: Gallimard, 1975.
4 Eugene D. Genovese, *Roll, Jordan, Roll: The World the Slaves Made*, New York: Pantheon, 1974; Herbert G. Gutman, *The Black Family in Slavery and Freedom, 1750–1850*, New York: Pantheon, 1976.
5 São Paulo today is Brazil's largest city and the world's second largest urban concentration with approximately 14 million inhabitants.

CHAPTER 1   DAILY LIFE AND POWER

1 *DI*, vol. 65 (1766), 106. *Atas*, IV (1632), 288; cf. Paulo Florencio Silveira Camargo, *A Igreja na História de São Paulo*, São Paulo: Instituto Paulista de História e Arte Religiosa, 1952–3, vol. 2, pp. 74–5.
2 'Bravas e decompostas' were the market women in Vicente's Maria Parda series, Marques Braga (ed.), *Obras Completas de Gil Vicente*, Coimbra, 1935; cf. Silveira Bueno, *O Auto das Regateiras de Lisboa*, São Paulo: Livraria Acadêmica, 1939; Mikhail Bakhtin, 'The language of the marketplace', in *Rabelais and His World*, Cambridge, Mass.: MIT Press, 1968; the essay on women troublemakers in Natalie Zemon Davis, *Society and Culture in Early Modern France*, Berkeley: Stanford University Press, 1975, p. 124.
3 Afonso de Freitas, *Tradição e Reminiscências Paulistanas*, São Paulo: Martins, 1955, p. 164.
4 Eduardo Freire de Oliveira, *Elementos para a História do Município de Lisboa*, Lisbon, 1911, vol. 17, p. 23 (12 Feb. 1765).
5 DAE, Processos Crimes da Capital, 0870-c75-P03-d09.
6 DAE, Processos Crimes da Capital, 0870-c75-P02-d64; 0864-069-P03-d06 and P01-d89 and c70-P1-d06; cf Ofícios Diversos, 0871-c76-P1-d93 and 94 (complaint lodged by Angélica Pedrosa).
7 DAE, Ofícios Diversos, 0871-c75-P02-d45 and Autos Crimes, 3902-c2-d1 (15 Apr. 1850). See E. P. Thompson, 'Patrician society, plebeian culture', *JSH*, vol. 7, no. 4, 1974, p. 382; André Leroi Gourhan, *Le Geste et la parole*, Paris: Albin Michel, 1964; Michel de Certeau, 'Systèmes de sens: l'écrit et l'oral', in *L'Écriture de l'histoire*, Paris: Gallimard, 1975, p. 215; 'Usages de la langue', in *L'Invention du quotidien*, Paris, 1980, vol. 1, p. 231; Thomas Luckmann, 'Philosophy, social science and everyday life', in *Phenomenology and Sociology*, Harmondsworth: Penguin, 1978, p. 217.
8 Gil Vicente (1465–1536) is a famous Portuguese Renaissance playwright; Fernando de Rojas (1475–1541) is a Spanish Renaissance playwright, author of *Celestina*.
9 'And in her confession, she said that about two months ago, she was going angrily through the thickets, towards the estates in this region, and seeing her difficulty in crossing to the river bank, and the likelihood of getting wet, she said that she cursed God, and repeated this blasphemy twice, there and then ... she also said angrily that because it was raining hard, that God was peeing on her and wanted to soak her ...' Capistrano de Abreu (ed.), *Primeira*

Visitação do Santo Ofício: Confissões da Bahia 1591–92, Rio de Janeiro, 1935, pp. 57–8.

10 *Atas*, XVI (1820), 16; X, 328; XIII, 345; XIV, 107; XVIII, 414; DAE, Ofícios Diversos, 0881-c91-P02-d41 (20 Aug. 1845 about the bridge repairs for Catarina Dias, on the road to the parish of Guarulhos), *Atas*, XXI (1813), 405 (about the hut of Quitéria Maria Gertrudes).

11 Augusto Emilio Zaluar, *Peregrinação pela Província de São Paulo 1860–61*, São Paulo: EDUSP, 1975, p. 125.

12 Pessanha Povoa, 'Anos Acadêmicos', in Ernani da Silva Bruno, *História e Tradições da Cidade de São Paulo*, Rio de Janeiro: José Olympio, 1954, vol. 2, p. 510.

13 Francisco de Assis Vieira Bueno, 'A Cidade de São Paulo', *Revista do Centro de Sciencias, Letras e Artes de Campinas*, no. 3, 1903, p. 31.

14 Auguste de Saint-Hilaire, *Voyage dans les Provinces de St. Paul et Ste Catherine*, Paris: Albin Michel, 1851, vol. 1, p. 271; Daniel P. Kidder, *Reminiscências de Viagens e Permanência no Brasil: Rio de Janeiro e São Paulo*, São Paulo: Martins, n.d., p. 192; Afonso de E. Taunay, *Memórias para a História da Capitania de São Vicente*, São Paulo: Melhoramentos, 1946, p. 114, refers to them as 'little black beetles'.

15 *Atas*, XVI (13 Dec. 1744), 362; XXII (1821), 568; XXIII (1823), 367; XXIV (1828), 449. Cf. Nuto Sant'Anna, *Metrópole*, São Paulo: Dep. de Cultura, 1953, p. 257 ('Rua do Cotovelo e Quitanda'); A. de Freitas, 'A Cidade de São Paulo no Dia 7 de Setembro de 1822', *RIHGSP*, vol. 22, 1923, p. 3.

16 *Atas*, XXII (2 Mar. 1822), 258; *Registro*, XVI, 339; Sant'Anna, *Metrópole*, p. 258.

17 'The introduction of customs from the more civilized Nations of Europe where the fair sex is employed in selling in shops, and involved in all the arts, which do not require great strength, would not only double the annual sum of wealth produced by human labour, but also the population.' Rodrigues de Brito, *Cartas Econômico-políticas da Bahia*, Salvador, 1806, p. 39; Thomas Ewbank, *Life in Brazil*, New York: Harper, 1856, p. 71.

18 Relations between women store owners and wine stores: *Registro*, XX (1829), 321 (Penha), 329 (Santo Amaro),388 (N. S. do Ó); at the festival of the patroness of Penha, 487; women who did not pay their dues, 408 and 511.

19 Antonio Rodrigues de Oliveira Velloso, *Memória Sobre o Melhoramento da Província de São Paulo*, Rio de Janeiro: Typ. Nacional, 1822, p. 113.

20 Antonio Egídio Martins, *São Paulo Antigo (1554 a 1910)*, São Paulo: Francisco Alves, 1911, vol. 2, p. 184.

21 DAE, ordem 37 A, lata 37 A, Maços, 1836.

22 Freitas, 'A Cidade de São Paulo no Dia 7 de Setembro de 1822', p. 33.

23 *Atas*, XXIX, 30–1; Vieira Bueno, 'A Cidade de São Paulo', p. 26.

24 Saint-Hilaire, *Voyage dans les Provinces de St Paul et Ste Catherine*, vol. 1, pp. 225, 257; *Atas*, XIII (1804), 235, and *Registro*, XIII, 140 and 188.

25 *Atas*, XXXVII, 32; Bruno, *História e Tradições da Cidade de São Paulo*, vol. 2, p. 621.

26 Francisco de Paula Ferreira de Rezende, *Minhas Recordações*, Rio de Janeiro: José Olympio, 1944, p. 265; Kidder, *Reminiscências de Viagens*, p. 252.

27 Maços, 1836.

28 *Registro*, XV (1818), 394; *Atas*, XXII (1821), 298; *Atas*, XXIII (1826), 525.

29 Saint-Hilaire, *Voyage dans les Provinces de St. Paul et Ste Catherine*, p. 293.

30 Zaluar, *Peregrinação pela Província de São Paulo (1860–61)*, p. 169.

31 *Registro*, XV, 79.

32 *Atas*, XXVI (1832), 422.

33 *Registro*, XVI, 359. Prince Dom Pedro visited São Paulo in 1822 and during this visit proclaimed Brazil's independence from Portugal. Rio de Janeiro was the capital of Brazil from 1763 to 1960.

34 *Atas*, XXII (4 May 1822), 580; *Registro*, XVI, 367–78.

35 *Registro*, XV, 453; *Registro*, XVI (1821), 192 and 196.

36 These were times of acute crisis, when the statue was brought from N. S. da Penha (Our Lady of the Rock): *Registro*, XV (1818), 462–7; *Atas*, XXIII (1823), 106; *Atas*, XXVI (1826), 184 and 214; *Atas*, XXIV (1828), 184; *Registro*, XX (1829), 138 and *Registro*, XXI (1830), 235 and 288.

37 The dollar sign signifies the nineteenth-century *real*, before the sign, with *réis* after the sign.

38 *Registro*, XVII, 104; *Atas*, XXIII, 20. João Carlos Augusto de Oeynhausen Grovenburg was appointed governor of the province of São Paulo by the court of Rio de Janeiro. Martim Francisco headed the opposition party against his brother José Bonifácio, who was then the prime minister of the young prince.

39 *Atas*, XXII, 568; *Registro*, XV, 464; *Atas*, XXIII (1826), 494.

40 Gilberto Freire, *Sobrados e Mocambos*, vol. 1, p. 112. The Brazilian empire began in 1822 with the Braganza monarchy and was overthrown by the Republican party in 1889.

41 *Registro*, XVII (May 1824), 425.

42 *Registro*, XV, 210, and *Registro*, XVII, 272.

43 'The people of this diocese live mostly on a continual circuit of the neighbouring districts. V.A.R. understands the reasoning behind this trade that the district has with those of Rio de Janeiro, Geraes, Goyazes and Matto Grosso. Some men grow old on this circuit and spend more of their lives in other districts than in their own.' D. Matheus de Abreu Pereira to the Prince Regent, São Paulo, 30 August 1810, *Registro*, XIV, 261. Cf. Manoel Cardoso de Abreu, 'Divertimento Admirável' (1783), *RIHGSP*, VI, 1900, p. 285; letter of Morgado de Matheus of 31 Jan. 1768, *DI*, vol. 23, 379.

44 *Registro*, XVII, 43 and 213 (on the plan of the house for foundlings); *Atas*, XXII (1822), 498.

45 Thales de Azevedo, *O Povoamento da Cidade de Salvador*, São Paulo, 1950, p. 212; Donald Ramos, 'Marriage and the family in colonial Vila Rica', *HAHR*, 55, 1975, p. 200; Donald Ramos, 'A Estrutura Demográfica de Vila

Rica às Vésperas da Inconfidência', *V Anuário do Museu da Inconfidência*, Ouro Preto, 1978, p. 41; Iraci del Nero Costa, *Vila Rica: População (1718–1826)*, São Paulo: IPE, 1979, pp. 36, 116ff.; Maria Luisa Marcílio, *A Cidade de São Paulo: Povoamento e População 1750–1810*, São Paulo, 1968, pp. 106 and 123; Eni de Mesquita Samara, 'A Família na Sociedade Paulista no Século XIX (1800–1860)', doctoral thesis, São Paulo, 1980, pp. 39, 43; Elizabeth Kuznetsof, 'The role of the female-headed household in Brazilian modernization (São Paulo, 1765 to 1836)', *JSH*, vol. 13, no. 4, 1980, p. 588.

46   *Registro*, XV, 79 and 498 (bridge at Juqueri); *Registro*, XVI, 659 (the plain of Carmo); Bruno, *História e Tradições da Cidade de São Paulo*, vol. 2, pp. 213, 241, 246; Theodoro Sampaio, 'A Cidade de São Paulo no Século XIX', *RIHGSP*, vol. 6, 1900, p. 168; Beatriz Westin de Cerqueira Leite, *Região Bragantina: Estudo Econômico Social (1653–1836)*, Marília: Faculty of Philosophy, n.d.

47   Households of women on their own in districts of São Paulo, 1836, by civil status (DAE, Maços, 1836):

District	Unmarried women (no. and %)	Married women (no. and %)	Widows (no. and %)
N. of cathedral	80 (55.9)	15 (10.4)	48 (33.5)
S. of cathedral	114 (60.9)	17 (9.0)	56 (29.9)
Ifigênia	50 (37.5)	20 (15.0)	63 (47.3)
Penha	28 (36.3)	4 (5.1)	45 (58.4)
N. S. do Ó	25 (54.3)	7 (15.2)	14 (30.4)
Total	297 (50.7)	63 (10.7)	226 (38.6)

48   Maços, 1804 and 1836; E. A. Wrigley, *Population and History*, New York: McGraw Hill, 1969, p. 90: 40 to 60 per cent of women remained unmarried in Europe under the ancien régime; cf. Marcílio, *A Cidade de São Paulo*, p. 181.

49   Marcílio, *A Cidade de São Paulo*, p. 158.

50   In 1836, among single mothers who were heads of households, there were 76 white (*brancas*), 51 dark-skinned or mulatta (*pardas*), 11 black (*negras*), 3 Indian (*indias*).

51   Governor of the captaincy of São Paulo appointed by the Queen of Portugal.

52   *DI*, vol. 23, 380 (letter of 31 Jan. 1768).

53   DAE, Requerimentos, ordem 341-c93-pasta 2-f.75 (5 Oct. 1810).

54   Ibid.

55   In the registers of 1829, from a sample of 200 villages, the women were an average of twelve years younger than their husbands. DAE, Maços.

56   Amadeu Amaral, *Tradições Populares*, São Paulo: Instituto de Progresso Editorial, n.d., p. 136.

57   Maços, 1804 and 1836.

58 Marcílio, *A Cidade de São Paulo*, p. 164.
59 DAE, Maços, 1804 and 1836.
60 *Registro*, XII (1798), 54.
61 ACM, Livro de Tombo do Braz 1818–85, f. 71 (enquiry of Bishop D. Antonio Joaquim de Mello, on 23 Nov. 1852); Visita Pastoral de 1801, portfolio of Bishop D. Matheus de Abreu Pereira, d. l; *Correio Paulistano*, 1854, on witchcraft, cf. *RIHGSP*, vol. 37, p. 328; 'Correição de um Desembargador em Taubaté' (1816), *RAMSP*, vol. 6, p. 133.
62 *DI*, vol. 20, 30; vol. 46, 262, 357; vol. 64, 102, 151.
63 Daughter of Emperor Francisco I of Austria, she married Pedro I of the Braganza family in 1817 at the court of Rio de Janeiro.
64 Inez de Castro (1323–1355) was a queen of Portugal who became a legendary martyr and was immortalized in the Renaissance epic of the Portuguese poet Luis de Camoës.
65 References to the Marquesa de Santos: *Atas*, XXVII (1834), 517; *Atas*, XXVIII (1835), II, 83; *Atas*, XXIX (1836), 53.
66 Antonio Vieira, *Sermões*, São Paulo: Ed. Anchieta, 1945, vol. 2, p. 1; vol. 12, p. 170; vol. 14, p. 5. A well-known Baroque Portuguese religious writer and Jesuit, Antonio Vieira was born in Lisbon in 1608 and died in Bahia in 1697.
67 Oswaldo Elias Xidieh, *Narrativas Pias Populares*, São Paulo, 1967, pp. 40, 44.
68 Francisco Montalverne, *Obras Oratóricas*, Rio de Janeiro: Garnier, n.d., vol. 2, p. 192 (eulogy of Sta Rosa de Viterbo). Frei Francisco de Monte Alverne (1754–1858) was a writer and great orator.
69 *RIHGSP*, vol. 20, p. 194.
70 Alcântara Machado, *Vida e Morte do Bandeirante*, São Paulo: Martins, n.d., p. 103; Leda Maria Pereira Rodrigues, *A Instrução Feminina em São Paulo: Subsídios para a Sua História*, São Paulo, 1962; *Atas*, XV (2 Feb. 1767), 239: 'and if the cattle are sold by a woman or a person who cannot read, a trustworthy person shall vouch for them before the weights and measures inspectors.'
71 DAE, Seçao de Periódicos, *O Publicador Paulistano*, no. 4, 5 Aug. 1854.
72 Luís Edmundo, *A Corte do D. João no Rio de Janeiro*, 3 vols, Rio de Janeiro: Imprensa Nacional, 1939, vol. 1, p. 296.
73 DAE, Ofícios Diversos, 871-c76-P01-d58.
74 Luís Joaquim dos Santos Marrocos, Letter of 1 Nov. 1814, *ABN*, vol. 56, p. 213.
75 Gonçalo Fernandes Trancozo, *Histórias Proveitosas*, Lisbon, 1681, conto XIX, p. 99 (the first edition, dated Lisbon 1575, was called *Histórias de Proveito e Exemplo*).
76 Luis da Câmara Cascudo, *Cinco Livros do Povo*, Rio de Janeiro: José Olympio, 1953, p. 88.
77 C. R. Boxer, *Mary and Misogyny: Women in Iberian Expansion Overseas 1415–1815, Some Facts, Fancies and Personalities*, London: Duckworth, 1975, p. 109.

78 José Cardoso Pires, *Cartilha de Marialva*, Lisbon: Moraes, 1973, p. 51; Francisco Manuel de Mello, *Carta de Guia de Casados*, Oporto: Livraria Chardron, n.d.

79 Paulo Prado, *Província e Nação: Retrato do Brasil*, Rio de Janeiro, 1972, p. 167.

80 Freire, *Sobrados e Mocambos*, vol. 1, p. 94.

81 Kurt H. Wolff (ed.), *Georg Simmel: A Collection of Essays*, Columbus: Ohio State University Press, 1959, p. 44.

82 DAE, Ofícios Diversos, 870-c75-P03-d01.

83 *Atas*, XXII (1821), 433, and *Atas*, XXIII (1822), 16.

84 ACM, Livro de Óbitos da Sé (1830–44), f. 5.

85 Antonio Manuel de Mello e Castro, 'Memória Econômica e Política da Capitania de São Paulo', *Anais do Museu Paulista*, XV, 1961, p. 98.

86 Assis, *Obra Completa*, 1959, vol. 1, pp. 321, 764.

87 Ibid., pp. 1108, 965; Erich Neumann, *The Great Mother*, London, 1955.

88 José de Alencar, *A Pata da Gazela*, in *Ficção Completa*, Rio de Janeiro: Aguilar, 1965, vol. 1, p. 419. Alencar (1829–1878) was a Brazilian romantic writer and politician.

89 Alencar, *Ficção Completa*, vol. 1, pp. 391, 836.

90 APJ, Juízo da Provedoria da Imperial Cidade de São Paulo, Testamentos: of Gertrudes Teresa de Jesus, 26 July 1880, Guarulhos, Ag. proc. 1/33, cx. 001; of M. Luisa de Barros, N. S. do Ó, Ag. proc. 35/36, cx. 002; of Anna da Anunciação, Sto. Amaro, 1853, proc. ag. 1/33 – cx. 003, etc.

91 ACM, Processos de Divórcio, estante 15, gaveta 27, proc. n. 357 and 365.

92 Yolanda Murphy and Robert Murphy, *Women of the Forest*, New York, 1974; Ernestine Friedl, 'The position of women: appearance and reality', *Anthropological Quarterly*, vol. 40, 1974, pp. 95ff.; Joyce F. Riegelhaupt, 'Saloio women: an analysis of formal and informal political roles of Portuguese peasant women', *Anthropological Quarterly*, vol. 40, 1974, p. 109; Beverley Chinas, *The Isthmus Zapotecs: Women's Role in Cultural Context*, New York, 1973.

93 Ladurie, *Montaillou*; Genovese, *Roll, Jordan, Roll*; Thompson, *The Making of the English Working Class*; Olwen Hufton, *The Poor in Eighteenth Century France*, Oxford: Clarendon Press, 1976.

94 Charles Valentine, *The Culture of Poverty*, New York, 1972; Tamara K. Hareven, 'Modernisation and family in history: perspectives on social change', *Signs*, vol. 2, no. 1, 1972, p. 190; Theodore Hershberg and John Modell, 'The origins of the female-headed black family: the impact of the urban experience', *Journal of Interdisciplinary History*, vol. 6, no. 2, 1975, p. 211; Marianne Schmink, 'A survey of anthropological approaches to the analysis of sex roles in Latin America' (with a review of the work of Oscar Lewis), University of Texas (mimeo.).

95 Judith Allen, 'Sitting on a man: colonialism and the lost political institutions of Igbo women', *Canadian Journal of African Studies*, vol. 6, no. 2, 1972, p. 165.

96 The war of the Mascates or pedlars (1710–14) in north-eastern Brazil was a conflict between local sugar merchants and planters.

97 José Bernardo Fernandes Gama, *Memórias Históricas da Província de Pernambuco*, Recife, 1844, vol. 4, p. 137.

98 '. . . I shall certainly marry / If you supply me / With meat, flower and fish, / And anything else I need.' Sílvio Romero, *Contos Populares do Brasil*, Rio de Janeiro: José Olympio, 1954, vol. 1, p. 294.

99 DAE, Maços, 1804 and 1836.

100 DAE, Requerimentos, ordem 341, cx. 93, pasta 2, doc. 74 (5 Oct. 1810).

101 ACM, Processos de Divórcio, estante 15, gaveta 27, nos 357 and 363.

102 Gabriel Soares de Souza, *Tratado Descritivo do Brasil em 1587*, São Paulo: Nacional, 1971, p. 252.

103 Pedro Taques de Almeida Leme, *Nobiliarquia Paulistana: Histórica e Genealógica*, São Paulo: Comissão da IV Centenário, 1954, vol. 1; Sérgio Buarque de Holanda, *Caminhos e Fronteiras*, Rio de Janeiro: José Olympio, pp. 262, 277.

104 DAE, Requerimentos, ordem 341, cz. 92-2-33 (Itapeva, 6 Apr. 1814).

105 Frei Vicente do Salvador, *História do Brasil (1500–1627)*, São Paulo: Melhoramentos, 1954, p. 273.

106 DAE, Seção de Periódicos, *Diário Popular*, 23 Dec. 1884, f. 4.

107 Tomàs Antônio Gonzaga, *Obras Completas*, ed. Rodrigues Lapa, São Paulo: Nacional, 1942; *Cartas Chilenas*, p. 284.

108 Provinces in central and south-eastern Brazil, now states, Goiás is the state in central Brazil where the present capital Brasilia is located.

109 Governador Antonio Paes de Sande (1698), 'Inventário dos Documentos do Arquivo Ultramarino', *ABN*, vol. 39, 1921, p. 199.

110 DAE, Seção de Periódicos, *O Governista*, 26 June 1847, f. 2 (customs registers).

111 Museu das Bandeiras, Goiás, Livros das Entradas, pacote 104, caderno 6, 1? volume, rolo 28, livro 10 (data kindly copied by Prof. Dra. Suely Robles Reis de Queiroz).

112 *Registro*, XX (1830), 511; *Registro*, XXI (1831), 23; *Atas*, XXIII, 345.

113 *Atas*, XXXV (1844), 23.

114 DAE, Ofícios da Capital, 31, cx. 31.

115 Katia Queiroz Mattoso, *Bahia: A Cidade de Salvador e seu Mercado no Século XIX*, São Paulo: Hucitec, 1978, p. 215. Salvador is the capital of the state of Bahia on the central coastline of Brazil.

116 Domingos Olympio, *Luzia Homem*, São Paulo: Gráfica Editora Brasileira, 1949.

117 DAE, Seção de Periódicos.

118 *Registro*, XX (1829), 31 (pigs loose in the Largo do Carmo); *Atas*, XXVII (1834), 340 (measures concerning rubbish); *Atas*, XIX, 149; *Registro*, XIV (1813), 511; XXI (1831), 54, 98; *Atas*, LVI (1870), 135 (loose animals), etc.

119 *Atas*, XIX, 216 and 454; *Registro*, XIV, 293, etc.

120 *Atas*, XXXVI (1846), 36.

121 *Atas*, XXIX (1836), 57.
122 *Atas*, XXVIII (1835), 13.
123 *Atas*, XXVIII (1835), 163.
124 Bueno, 'A Cidade de São Paulo', p. 29.
125 Marcel Detienne and Jean-Pierre Vernant, *Les Ruses de l'intelligence: la métis des grecs*, Paris: Flammarion, 1974.
126 Edison Souza Carneiro, *Antologia do Negro Brasileiro*, Porto Alegre: Globo, 1950, pp. 154–7.
127 Oswaldo Elias Xidieh, *Semana Santa Cabocla*, São Paulo: IEB, 1972, pp. 70–86.
128 J. R. Amaral Lapa (ed.), *Livro da Visitação do Santo Ofício da Inquisição ao Estado do Grão-Pará(1763–1769)*, São Paulo: Vozes, 1978, p. 238.
129 *DH*, 34, 57; DAE, Ofícios Diversos 864-c69-P03-d06; 866-c72-P2-d6 and c76-P2-d69 and 80 (thefts, libel).
130 Bakhtin, 'The language of the marketplace', in *L'Oeuvre de François Rabelais et la culture populaire*, Paris: Gallimard, 1970, pp. 187–92.
131 *Capoeira* is a martial dance introduced by slaves of Angolan origin, currently in style in Brazil as a defensive sport.

CHAPTER 2   BAKERWOMEN AND WOMEN STALLHOLDERS: SURVIVAL AND RESISTANCE

1 *Atas*, X, 342; *Registro*, V (1744), 236; *Registro*, VI (1746), 106 and 356, 360; *Registro*, XII (1797), 169, etc. Cf. Otoniel Mota, *Do Rancho ao Palácio: Evolução da Civilização Paulista*, São Paulo: Nacional, 1941, p. 161; Nuto Sant'Anna, *São Paulo Histórico*, São Paulo: Dep. de Cultura, 1937, vol. 1, p. 135; Kurt Lange, 'As Danças Coletivas Públicas no Periodo Colonial', *Barroco*, Belo Horizonte, no. 1 (1969), p. 29.
2 *Atas*, XII (1746), 244.
3 Holanda, *Caminhos e Fronteiras*, 1957, p. 211.
4 *Atas*, X (1735), 490; X, 95; XIV (1763), 514; XV (1768), 341.
5 *Registro*, XII (1798), 198; *Atas*, XIX (1798), 67.
6 *Atas*, XI (1739), 222; XII (1747), 365.
7 *Atas*, XI (1739), 217.
8 *Atas*, XI (1739), 220 and 256.
9 *Atas*, X (1734), 328; XI (1739), 223.
10 *Atas*, XII (1746), 243.
11 *Atas*, XII (1746), 244.
12 Ibid.
13 *Atas*, XII (1746), 245–8.
14 *Atas*, XII (1747), 364.
15 *Atas*, XX (1798), 100.
16 Oliveira, *Elementos para a História do Município de Lisboa*, vol. XI, 1717, p. 196; vol. XIII, pp. 25–34; vol. XIV, p. 126; vol. XVII, p. 439.

17 *Registro*, V, 181–5; *Registro*, VI, 21. *Congada* is a traditional folk dance of African origin representing the coronation of a Congo king.
18 *Registro*, V, 237.
19 C. R. Boxer, *Portuguese Society in the Tropics: The Municipal Councils of Goa, Macao, Bahia and Luanda 1510–1800*, Madison: University of Wisconsin Press, 1965, p. 125.
20 A municipal order of 20 Feb. 1713, constantly renewed, just as in the Ofícios Diversos of the last century, forbade any person, blacks and Guarani Indians from interfering with the processions or from going alongside and causing commotion or playing drums. *Atas*, VIII, 275; cf. *Registro*, VI, 378.
21 Bueno, 'A Cidade de São Paulo', p. 83.
22 *Registro*, V, 237.
23 *Registro*, VI, 105.
24 *Registro*, VI, 356 and 359.
25 *Atas*, XI, 274; XII, 542; XIII, 43.
26 *Atas*, XIV, 13; XVI, 357 and 460; XVII, 113; XXII, 447; XXIV, 82.
27 *Aluá* is a cold drink made from fermented rice flour and maize.
28 DAE, Maços.
29 Aluísio de Almeida, '142 Histórias Paulistas', *RAMSP*, vol. 144, 1951, p. 113; 'Contos Populares do Planalto', *RAMSP*, vol. 147, 1952, p. 10.
30 *Atas*, XXI, 495.
31 *Atas*, X, 486. *Catimpuera* is a fermented drink of cooked manioc flour, water and limes.
32 *Registro*, V (1741), 293; *Atas*, XI (1741), 364.
33 'The women stallholders who proclaimed their wares in loud voices were, on the whole, slaves from various families who lived by this trade.' Martins, *São Paulo Antigo*, vol. 2, p. 54.
34 DAE, Maços, 1836.
35 Luís dos Santos Vilhena, *Recopilação das Notícias Soteropolitanas e Brasílicas*, Bahia: Imprensa oficial do Estado, 1921, vol. 1, p. 132. Vilhena was a Portuguese Greek teacher and chronicler of eighteenth-century Bahia.
36 *Atas*, XII, 366; XXI (1800), 198 and 206; XII, 435; cf. Roberto Simonsen, *História Econômica do Brasil*; Myriam Ellis, *O Monopólio do Sal* and *A Pesca da Baleia*; Katia M. Abud, *Autoridade e Riqueza*, São Paulo, 1978, pp. 94–114.
37 *Registro*, XVII (1823), 192–321; *Atas*, XXXIII, 106 and 185; *DI*, 44, 206; Elisabeth Darwiche Rabelo de Almeida, *As Elites na Sociedade Paulista na Segunda Metade do Século XVIII*, São Paulo: Safady, 1980; Abud, *Autoridade e Riqueza*, pp. 100–4.
38 *Atas*, XXI (27 Apr. 1811), 206; *Registro*, XIX (27 Apr. 1811), 365 and 232, 248. Cf. Maria Thereza S. Petrone, *O Barão de Iguape: Um Empresário da Época da Independência*, São Paulo: Nacional, 1976.
39 *Registro*, XVII, 339.
40 *Registro*, XII, 428–31.
41 *Registro*, XII, 614–18; *Atas*, XIV, 513; *Registro*, XV (1819), 464; *Atas*, XX (1798), 101.

42 APJ, inventory of Santo Amaro (1840), of a small shop, in debt, belonging to Catarina Brau (deceased). Judgement on orphans of Santo Amaro, Ag. Proc. 56/64, cx. 7. (An arroba is about 15 kg.)

43 DAE, Maços, 1836.

44 Bueno, 'A Cidade de São Paulo', p. 23.

45 Ibid., p. 31.

46 Sant'Anna, *São Paulo Histórico*.

47 Afonso de Freitas, 'Folganças Populares do Velho São Paulo', in *Tradição e Reminiscências Paulistanas*.

48 Moraes Filho Mello, *Histórias e Costumes*, Rio de Janeiro: Garnier, 1904, p. 50; Freire, *Sobrados e Mocambos*, vol. 2, pp. 584, 587.

49 Bueno, 'A Cidade de São Paulo', p. 31.

50 APJ, inventário de Ursula Pires de Oliveira, Santo Amaro (1833), Ag. Proc. 6 a 17 cx. 2 and José Vieira da Silva, Santo Amaro (1841), Ag. Proc. 73/8 cx. 9 no. 78. A Portuguese alqueire measure is 8.4 litres.

51 *Registro*, V, 121 and 193–200. (A vintém was approximately 1 penny.)

52 Royal charter of 21 February 1765. Cf. Oliveira, *Elementos para a História do Município de Lisboa*, vol. XVII, pp. 24, 601ff.; *Registro*, XII (1800), 436–43.

53 *Atas*, XVI (1773), 209, 240 and 278, 361.

54 *Atas*, XXI (29 May 1812), 297; *Registro*, XV, 451 and 464.

55 *Atas*, XXII (6 Oct. 1821), 521, 526.

56 In 1836, out of 30 who declare themselves businesswomen, only 6 have around 10 slaves and own some kind of shop or store: D. Ignácia, in Sta. Ifigênia, has 21 slaves and a material store; Maria Jesuina do Espírito Santo, a white widow, has a material shop south of the cathedral with 12 slaves; about 20 have small shops and poorer stalls with 1 or 2 slaves; the large majority make vague declarations, suggesting that they live from their work, business, stall or as intermediaries. DAE, Maços.

57 *Atas*, XVI, 13; *Atas*, XXIII (1828), 136, 149, 494.

58 *Atas*, X, 60; XI, 364; Holanda, *Caminhos e Fronteiras*, p. 238.

59 *Atas*, XX, 359; XXI, 206; *Registro*, XII, 96, 148, 158.

60 *Registro*, XII (1803), 614–19.

61 *Atas*, XXII, 447; *Registro*, XV, 27.

62 *Registro*, XV (1814), 28; XVI (1821), 150.

63 *Registro*, XVI (1821), 150.

64 *Atas*, XVI, 301 and 357; *Registro*, XVII (1823), 162; *Atas*, XXII, 360.

65 Municipal orders of 1828 and 1829; *Atas*, XXIII (2 Mar. 1820); *Atas*, XXIV, 425; *Atas*, XXVIII (1835), 24.

66 *Atas*, XXIV (1829), 425; *Atas*, XXIX (1836), 27–31; DAE, Maços, 1836.

67 In 1804, out of 302 women on their own, with jobs in the tertiary sector (commercialization of domestic services and small trade), 170 had slaves (56.2 per cent); in 1836, out of 245, only 90 had slaves (36.7 per cent). DAE, Maços. If we count only those who declared that they lived from their businesses, there were 136 in 1804, of whom 86 had slaves (63.2 per cent) and 162 in 1836, of whom 87 had slaves (53.7 per cent). DAE, Maços.

CHAPTER 3 THE MYTH OF THE ABSENT LADY

1 Bueno, 'A Cidade de São Paulo', pp. 21, 29.
2 Mário de Andrade, 'A Dona Ausente', *Rev. Atlantica*, Lisbon, 1929, p. 10.
3 Ibid., p. 12.
4 Ibid., p. 9.
5 'I swam across the river / I came up, I dived, / Just to see you, / Lips of ripe cashew nut . . .' Ibid., p. 11.
6 Jesuits opposed the São Paulo settlers' business of enslaving native Indians throughout the colonial period up to 1759, when they were expelled from Portugal and its colonies.
7 Frei Vicente do Salvador, *História do Brasil*, p. 202.
8 Basilio de Sáa Vedra, in *RAPM*, vol. 6, 1896, p. 145.
9 Leme, *Nobiliarquia Paulistana*, vol. 1, p. 9, and vol. 3, p. 137.
10 Ibid., vol. 3, p. 104, and vol. 2, p. 206.
11 Ibid., vol. 2, p. 86.
12 Lisbon, 12 June 1739, enquiry into lawsuit of Simão de Alvarenga and his son Ignácio José de Alvarenga Peixoto, in M. Rodrigues Lapa, *Vida e Obra de Alvarenga Peixoto*, Rio de Janeiro, 1960, p. 156.
13 Appeals judge José Vieira Fazenda, 'Legislação Portuguesa Relativa ao Brasil', *RIHGB*, vol. 105, p. 215; *Coleção Chronológica de Leis Extravagantes (1609–1761)*, Biblioteca Mário de Andrade, Seção de Livros Raros.
14 André João Antonil was an eighteenth-century Jesuit chronicler of the Brazilian colonies. Andrée Mansuy (ed.), *Antonil, André João, Cultura e Opulência do Brasil por suas Drogas e Minas (1711)*, Paris: Institut des Hautes Études de l'Amérique Latine, 1965, ch. 17, p. 464.
15 Carta Régia de D. Alvaro Siqueira de Albuquerque, *DI*, vol. 51, 210.
16 Azevedo, *O Povoamento da Cidade de Salvador*; Mafalda Zemella, *O Abastecimento da Capitania de Minas Gerais no Século XVIII*, São Paulo: Bulletin 118 of the Faculty of Philosophy, 1951, pp. 188, 206.
17 Joaquim Felicio dos Santos, *Memórias Históricas do Distrito Diamantino da Comarca de Serro Frio*, São Paulo: EDUSP, 1976, p. 124.
18 Oliveira Mello, *Minha Terra: Suas Lendas e Seu Folclore*, Belo Horizonte, 1970, p. 71.
19 *IeT*, XVII, 94; XXIII, 7.
20 Punished by expulsion from the white lay religious brotherhoods, which had been transplanted from Portugal and were an important symbol of social hierarchies. Leme, *Nobiliarquia Paulistana*, vol. 1, p. 19; vol. 2, p. 206, and vol. 3, p. 137.
21 Frei Vicente do Salvador, *História do Brasil*, p. 305.
22 Letter of 31 Jan. 1768; *DI*, vol. 23, 383.
23 Trade with England was still kept on a clandestine basis during this period, or depended on Portuguese intermediaries. Legal commerce was established only after the 1810 commercial treaty with Portugal.

24 The Morgado de Matheus, letter of 31 Jan. 1768; *DI*, vol. 23, 383.
25 *RIHGSP*, 6, 1900, p. 168.
26 Alice Canabrava, 'Uma Economia de Decadência: Níveis de Riqueza na Capitania de São Paulo 1765/67', *Revista Brasileira de Economia*, vol. 26, no. 4, 1972, p. 95.
27 Sampaio, 'A Cidade de São Paulo no Século XIX', p. 168.
28 The roads were paved with hard, red limonite (ibid.). Bueno, 'A Cidade de São Paulo', p. 28: 'as it is an ill wind that blows no one any good, the elegant manner in which São Paulo women walked was attributed to the habit they had acquired from the need to tread carefully on very uneven paths.'
29 Bueno, 'A Cidade de São Paulo', p. 30.
30 Ibid., p. 29.
31 Cf. note 17 of ch. 1 above.
32 'Tomorrow is a holiday, / Corpus Christi, / Those who have something to wear go to Mass, / Those who don't, do as I do . . .' Mota, *Do Rancho ao Palácio*, p. 152. It was a mark of prestige for a man to carry the canopy during the Catholic holy day procession, and they were expected to be prosperous and well dressed.
33 Paulo Cursino de Moura, *São Paulo de Outrora*, São Paulo: Melhoramentos, 1932, p. 34.
34 Kidder, *Reminiscências de Viagens*, p. 192.
35 Auguste de Saint-Hilaire, *Segunda Viagem do Rio de Janeiro a Minas Geraes e a São Paulo (1822)*, trans. A. de E. Taunay, São Paulo: Nacional, 1932, p. 185.
36 *DI*, vol. 18, 87; vol. 40, 120–33; the sister of Frei Gaspar da Madre de Deus carried out reforms in the convents of Ajuda, in Rio: 'throwing out everything that was superfluous and improper from the furniture with which the nuns adorn their cells, in many of which there were damask seats, hangings and frilled cloth. She also dismissed the surplus of mulatta servants whom the nuns used, a practice as superfluous as it was improper.' Leme, *Nobiliarquia Paulistana*, vol. 3, p. 128; cf. *DH*, vol. 90, 92, 96; concerning the convents in São Paulo, cf. *RIHGSP*, 65, p. 120.
37 Nilva R. Mello, 'De Como se Vestia a Gente de Piratininga nos Tempos Coloniais', *Rev. do Atheneo Paulista*, vol. 4, 1967, p. 75.
38 Alfonso d'Escragnolle Taunay (Viscount Taunay) was a nineteenth-century writer, statesman and memorialist. Taunay, *Memórias*, p. 114; Wanderley Pinho, *Salões e Damas do Segundo Reinado*, São Paulo: Martins, n.d., p. 96.
39 Alencar, *Senhora*, in *Ficção Completa*, vol. 1, p. 723.
40 Edmundo Amaral, *Rótulas e Mantilhas: Evocações do Passado Paulista*, Rio de Janeiro: Civilização Brasileira, 1932, p. 202.
41 Pinho, *Salões e Damas do Segundo Reinado*, p. 93.
42 Report of 17 Nov. 1755, *DI*, vol. 28, 4 and 42.
43 'Informação sobre os magistrados', of 6 May 1810, *DI*, vol. 59, 9, 67, 118; Nuto Sant'Anna, 'Como se Vestiam as Paulistas em Fins do Século XVIII', *RAPM*, vol. 11, 1935, p. 156.

44 *Registro*, XII, 33.
45 DAE, Maços, 1836.
46 Ibid.
47 Ibid.
48 Letter of 30 Jan. 1768, *DI*, vol. 23, 279.
49 Vilhena, *Recopilação das Notícias Soteropolitanas e Brasílicas*, vol. 1, p. 140.
50 J. J. Teixeira Coelho, 'Instruções', *RAPM*, vol. 8, p. 561.
51 Vilhena, *Recopilação das Notícias Soteropolitanas e Brasílicas*, vol. 1, p. 48.
52 Gold production began to fall after 1750, causing a local crisis which reached its most acute level between 1770 and 1810, when slaves were too expensive to be maintained.
53 Costa, *Vila Rica*, pp. 77, 96.
54 Cf. ch. 1 above.
55 Sérgio Buarque de Holanda, *Raízes do Brasil*, Rio de Janeiro: José Olympio, 1973, p. 88.
56 Boxer, *Mary and Misogyny*, p. 86; report by Franca e Horta, 24 June 1810, *DI*, vol. 59, 73 and 140.
57 Capistrano de Abreu (ed.), *Primeira Visitação do Santo Ofício às Partes do Brasil: Denunciações da Bahia 1591–1593*, São Paulo, 1925, pp. 255, 250.
58 Ibid., p. 384.
59 Ibid., p. 261.
60 Capistrano de Abreu (ed.), *Primeira Visitação do Santo Ofício: Confissões da Bahia 1591–92*, p. 24.
61 Letter from Manoel da Nóbrega to P. Simam Rodrigues from Bahia, 9 Aug. 1549. Nóbrega was a sixteenth-century Jesuit, one of the founders of São Paulo. In Serafim Leite (ed.), *Cartas dos Primeiros Jesuítas do Brasil*, São Paulo: Comissão do 4º Centenário, 1954, vol. 1, pp. 119–20.
62 Frei Vicente do Salvador, *História do Brasil 1500–1627*, p. 298.
63 The gold rush to Minas from the northern towns of Portugal started in 1701 and continued to 1736.
64 Costa, *Vila Rica: População (1719–1826)*, p. 81; 'Correspondência de D. Lourenço de Almeida', *RAPM*, vol. 7, 1906, p. 207; Desembargador Vieira Fazenda, 'Legislação Portuguesa Relativa ao Brasil', p. 207; *DI*, vol. 24 (1732), 86, 208; *DH*, vol. 6 (Jan. 1677); *DH*, vol. 7, 5.
65 Rodolfo Garcia, 'As Órfãs', *RIHGB*, vol. 192, 1946, p. 137; Afonso Costa, 'As Órfãs da Rainha', *RIHGB*, vol. 190, 1944, p. 105.
66 Fernando H. Mendes Almeida (ed.), *Ordenações Filipinas*, São Paulo: Saraiva, 1957, vol. 1, Livro 1, tit. 88 and 93; *DH*, vol. 16, 438 and 458; vol. 17, 42 and 199; vol. 47, 21, 86, 105ff.; Leme, *Nobiliarquia Paulistana*, vol. 3, p. 104.
67 Pious matrons were the founders of the Capela de Sant'Ana in S. Vicente; until the Bishop annexed it, they had the privilege of administering it and dealing with the funerals and weddings of slaves. Leme, *Nobiliarquia Paulistana*, vol. 3, pp. 124, 130. They were not simply women from the ruling classes who figured in the local stories as founders of chapels: 'The African

woman Jacinta de Siqueira, herself the fortunate discoverer of an abundance of gold in the stream, which since then has been called 'Four Pence', raised the first rustic Catholic hermitage, where today is the Church of Purificação.' *RAPM*, vol. 10, 1905, p. 171.

68 *RAPM*, vol. 1, 1896, p. 661. Cf. Boxer, *Mary and Misogyny*, p. 35.

69 Coriolano Pinto Ribeiro, *Dona Joaquina do Pompeu*, Juiz de Fora, 1947.

70 Pedro Nava, *Baú de Ossos: Memórias*, Rio de Janeiro: Ed. Sabiá, 1972, p. 175.

71 Almeida, *Ordenações Filipinas*, vol. 2, Livro 3, tit. 18, 47, 48, 86; tit. 31, 'women should not be arrested because of debts'; livro IV, tit.18, 61, 65, 66 and 95, on 'Senatus Velleano'.

72 Antonio Candido de Mello e Souza, 'The Brazilian family', in T. Lynn Smith, *Brazil: Portrait of Half a Continent*, New York: Dryden, n.d., p. 296.

73 Ibid., p. 296; *IeT*, XVII, 366–70, 418, 425; Souza, *Tratado Descritivo*, p. 63; Zaluar, *Peregrinação pela Província de São Paulo*, pp. 138, 160; Nava, *Baú de Ossos*, pp. 32–9, 172, 276; Helena Morley, *Minha Vida de Menina*, Rio de Janeiro: José Olympio, 1971, pp. 14, 36, 44, 54, etc.

74 Frei Vicente do Salvador, *História do Brasil*, p. 126; Leme, *Nobiliarquia Paulistana*, vol. 2, pp. 80–3; Luis da Costa Pinto, *Lutas de Família no Brasil Colonial*, Rio de Janeiro: Nacional, 1948.

75 Letter from Governor D. Rodrigo da Costa, dated Bahia, 19 Aug. 1705, *DH*, 41, 107 and 125.

76 Prado, *Província e Nação*, p. 59.

77 Boxer, *Mary and Misogyny*, p. 61; A. J. R. Russell Wood, *Fidalgos and Philanthropists* (*1550–1755*), London: Macmillan, 1968, pp. 311–15; cf. by the same author, 'Women and society in colonial Brazil', *JLAS*, vol. 9, no. 2, 1977, p. 28.

78 Governador Antonio Paes de Sande, 'Inventário dos documentos do Arquivo Ultramarino', *ABN*, vol. 39, 1921, p. 199; Leme, *Nobiliarquia Paulistana*, vol. 3, p. 104; Afonso de E. Taunay, 'Introdução à Obra de Frei Gaspar da Madre de Deus', in *Memórias para a História da Capitania de São Vicente*, São Paulo: Saraiva, n.d., pp. 13, 17, 25.

79 Susan Soeiro, 'The social and economic role of the convent: women and nuns in colonial Bahia 1677–1800', *HAHR*, 1976.

80 *IeT*, vol. 48, 198; 'Catálogo dos Documentos sobre a História de São Paulo Existentes no Arquivo Histórico Ultramarino de Lisboa', *RIHGB*, special issue for fourth centenary of São Paulo, 1956, vol. 2, documents of 13 Aug. 1801.

81 Curitiba is now the capital of the state of Paraná, south of the state of São Paulo.

82 *DI*, vol. 49, 111; vol. 59, 22; *DH*, vol. 43, 92; vol. 41, 13 and 164; *Atas*, VI, 59; *Atas*, XIII, 406 and 410. Elisabeth Darwiche Rabelo de Almeida, *As Elites na Sociedade Paulista na Segunda Metade do Século XVIII*, São Paulo, 1981, p. 78.

83 *DI*, vol. 30, 143 ('The Secretary of State for Marine Affairs and Overseas

Dominions orders the Colonel's widow ... to pay the Exchequer what she owed (1802)'); *DI*, vol. 41, 101; *DH*, vol. 30, 40, 34, etc.

84 'In this city, some plantation workers have their slaves selling provisions ...' *Atas*, XVI, 124.

85 DAE, Maços, 1836.

86 *DH*, vol. 8, 381; vol. 5, 63. In 1706, D. Ana da Silva, widow of Captain Fernão P. da Rocha, received orders from the Exchequer to make ten 'champrões' for the restoration of the Artillery. *DH*, vol. 41, 190.

87 'Catálogo dos Documentos sobre a História de São Paulo', vol. 13, 1766; *DH*, vol. 34, 50; vol. 23, 46; vol. 30, 311; *DH*, vol. 3, 333–40.

88 Leme, *Nobiliarquia Paulistana*, vol. 3, p. 104; *DH*, vol. 27, 28.

89 *DH*, vol. 1, 365; *DH*, vol. 23, 46 (The King concedes to the mother the right to nominate a substitute for her son in the job of customs superintendent in S. Vicente); *DH*, vol. 24, 33 (Maria Dourado de Bulhões nominated a son of heirs to be customs purveyor); *DH*, vol. 30, 93 (D. Joana de Vasconcelos, while her son is a minor, could nominate persons for the job of customs inspector in the Appeals Court in Bahia); *DH*, vol. 30, 277 (the favour of the job of main clerk to the bailiff for the executions of the Treasury of Bahia as a dowry for her sister, 'on condition that she marries within two years and that her husband must personally go to serve in said office').

90 *RAMSP*, vol. 7, p. 72.

91 Fernandes Gama, *Memórias Históricas de Pernambuco*, vol. 4, pp. 249, 271–5.

92 'Catálogo dos Documentos ...', vol. 10, 97.

93 Nava, *Baú de Ossos*, pp. 251–6.

94 In 1836, of 189 slave owners (women on their own), 167 were white, 17 dark-skinned and 5 black. DAE, Maços, 1836.

95 In 1836, of 110 women on their own with servants, 67 were white, 29 dark-skinned, 4 black and 2 Indian. DAE, Maços, 1836.

96 Eny Mesquita, 'O Papel do Agregado em Itu', Master's thesis, São Paulo, 1975; Francisco Luna and Iraci del Nero Costa, 'A Presença do Elemento Forro no Conjunto dos Proprietários de Escravos', *Ciência e Cultura*, vol. 32, 1980, p. 836.

97 DAE, Testamentos da Capital, 1858, n. 1525; cf. Samara, 'A Família na Sociedade Paulista', p. 80.

CHAPTER 4   LADIES AND WOMEN SLAVES AT A PRICE

1 DAE, Maços, 1804.

2 DAE, Maços, 1836.

3 Orôncio Vaz Arruda Filho, *Memorando*, São Paulo, 1973, pp. 11, 52.

4 Samara, 'A Família na Sociedade Paulista', pp. 110, 114.
5 In households with domestic help in 1836, the family structure of women on their own was the following: solitary 67; nuclear 108; extended 50; sorority 24. DAE, Maços, 1836.
6 A slave as a gift for bearing a son was a custom among the 'signaras' (mistresses) of Senegal. George E. Brooks Jr, 'The signaras of Saint Louis: women entrepreneurs in eighteenth century Senegal', in Nancy J. Hafkin and Edna G. Bay, *Women in Africa: State and Society in Economic Change*, Stanford, Calif.: Stanford University Press, 1976, p. 34; DAE, Maços, 1804.
7 DAE, Maços, 1836.
8 Almeida, *As Elites na Sociedade Paulista na Segunda Metade do Século XVIII*; Francisco Vidal Luna, *Minas Gerais: Escravos e Senhores*, São Paulo: IPE, 1981; Costa, *Populações Mineiras*, pp. 75ff.; Samara, 'A Família na Sociedade Paulista', p. 109; Francisco V. Luna and Iraci del Nero Costa, 'Posse de Escravos em São Paulo no Início do Século XIX', *Estudos Econômicos*, vol. 13, no. 1, 1983, p. 211; Stuart B. Schwartz, 'Padrões de Propriedade de Escravos nas Américas: Nova Evidência para o Brasil', *Estudos Econômicos*, vol. 13, no. 1, p. 259. The period of the empire refers to the years 1822 to 1889.
9 According to Maria Luísa Marcílio, the average size of household in de São Paulo was 5.39 inhabitants per household. Marcílio, *A Cidade de São Paulo*, p. 128.
10 In 1804 there were 216 heads of households of women with slaves, and in 1836 about 190. The documents contain the following figures (DAE, Maços, 1804 and 1836).

Numbers of slaves kept	1804 (no. and %)	1836 (no. and %)
Only 1 slave	57 (30.7)	56 (34.1)
2 to 4 slaves	67 (37.9)	66 (38.4)
5 to 10 slaves	51 (28.4)	38 (23.1)
20 or more slaves	5 (2.7)	7 (4.2)
Total	180 (98.7)	167 (99.8)

11 The proportions of women on their own with slaves and servants, per district of São Paulo, are shown for 1804 and 1836 in the following table (DAE, Maços).

Districts	Total households in districts	Total households of women on their own	Households of women with slaves (no. and %)
1804			
1st	506	206	100 (48.5)
2nd	378	169	38 (22.4)·
3rd	301	146	59 (40.4)
N. S. do Ó	165	36	18 (50.0)
Total for 1804	1,350	557	215 (38.6)
1836			
North of cathedral	340	147	60 (40.8)
South of cathedral	570	173	52 (30.0)
Ifigênia	442	135	38 (28.1)
Penha	208	81	17 (20.9)
N. S. do Ó	183	47	18 (38.3)
Total for 1836	1,743	583	185 (31.7)

12 The collective make-up of the population in households headed by women with slaves was as follows:

	1804 (no. and %)	1836 (no. and %)
Heads (free)	215 (12.1)	189 (12.4)
Slaves	941 (53.1)	782 (51.3)
Servants (free)	204 (11.5)	138 (9.1)
Dependants (free)	413 (23.3)	414 (27.2)
Total	1,773 (100.0)	1,523 (100.0)

13 Bueno, 'A Cidade de São Paulo', p. 30; Martins, *São Paulo Antigo*, vol. 1, p. 6.
14 Ibid., p. 31; ibid., vol. 2, p. 54.
15 *Atas*, XII (1821), 356 (subject to a fine of $640).
16 Bueno, 'A Cidade de Sao Paulo', p. 29.
17 Of the total population of the city of São Paulo, slaves were in 1798, 28.5 per cent; in 1803, 25.6 per cent; in 1836, 24.2 per cent. Marcílio, *A Cidade de São Paulo*, p. 107. In 1854, slaves were 28.4 per cent; in 1872, 18.7 per cent; in 1886, 8.7 per cent. Roger Bastide and Florestan Fernandes, *Brancos e Negros em São Paulo*, São Paulo: Nacional, 1971, p. 49.
18 Costa, *Vila Rica: População*, pp. 25, 137; Luna, *Minas Geraes: Escravos e*

Senhores, p. 123; Kátia Queiroz Mattoso, *Être esclave au Brésil (XVIe–XIXe)*, Paris: Hachette, 1979, pp. 162, 235; Mary Catherine Karrasch, *Slave Life in Rio de Janeiro: 1808–1850*, Princeton: Princeton University Press, 1987.

19 The Andradas were a family from Santos known mainly because of the political influence of the oldest of the three brothers, José Bonifácio, who became Pedro I's minister and afterwards the tutor of Pedro II. His brother Martim Francisco was a local magistrate and politician in São Paulo of very conservative tendencies, as opposed to the younger brother Antonio Carlos, who took part in native liberal revolutions in Bahia and Pernambuco. Hélio Viana (ed.), 'Cartas de José Bonifácio', dated 3 Sept. 1813, *Revista de História*, vol. 55, pp. 224ff.; cf. Sérgio Buarque de Holanda, 'A Província de São Paulo', in *História Geral da Civilização Brasileira*, vol. 2: *O Brasil Monárquico*, São Paulo: Difusão Européia do Livro, 1964, p. 453; Martins, *São Paulo Antigo*, vol. 1, p. 6 and vol. 2, p. 84.

20 DAE, Maços.

21 In the registers of 1804 they record 302 women heads of households with jobs in the tertiary sector, of whom 170 have slaves; in the registers of 1836 they record in the tertiary sector 342 heads, of whom 90 have slaves. DAE, Maços.

22 DAE, Maços, 1836.

23 Ibid.

24 Ibid.

25 Ibid..

26 Ibid.

27 Ibid.

28 Ibid.

29 Ibid.

30 Ibid.

31 *DI*, vol. 23, 278.

32 *DI*, vol. 23, 393 (4 Feb. 1768).

33 Jaime Cortesão (ed.), *Obras Várias de Alexandre de Gusmão*, Rio de Janeiro, 1950, p. 124.

34 Luís Lisanti (ed.), *Negócios Coloniais: Correspondência de um Comerciante do Século XVIII*, Brasília: Ministério da Fazenda, 1965, vol. 2, p. 258 (letter of 22 May 1726). Sabará is an old Baroque town in central Minas Gerais, an important gold mining area in the first half of the eighteenth century.

35 Luis Viana Filho, *O Negro na Bahia*, Rio de Janeiro: José Olympio, 1946, p. 107.

36 Jorge Benci, *Da Economia Cristã dos Senhores no Governo de Seus Escravos (1700)*, ed. Serafim Leite, Porto: Livraria Apostolado da Imprensa, 1954, p. 99. Jorge Benci was an eighteenth-century Jesuit writer on slavery.

37 Cf. critique by Herbert G. Gutman of book by Genovese, in *The Black Family in Slavery and Freedom 1750–1850*, p. 311; Genovese, *Roll. Jordan, Roll*, pp. 3, 597.

38 Maria Graham, *Diário de uma Viagem ao Brasil e de uma Estada nesse pais durante parte dos anos 1821, 1822 e 1823* (trans.), São Paulo: Nacional, 1956, pp. 117, 323; John Barrow, *A Voyage to Cochinchina in the Years 1792 and 1793*, London: Caldwell and Davies, 1806, pp. 112–13; J. M. Rugendas, *Viagem Pitoresca Através do Brasil* (trans.), São Paulo: Martins, 1941, pp. 187–8, 113; Ferreira de Rezende, *Minhas Recordações*, p. 279.

39 Paul Bohannan and G. Dalton, *Markets in Africa*, Evanston, Ill.: Northwestern University Press, 1962, p. 120.

40 DAE, Maços, 1836.

41 *Atas*, XXVIII (19 Jan. 1835), 120; Martins, *São Paulo Antigo*, vol. 2, pp. 82–4.

42 DAE, Maços, 1804 and 1836.

43 Bueno, 'A Cidade de São Paulo', p. 31.

44 For different points of view on this subject, see Maria Beatriz Nizza Silva, 'Casamentos de Escravos na Capitania de São Paulo', *Ciência e Cultura*, vol. 32, no. 7, 1980, p. 816; Richard Graham, 'Brazilian slavery re-examined: a review article', *JSH*, vol. 3, no. 4, 1970, p. 431.

45 DAE, Maços.

46 Ibid.

47 Contas do Seminário de Meninos Órfãos São Luís do Sagrado Coração de Jesus, DAE, Ofícios Diversos, 870-c75-P03-d49 to 58.

48 Daniel Pedro Muller, *Ensaio d'um Quadro Estatístico da Província de São Paulo (1838)*, São Paulo, 1923.

49 Cf. tables of weights and measures in Simonsen, *História Econômica do Brasil*, pp. 462–3; Harold Johnson, 'A preliminary inquiry into money, prices and wages in Rio de Janeiro, 1763–1823', in Dauril Alden (ed.), *Colonial Roots of Modern Brazil*, Berkeley: University of California Press, 1973, p. 238.

50 J. B. Debret, *Viagem Pitoresca e Histórica ao Brasil*, São Paulo: Martins, vol. 1, p. 224. Debret was a French traveller and artist, renowned for his portrayal of Brazilian social life.

51 J. J. Tschudi, *Viagem às Províncias do Rio de Janeiro e São Paulo*, São Paulo: EDUSP, 1980, p. 58; D. Sutch, 'The care and feeding of slaves', in Paul A. David et al., *Reckoning with Slavery: A Critical Study in the Quantitative History of American Negro Slavery*, New York: Oxford University Press, 1976, pp. 261–80.

52 Tschudi, *Viagem às Províncias do Rio de Janeiro e São Paulo*, p. 67. J. J. Tschudi was a German traveller who documented the first experiments of coffee planters with European immigrants as labourers.

53 Ibid.

54 APJ, 2? Vara da Família, Juízo da Provedoria da Imperial Cidade de São Paulo, inventories from N. S. do Ó (1853), ag. proc. 35/33 – cx. 002; 1-33-cx. 001 to 5; processos de Sto. Amaro (1847–1873), 73/8-cx. 9; 1-6 to 7-cx. 2 (1883); Penha, proc. 56/64-cx. 007; Cotia (1842) 51/89-cx. 010 (n. 1215); Juízo dos Órfãos (1820 to 1842) 81-89-cx. 10-85 e 18-23-cx. 3

n. 1370. Sums do not always add up or multiply out but these errors are common in the sources.

55 *Atas*, XII, 435.

56 *Atas*, XXV (1829), 36.

57 *Registro*, V, 54; *Atas*, XIX, 366.

58 *Registro*, V, 54.

59 *Atas*, XVIII, 366.

60 *Atas*, XXXV (1845), 21.

61 Daily pay of wage-earning slaves, based on indications in the Maços; Debret, *Viagem Pitoresca e Histórica ao Brasil*, vol. 1, p. 160; John Luccock, *Notas sobre o Rio de Janeiro e Partes Meridionais do Brasil*, São Paulo: Martins, 1942, p. 427; Ernst Ebel, *O Rio de Janeiro e Seus Arredores em 1824*, São Paulo: Nacional, 1972, p. 17 (about 370 réis a day); Ferreira de Rezende, *Minhas Recordações*, pp. 47, 279 (in São Paulo, in 1840, 400 réis a day).

62 Ibid.

63 Cf. ch. 6 below.

64 Ferreira de Rezende, *Minhas Recordações*, p. 49.

65 DAE, Escravos, 1830–82, ordem 5534 cx. 1–2. Report by Antonio Joaquim de Oliveira, to the vice-president of the province of São Paulo, dated 29 Sept. 1829: 'I report to Your Excellency that on the 28th, eight local slaves employed on this road disappeared from the group, and, I am fairly certain, will go and present themselves to Your Ex. to claim the holidays granted, which, according to Your Ex.'s orders, I have made them work; if on the 21st of the same month they do not turn up for work, because it is a holiday, they will not be punished, only reprimanded and threatened with a severe punishment if they do it again.'

66 Emilia Viotti, *Da Senzala à Colônia*, São Paulo: Difusão Européia do Livro, 1966, p. 389; Robert Conrad, *The Destruction of Brazilian Slavery, 1850–1888*, Berkeley: California University Press, pp. 131, 134.

67 Rugendas, *Viagem Pitoresca*, p. 179.

68 Barbara C. Lewis, 'The limitations of group action entrepreneurs: the market women of Abidjan, Ivory Coast', in Hafkin and Bay, *Women in Africa*, pp. 135, 141; Raymond Firth and B. S. Yamey, *Capital Saving and Credit in Peasant Societies*, Chicago: Aldine, 1964.

69 *Atas*, XXII (1820), 357.

70 Richard C. Wade, *Slavery in the Cities: The South, 1820–1860*, New York: Oxford University Press, 1972, pp. 19–27; Hélio Oliveira de P. Castro, 'Viabilidade Econômica da Escravidão no Brasil (1850–1888)', *Revista Brasileira de Economia*, vol. 27, no. 1, 1973, p. 43. Cf. Thomas Weiss, *A Deplorable Scarcity: The Failure of Industrialization in the Slave Economy*, Chapel Hill: University of North Carolina Press, 1981.

71 The abolition of the trade in slaves was formally decreed in 1831 under British pressure, but the slave trade continued as an illegal activity until finally the British succeeded in securing the enforcement of the law in 1850.

The sudden release of capital invested in this trade caused inflation and the rise of foodstuff prices between 1850 and 1854.

72   Canabrava, 'Uma Economia de Decadência: Níveis de Riqueza em 1765/ 67'; Mattoso, *Être esclave au Brésil*, pp. 106–10; Warren Dean, *Rio Claro: um Sistema de Grande Lavoura*, São Paulo: Paz e Terra, 1977; *IeT*.

73   The first textile factory was established in 1811 by Antonio Maria Quartim. It functioned in the basement of the government palace until 1824 and employed about 20 seamstresses in work at home. The second, belonging to João Marcos Vieira, established in 1828, employed 34 seamstresses. Bruno, *História e Tradições da Cidade de São Paulo*, vol. 1, p. 342. According to information in the Ofícios Diversos in the Arquivo do Estado, in 1831 this passed into the hands of Tomé Manoel de Jesus, and in March 1832 it was discontinued, because of the high cost of raw materials. DAE, Ofícios Diversos, 866-c73-P01-d27. The spinning machines 'which dispensed with women spinners' were sold by public auction. 865-c70-P02-doc. 26 to 31.

74   Maria Eulália Lahmeyer Lobo et al., 'Estudos das Categorias Sócio-profissionais dos Salários e do Custo de Alimentação no Rio de Janeiro de 1820 a 1920', *Revista Brasileira de Economia*, vol. 27, no. 4, 1973, pp. 154–60, Johnson, 'A preliminary inquiry into money, prices and wages in Rio de Janeiro, 1763–1823', p. 231.

75   In 1804, of 941 slaves in households of women on their own, 563 were women and 378 men. In 1836, of 782 slaves, 447 were women and 305 men. DAE, Maços.

76   *Farol Paulistano*, no. 410, 2 Nov. 1830, DAE, Seção de Periódicos.

77   *Atas*, XVI (1773), 210 and 278.

78   Sant'Anna, *São Paulo Histórico*, vol. 4, p. 123.

79   Ibid., p. 190.

80   DAE, Maços, 1804.

81   The proportion indicated in the text refers to households of black women in relation to the total of slave women in houses of women owners. DAE, Maços.

82   DAE, Maços

83   The first law to abolish slavery itself was voted in in 1871, and declared free all slave children born from that date on.

84   DAE, Ofícios Diversos (2 Sept. 1837), 875-c80-P1-d43; cf. Machado de Assis's story, 'O caso da vara', in *Obra Completa*, vol. 2, pp. 559ff.

85   *Diário Popular*, 1 Feb. 1886; cf. Viotti, *Da Senzala à Colônia*, p. 293. After the end of the slave trade in 1850, slavery continued until 1888 and prospered mainly in the southern region of Brazil, where coffee plantations were being opened. The abolitionist campaign of 1884 to 1888 was concentrated mainly in the press.

86   DAE, Ofícios Diversos, 876-c81-P1-d27 (list of prices for public auction of free Africans). DAE, Escravos (1830–1882) – ordem 5534, cx. 1 – doc. 30 Mar. 1830: 'Report on slaves who are in my charge, with declarations

required by the Treasury Council, belonging to Armação de Vila Bela da Princeza:

Names	Monthly hire (25 days)
Francisco Mulato	1$600
Antonio Jacaré	1$200
Miquelina Mulata	1$280
Benedita Mulata	2$000
Maria Negra	1$600
Maria	1$280
Ana and two young daughters	2$000
Catharina preta	1$600
Perpétua Mulata with two children	2$000

87 DAE, Ofícios Diversos, 876-c81-P1-doc. 43.
88 DAE, Ofícios Diversos, 877-c83-P02-d17.
89 DAE, Ofícios Diversos, 881-c87-P1-d91.
90 DAE, Ofícios Diversos, 881-c87-P1-d100; c91-P1-d48; c93-P1-d87 and 87a; 888-c94-P1-d16.
91 DAE, Seção de Periódicos: *O Amigo do Povo e da Pátria*, n. 58, 16 Jan. 1830, p. 4.
92 Bueno, 'A Cidade de São Paulo', p. 30.
93 Debret, *Viagem Pitoresca e Histórica ao Brasil*, vol. 1, pp. 123, 144, 228 (prints 5, 6, 9 (Largo do Palácio), 12); Charles Ribeyrolles, *Brasil Pitoresco*, São Paulo: Martins, 1941, vol. 1, p. 166.
94 Postura Municipal of Jan. 1870; cf. Viotti, *Da Senzala à Colônia*, p. 228.
95 DAE, Maços, 1836.
96 DAE, Ofícios Diversos, 881-c86-P02-d62 (28 Sept. 1841).
97 Luccock, *Notas sobre o Rio de Janeiro*, p. 74; Ewbank, *Life in Brazil*, p. 92.
98 DAE, Ofícios Diversos, 860-c75-P02-d51.
99 DAE, Ofícios Diversos, 870-c75-P02-d28.
100 DAE, Seção de Periódicos, *O Novo Farol Paulistano*, 12, no. 3, 1834; cf. Suelly R. Reis Queiroz, *A Escravidão Negra em São Paulo: Um Estudo das Tensões Provocadas pelo Escravismo no Século XIX*, Rio de Janeiro: MEC/ José Olympio, 1977. Cabinda is a small region in northern Angola.
101 DAE, Crimes da Sé, 870-c75-P02-d45 (4 Aug. 1834); c75-P03-d16 (July 1834).
102 DAE, Ofícios Diversos, 870-c75-P01-d27 (12 Feb. 1834).
103 DAE, Ofícios Diversos, 866-c72-P02-d93 (16 Nov. 1830).
104 *Atas*, XXII (1822), 433; XXIII (1823), 16.
105 *O Publicador Paulistano*, no. 10 (1858), p. 3; DAE, Seção de Periódicos.
106 DAE, Ofícios Diversos, Ocorrências policiais 1824–1825, 866-c69-P02-d56, 41, 82, etc.; 866-c72-P01-d38 (23 June 1830); 866-c72-P02-d72 (13 Nov. 1831), etc.

107 DAE, Autos Crimes 1850–59, ordem 390 2-C2-1857; Escravos – 5534 – cx. i – doc. 15, etc.
108 Bruno, *História e Tradições da Cidade de São Paulo*, vol. 2, p. 487; Martins, *São Paulo Antigo*, vol. 1, p. 80.
109 DAE, Ofícios Diversos, 866-c73-P02-d93 (incident between parish priest and delegate of Justice of Peace of cathedral district, 11 Oct. 1832); 866-c74-P02-d24; 866-c74-P03-d57; 875-c83-P01-d72 (July 1838); *Registro*, XX (1829), 93.
110 ACM – Divórcios, processo 15-7-106 (1811). Cf. Maria Beatriz Nizza da Silva, 'O Divórcio na Capitania de São Paulo', in Maria Cristina Bruschini and Fulvia Rosemberg (eds), *Vivência: História, Sexualidade e Imagens Femininas*, São Paulo: Brasiliense, 1980, p. 174.
111 Ibid., p. 185.
112 The first railroad in São Paulo, inaugurated after 1867, brought many changes and was crucial to the spread of the abolitionist movement.
113 *Atas*, XXVII (1832), 348; *Atas*, XXVIII (1835), 13.
114 Moura, *São Paulo de Outrora*, p. 87.
115 *Atas*, XXVIII (1835), 111.
116 *Atas*, XXXIV (1843), 197.
117 Ferreira de Rezende, *Minhas Recordações*, p. 279.
118 Conrad, *The Destruction of Brazilian Slavery, 1850–1888*, p. 214. Many of the first abolitionist laws, such as this municipal decree of 1871 in São Paulo, had the ambiguous aim of attracting slaves towards the plantations by over-taxing them in urban areas.
119 Viotti, *Da Senzala à Colônia*, pp. 208–10.
120 Bastide and Fernandes, *Brancos e Negros em São Paulo*, p. 49.
121 *Atas*, X (1730), 60.
122 *Atas*, XI (1741), 364; *Atas*, XVIII, 202, 414.
123 *Registro*, V, 293; *Atas*, XIII (1749), 29 and 34; *Registro*, XII (12 Feb. 1803), 615.
124 *Registro*, V (1741), 312; *Registro*, XVII (1823), 79, etc.; XII (1798), 198 and 240.
125 'The women slaves shall not wear baize on their heads and any found doing so will be imprisoned at my discretion' (21 Sept. 1810), *Registro*, XIV, 306; drying clothes in an unseemly way, *Atas*, XIX, 149; *Registro*, XIV, 551; XXI, 54, 98; *Atas*, LI, 39 (on the bridge of Piques); municipal order concerning indecent language, 11 Jan. 1830, Debret, *Viagem Pitoresca e Histórica ao Brasil*, vol. 1, p. 234; APM, 'Posturas', CM 1-39-v. 73.
126 *Atas*, LVIII (1869), 82.
127 Viotti, *Da Senzala à Colônia*, pp. 231–3; Taunay, *História da Cidade de São Paulo no Império*, vol. 6, p. 354; Bruno, *História e Tradições da Cidade de São Paulo*, vol. 2, p. 741.
128 Viotti, *Da Senzala à Colônia*, p. 312.
129 Cf. Luna and Costa, 'A Presença do Elemento Forro no Conjunto dos Proprietários de Escravos', *Ciência e Cultura*, vol. 32, no. 7, 1980, p. 836;

Schwartz, 'Padrões de Propriedade de Escravos nas Américas: Nova Evidência para o Brasil', p. 259.

CHAPTER 5   SLAVES AND FREEDWOMEN VENDORS

1   *Registro*, V, 428; *Atas*, IX, 31; *Atas*, XVI, 454; XII, 455.
2   On slave hideouts in São Paulo: *Registro*, V, 427; VI, 359; XVII, 455 (about Catarina Correia); *Registro*, XVII, 77 and 117; XXII (1834), 423 and 457; *Atas*, XXVI, 62 (Anhangabaú and Bexiga); in Pinheiros, *DI*, vol. 84, 70; cf. Moura, 'Revoltas de Escravos em São Paulo', *RAMSP*, vol. 181, 1970, p. 103; Bruno, *História e Tradições da Cidade de São Paulo*, vol. 2, pp. 333, 556, 571, 738; Martins, *São Paulo Antigo*, vol. 2, p. 82. Anhangabaú, then an unoccupied valley with forest, is now a main access avenue to the business centre, and there is now an important access route to the city along the Pinheiros river.
3   Bueno, 'A Cidade de São Paulo', p. 30; Martins, *São Paulo Antigo*, vol. 2, p. 54.
4   Debret, *Viagem Pitoresca e Histórica ao Brasil*, vol. 1, pp. 179, 228; vol. 2, engraving 11; Ribeyrolles, *Brasil Pitoresco*, vol. 1, p. 166; cf. Roger Bastide, *As Religiões Africanas*, São Paulo: EDUSP, vol. 2, pp. 412, 454; Bruno, *História e Tradições da Cidade de São Paulo*, vol. 2, p. 304; Martins, *São Paulo Antigo*, vol. 2, pp. 54, 82–4.
5   Holanda, *Caminhos e Fronteiras*, p. 64.
6   Bastide, *As Religiões Africanas*, vol. 2, p. 315. What also stands out are the syncretism and confluence of the cults of Iemanjá, Iansã, St Barbara and Joan of Arc, underlining the image of strong women. Ruth Landes, *A Cidade das Mulheres*, Rio de Janeiro: Civilização Brasileira, 1967; Hafkin and Bay, *Women in Africa*; 'Images of women in society', *International Social Science Journal* (UNESCO), special issue, XIV, 1962, p. 148.
7   Bohannan and Dalton, *Markets in Africa*, pp. 13, 93, 111.
8   Karrasch, *Slave Life in Rio de Janeiro*, p. 107.
9   Dora Emily Earth, *Vallenge Women: The Social and Economic Life of the Vallenge Women of Portuguese East Africa, An Ethnographic Study* (1933), London: Cass, 1968; Maria Theresa S. Petrone, *A Lavoura Canavieira em São Paulo*, São Paulo: Difusão Européia do Livro, 1969, p. 116; F. A. Curtin, *The African Slave Trade: A Census*, Madison: University of Wisconsin, 1969; Herbert S. Klein, 'The trade to Rio de Janeiro', *Journal of African History*, vol. 10, no. 4, 1969, p. 540.
10 William Hodder, 'The Yoruba rural market', in Bohannan and Dalton, *Markets in Africa*, p. 103; Robert Le Vine, 'Sex roles and economic change in Africa', in John Middleton (ed.), *Black Africa*, London: Macmillan, 1970, p. 174; Collette La Cour Grandmaison, 'Les Activités économiques des femmes dakaroises', *Africa*, vol. 31, no. 2, 1969, p. 138; Sidney Mintz, 'The employment of capital by market women in Haiti', in Raymond Firth and B. S. Yamey, *Capital, Saving and Credit in Peasant Societies*, p. 256.

11   Dorothy Hammond, 'Women: their economic roles in traditional societies', an
      Addison-Wesley Module in Anthropology no. 35, Reading, Mass., 1973,
      p. 35; Richard Gray and David Birmingham (eds), *Pre-colonial African
      Trade*, London, 1973; F. Balsan, 'Chez les femmes à crinières au Sud Angola',
      African Women, 1, 1956, p. 24; Bohannan and Dalton, *Markets in Africa*,
      p. 15; Melville Herkovits Jr, *The Economic Life of Primitive People*, New
      York: Knopf, 1940; Middleton, *Black Africa*; Hodder, 'The Yoruba rural
      market', p. 103; Gloria A. Marshall, 'Women, trade and the Yoruba family',
      doctoral thesis, Columbia University, 1964; Claudine Tardits and Claude
      Tardits, 'Traditional market economy in South Dahomey', in Bohannan and
      Dalton, *Markets in Africa*, p. 89.

12   Audrey Wipper, 'The roles of African women: past, present and future',
      Canadian Journal of African Studies, vol. 6, no. 6, 1972, p. 17; Jack Goody
      and Joan Buckley, 'Inheritance and women's labour in Africa', *Africa*, vol. 43,
      1973; Paul Bohannan and John Middleton, *Marriage, Family and Residence*,
      New York, 1968; Sidney Mintz, 'Men, women and trade', *Comparative
      Studies in Society and History*, 13, 1971; G. Calame-Griaule, 'The spiritual
      and social role of women in traditional Sudanese society', *Diogenes*, vol. 37,
      1962.

13   Bastide, *As Religioes Africanas*, vol. 1, pp. 85ff., Genovese, *Roll, Jordan,
      Roll*, p. 311; Gutman, *The Black Family in Slavery and Freedom*, pp. 260ff.

14   *Registro*, V, 181 (forbidding seizure of objects stolen by slaves in the inns);
      Atas, XIV (1763), 457; XVII (1778), 107 and 113; *Registro*, VI, 389; *Atas*,
      XXI (1831), 241; *Registro*, XXI, 139; *Atas*, XXII (1831), 498 and 666 (thefts
      in the storehouses); *Registro*, XXII, 63.

15   'Transfer proposed to Manuel da Silva Ferreira for his slaves, at a time when
      they are still in rebellion', Ilhéus (1806), Arquivo Público da Bahia, in Stuart
      Schwartz, 'A Resistência dos Escravos Contra o Regime Açucareiro',
      Minneapolis: University of Minnesota (mimeo.), 1977.

16   Bastide, *As Religiões Africanas*, vol. 2, pp. 261, 285ff.

17   Roger Bastide, 'A Macumba Paulista', in *Estudos Afro-brasileiros*, São Paulo:
      Perspectiva, 1973, p. 193; *As Religiões Africanas*, vol. 2, p. 387, 407.

18   Martins, *São Paulo Antigo*, vol. 2, pp. 84–5. Our Lady of Rosário was a slave
      Catholic lay brotherhood.

19   Xidieh, *A Semana Santa Cabocla*, p. 25.

20   Mattoso, *Bahia: A Cidade de Salvador e seu Mercado no Século XIX*, p. 215.

21   APJ, 2.ª Vara de Família, Juízo da Provedoria de Capellas e Resíduos,
      Testamento de Maria Joaquina das Chagas, 10 Jan. 1873 (Processos 1-33-cx.
      001, f. 1). Wills always indicate the relationship between the burial and the
      religious lay brotherhood: 'his body wrapped in a habit and buried in the
      cemetery of Nossa Senhora do Ó, his funeral with a decorum fitting his
      person' (testament of Anna Emília da Silva, processo L/33 cx. 001). At times,
      in the margins, some observations by the vicar, as on 22 Sept. 1846, those
      of José Manuel de Oliveira: 'On 2nd September 1846, in the district of
      Lages, in this parish of Cotia, there died without sacrament, for he had no

time . . . the slave Caetano, thirty years of age . . . wrapped in the habit of St Francis, he was buried in the graveyard of Rosário, since he was a Brother and recommended.' Also on 2 Sept. 1845: 'twelve-year-old Benedicta died, the daughter of Caetano . . . wrapped in a white cloth, buried in the graveyard of Rosário, since her parents belonged to the brotherhood and were recommended' (proc. 1/33 cx. 002).

22 Testamento de Josepha de Souza, DAE, 456, fls. 93; cf. Alzira Lobo de Arruda Campos, *Os Agregados no Tempo dos Capitães Generais*, University of São Paulo, 1978, p. 13 and 248.

23 See note 21 above.

24 Martins, *São Paulo Antigo*, vol. 2, pp. 78ff.; Taunay, *História da Cidade de São Paulo no Império*, vol. 4, p. 370 (chapter on the Negro lay orders); see also ch. 6, p. 365.

25 DAE, Ofícios Diversos da Capital, 870-c75-P02-d55 (Aug. 1834).

26 *Atas*, IX, 31.

27 *Registro*, XIV, 457; XVII, 107 and 113.

28 DAE, Ofícios Diversos, 870-c81-P01-d64 and c82-P01-d14 (measures taken in 1838 against vagrants and thieves in the city); *Atas*, XI (1763), 96 and 308; XIX (1793), 385.

29 *Registro*, XVII, 455.

30 *Atas*, XXVI, 82.

31 *Atas*, XXI, 241.

32 *Registro*, VI (1743), 21–3; *Atas*, XIV (1763), 471; *Registro*, XXI (1831), 158 to 163; DAE, Ofícios Diversos, 866-c72-P1-d38 (measures to arrest people carrying arms, 1838).

33 Taunay, *História da Cidade de São Paulo no Império*, vol. 4, p. 475 (exemption for woodcutters).

34 DAE, Ofícios Diversos, 866-c73-P2-d58 (17 Nov. 1832) and 820-c76-P03-d03 (11 Dec. 1834) and d02 (more measures against assaults, 13 Dec. 1834); *Atas*, XXVII (1832), 7.

35 Police measures against meetings, gambling, drum-playing and assaults. DAE, Ofícios Diversos, 866-c71-P02-d80 (May 1829); 72-P02-d6 (27 Nov. 1831) and 870-c75-P01-d9-94 (investigation of slaves arrested on the farm belonging to Joaquina Ferreira), etc.; *Atas*, XXXVI (1845), 59; *Registro*, XXI, 23 and 159; *Registro*, XXII (1831), 63 (in Rua da Cruz Preta).

36 *Registro*, XXII (4 Feb. 1832), 63.

37 Permission for slaves of African origin to celebrate Our Lady of the Conception for Black Men (25 Dec.1829); DAE, Ofícios Diversos, 866-c71-P03-d85; authority and municipal order for masked entertainment on 19 April 1833 (866-c74-P1-d43).

38 Arrangements for the carnival in Largo do Chafariz, DAE, Ofícios Diversos, 866-c73-P01-d25 and 25a (29 Feb. 1832); order forbidding masked entertainments, 870-c85-P02-d32 and 32a (30 Jan. 1834); *Registro*, XXII, 63; XXI, 53 and 23.

39 *Registro*, V, 427.
40 *Registro*, VI, 359; *Atas*, XVI, 460; XVII, 113; XVIII, 117, 225; *Atas*, XIX, 77.
41 *Atas*, XVIII (1835), 120.
42 *Atas*, XVIII, 117; XIX, 77; XXIV (1828), 184 and 298.
43 *Registro*, XII, 542; *Atas*, XXII, 525; XXIII, 307; XXXIV (1842), 9; *Registro*, XX (1829), 321, 388, 408, 487.
44 *Registro*, XV, 394; *Atas*, XXXVI (1847), 114 and 120.
45 *Registro*, XVI, 15.
46 *Registro*, XIV (1809), 147.
47 'Correspondência de D. Lourenço de Almeida (1732)', *RAPM*, vol. 7, 1906, pp. 276, 296, 298, 341.
48 *Registro*, VI, 359 (6 May 1744); Correspondence of D. Pedro de Almeida, letter of 20 April 1719, *RAPM*, vol. 3, 1898, p. 263.
49 *Registro*, XIV (1809), 147; *Atas*, XIV (1763), 463 and 498; *Atas*, XXI, 55; *Atas*, XII, 523; *Registro*, VI, 389; *Atas*, XII, 613.
50 'Black women stallholders shall only do business on their stalls until angelus and thereafter any black women or man who is found there will be condemned to 6$ fine and thirty days in prison, as well as lashing at the public whipping post' (*Atas*, XIV (1763), 498; *Registro*, XIV, 147; *Atas*, XXI, 551).
51 Cf. note 35 above.
52 *Registro*, VI, 359.
53 *Atas*, XXIV (25 June 1828), 184.
54 *Atas*, XXII (1818), 356–8.
55 *Atas*, XXIX (1836), 27.
56 *Atas*, XXXVI (1847), 94.
57 *Atas*, XXII (1820), 357.
58 See Samara, 'A Família na Sociedade Paulista', p. 45.
59 In households of women on their own in 1804, 9 per cent were of black or mulatta women; in 1836, the figure reached 39 per cent (DAE, Maços, 1836); on the predominance of freedwomen in Minas Gerais, see Costa, *Populações Mineiras*, pp. 77, 96.
60 Stuart B. Schwartz, 'The manumission of slaves in colonial Brazil: Bahia 1685–1745', *HAHR*, vol. 54, no. 4, 1974, p. 3; Mattoso, *Être esclave au Brésil*, pp. 201ff.; James Kiernan, 'Slavery and manumission in Paraty, Brazil, 1789–1822', New York: Columbia University (mimeo).
61 Samara, 'A Família na Sociedade de Paulista', pp. 98, 115; Mattoso, *Être esclave au Brésil*, pp. 238ff.
62 *Atas*, XVI, 454.
63 DAE, Maços, 1804.
64 *Atas*, XVII, 159.
65 *Atas*, XXVIII (1835), 120.
66 DAE, Ofícios Diversos 870-c75-P02-d55 (Aug. 1834).
67 DAE, Ofícios Diversos 870-c75-P02-d92 (7 Sept. 1834).
68 DAE, Ofícios Diversos 870-c75-P02-d64 (3 Sept. 1834).

69   Debret, *Viagem Pitoresca e Histórica ao Brasil*, vol. 1, p. 184 (grav. XVI).
70   Ibid., p. 126 (prints 5 and 6); Ribeyrolles, *Brasil Pitoresco*, vol. 1, pp. 166–7.
71   *DH*, vol. 106, 92.
72   *Atas*, LVIX (1873), 45.

CHAPTER 6   THE LOCAL COMMUNITY

1   DAE, Maços, 1836.
2   Ibid.
3   Xidieh, *Narrativas Pias Populares*, p. 62.
4   DAE, Maços, 1804 and 1836.
5   Arruda Campos, *Agregados no Tempo dos Capitães Generais*.
6   'And it is my wish that this Tuesday she should enter my house at 10 Rua
     Piques, with great gratitude, and that my daughter Guilhermina, while she
     remain unmarried, should stay with her and with her husband, Sr Lima,
     whom I trust will look after her in her trouble, and feed and clothe her, as if
     she were their daughter, caring for her person and interests as best they can.'
     Samara, 'A Família na Sociedade Paulista', p. 93.
7   Amaral, *Tradições Populares*, p. 253.
8   Ibid., pp. 153, 169.
9   Xidieh, *Narrativas Pias Populares*, p. 41.
10   Amadeu Amaral, *Ensaios e Conferências*, São Paulo: Hucitec, 1976, p. 123.
11   Carneiro, *Antologia do Negro Brasileiro*, pp. 211–14.
12   Almeida, '142 Histórias Brasileiras': 'As Três Cidras do Amor', p. 281; 'A
     Princeza da Pedra Lisa', p. 299. Romero, *Contos Populares do Brasil*: 'A
     Moura Torta', p. 50.
13   Almeida, '142 Histórias Brasileiras', p. 284. *Cafuné* was the custom of
     caressing the hair, originally for taking out lice. It was not specifically Brazil-
     ian but was practised in Europe in the Middle Ages.
14   Ibid.: 'Maria e a Pele da Negra', p. 193; 'O Príncipe Lagarto', pp. 253–7;
     'Destino de uma Jovem', p. 271. Romero, *Contos Populares do Brasil*: 'O
     Pássaro Negro', p. 69; 'O Homem Pequeno', p. 87; 'Dona Pinta', p. 95.
15   Almeida, '142 Histórias Brasileiras', p. 268; for the same theme in Gil
     Vicente, see Sigismundo Spina, *Obras-primas do Teatro Vicentino*, São
     Paulo: Difel, 1975, p. 97. Dona Orgulina refers to *orgulho*, which means
     'pride' in Portuguese.
16   Of 589 households of women on their own in 1836, there were 156 women
     totally alone; of the 344 without slaves there were 90 totally alone. DAE,
     Maços, 1836.
17   DAE, Maços, 1836.
18   Ibid.
19   Waldemar Iglésias Fernandes, *82 Histórias Populares Colhidas em Piraci-
     caba*, São Paulo: Comissão de Literatura, Conselho Estadual de Cultura,
     1969: 'O Prato de Estanho', p. 31; 'As Três Irmãs Bobas', p. 67. In the tale of

the tin plate a child sees his parents give his grandfather a tin plate instead of a china plate because the old man breaks the china ones; the child hides a tin plate and, when questioned by his parents, replies that it is for *their* old age.

20 Hershberg and Modell, 'The origins of the female-headed black family: the impact of the urban experience', *Journal of Interdisciplinary History*, vol. 6, no. 2, 1975, p. 211. See note 94 in ch. 1 above.

21 DAE, Maços, 1836.

22 Ibid.

23 Ibid.

24 Ibid.

25 DAE, Ofícios Diversos, 877-c82-P02-d8 and 8a (20 July 1838).

26 DAE, Maços, 1836.

27 DAE, Ofícios Diversos, 870-c75-P01-d20 (8 Feb. 1834).

28 DAE, Ofícios Diversos, 874-c83-P02-d61 (9 Aug. 1839); 870-c75-P02-d06 (16 Jun. 1834: 'The slave who was to be sent to the front lines, and who belongs to Regina Mendes Lustosa, has been locked in the barracks' (11 May 1842, 881-C89-P2-d19).

29 *Registro*, XIV (1808), 31 and 178; *Atas*, XXIII (1823), 185.

30 DAE, Requerimentos, 341-c92-P03-d76.

31 DAE, Requerimentos, 341-c93-P02-d25 (17 Aug. 1814).

32 *DI*, vol. 37, 223, 271.

33 DAE, Requerimentos, 341-c93-P01-d61 (1816).

34 DAE, Ofícios Diversos, 864-c90-P01-d50 (31 July 1843).

35 Arruda Campos, *Agregados no Tempo dos Capitães Generais*, p. 116.

36 DAE, Maços, 1836.

37 Lia de Freitas Garcia Fukui, *Sertão e Bairro Rural: Parentesco e Família entre Sitiantes Tradicionais*, São Paulo: Ática, 1979, p. 140.

38 In Maços, they declared they were 'nationals', 'of the borough', and after 1831 described themselves 'as Brazilians'. DAE, Maços, 1836.

39 Lists of agreements of persons who pledged a 'period of good behaviour'. DAE, Ofícios Diversos, 870-c75-P02-d41, 51, 77, 59 and 92; and also 871-c76-P02-d72 and 72a (April/June 1835).

40 DAE, Ofícios Diversos, 864-c69-P02-d14 (21 June 1823).

41 DAE, Ofícios Diversos, 865-c70-P02-d1.

42 Arruda Campos, *Agregados no Tempo dos Capitães Generais*, p. 116.

43 Translations of quarrels and disputes: DAE, Ofícios Diversos, 871-c76-P01-d93 and 93a, and 871-c73-P01-d19, etc.; *DI*, vol. 46, 262, 357, 359, etc.

44 Samara, 'A Família na Sociedade Paulista', pp. 69, 75; Kuznetsof, 'The role of the female-headed household in Brazilian modernization (São Paulo, 1765 to 1886)', *JSH*, vol. 13, no. 4, 1980, p. 599.

45 Marcílio, *A Cidade de São Paulo*, p. 106.

46 Ibid., p. 157.

47 DAE, Maços, 1836, gives the domestic structure of 344 households of

women on their own without slaves as follows: 90 solitary; 56 nuclear (with small children); 72 nuclear (with adult children); 74 extended; 52 sorority.

48 Martins, *São Paulo Antigo*, vol. 1, p. 82; Laima Mesgravis, 'A Assistência à Infância Desamparada e a Santa Casa de São Paulo: a Roda dos Expostos no Século XIX', *Revista de História*, 103, 1975, p. 413.

49 Mesgravis, 'A Assistência',p. 418.

50 DAE, Maços, 1836; about 68 out of 589 women on their own.

51 Alfredo Mesquita, *Sílvia Pelica na Liberdade*, São Paulo: Duas Cidades, 1979, p. 4.

52 DAE, Autos Crimes da Capital, 1850–59, ordem 3902-c2-24, Dec. 1851.

53 DAE, Ofícios Diversos, 881-c93-P02-d95ff.

54 DAE, Ofícios Diversos, 881-c93-P02 documents 30, 30a, 38, 38a and following.

55 Amaral, *Tradições Populares*, p. 259.

56 DAE, Ofícios Diversos, 870-c75-P01-d15.

57 See Castro, 'Memória Econômica e Política da Capitania de São Paulo'.

58 DAE, Autos Crimes da Capital, 1850–1859, ordem 3902-c2-d8ff. (opinions of judges in proceedings).

59 DAE, Ofícios Diversos, 864-c69-P02-d73 (Sept. 1824); 881-c85-P01-d1 (2 Jan. 1840); Biblioteca Nacional, 'Avulsos', *Coleção de Leis Extravagantes (1710–1822)*, 89, 5, 6, n. 4ff. (law of 6 Oct. 1784), with index by M. Weinberger Teixeira.

60 Samara, 'A Família na Sociedade Paulista', p. 80.

61 Amaral, *Tradições Populares*, pp. 78–9.

62 Ibid., p. 110.

63 Almeida, '142 Histórias Brasileiras', p. 297.

64 Ibid.: 'Pão com Mel, Pão com Fel', p. 176; 'O Príncipe Lagarto', p. 254. L. Gomes, *Contos Populares: Episódios, Cyclicos e Sentenciosos, Colhidos da Tradição Oral, no Estado de Minas*, São Paulo: Melhoramentos, n.d., vol. 1, pp. 55, 58, 65, 82; Romero, *Contos Populares do Brasil*: 'Os Três Coroados', 'O Homem Pequeno'.

65 Almeida, '142 Histórias Brasileiras': 'O Príncipe Lagarto', pp. 253–7. Erich Neumann, *Amor and Psyche: The Psychic Development of the Feminine, A Commentary on the Tale by Apuleius*, Princeton: Princeton University Press, 1973; Marie Louise von Franz, *An Introduction to the Interpretation of Fairy Tales*, New York: Spring, 1971.

66 Almeida, '142 Histórias Brasileiras': 'O Príncipe Encantado', pp. 256, 271; 'Maria Borralheira', p. 175; 'Maria e a Pele Negra', p. 193. Romero, *Contos Populares do Brasil*: 'O Príncipe Cornudo', p. 301; 'O Homem Pequeno', p. 91; 'Destino de uma Jovem', p. 272; 'Os Dois Amigos' (Boccaccio), p. 277.

67 Almeida, '142 Histórias Brasileiras': 'A Filha do Pescador', p. 219; 'O Príncipe Lagarto', p. 253. Cascudo, *Cinco Livros do Povo*: 'A Peregrina Magalona'. Romero, *Contos Populares do Brasil*: 'O Homem Pequeno', p. 91; 'O Sargento Verde', p. 58; 'Dona Lobismina', 'O Rei Andrada'.

68 Almeida, '142 Histórias Brasileiras': 'Joãozinho e Maria', p. 295; 'A Gata Borralheira', p. 175; 'A Princeza da Pedra Lisa', p. 300; 'História das Três Irmãs', p. 184; 'O Espelho Cristalino', p. 249.
69 Ibid., pp. 193, 178, 254; Romero, *Contos Populares*: 'O Sargento Verde', p. 55; 'Dona Pinta', p. 94; 'O Príncipe Cornudo', p. 103.
70 Gomes, *Contos Populares*, vol. 1, p. 27.
71 Spina, *Obras-primas do Teatro Vicentino*, pp. 186, 195.
72 Ibid., p. 217.
73 Gomes, *Contos Populares*, p. 187.
74 José Leite de Vasconcelos, *Tradições Populares em Portugal*, Lisbon, 1910, p. 84.
75 Cf. Florestan Fernandes, *Folclore e Mudança Social na Cidade de São Paulo*, Petrópolis: Vozes, 1979, p. 28.
76 Almeida, '142 Histórias Brasileiras', p. 295.
77 Arthur Ramos, *O Folk-lore do Brasil*, Rio de Janeiro, 1935, p. 209.
78 Almeida, '142 Histórias Brasileiras', pp. 166, 168, etc.
79 DAE, Ofícios Diversos, 881-c93-P01-d69.
80 DAE, Ofícios Diversos, 878-c84-P02-d37, 62 and 79; c88-P02-d107.
81 Almeida, '142 Histórias Brasileiras', p. 253.
82 Abreu, *Primeira Visitação do Santo Ofício às Partes do Brasil: Confissões da Bahia*, p. 119.
83 Lapa, *Vida e Obra de Alvarenga Peixoto*, p. 61.
84 Lisanti, *Negócios Coloniais*, vol. 2, p. 265.
85 Gil Vicente, *Dom Duardos*; Menéndez Pelayo, *Orígenes de la novela*, vol. 2, p. 189.
86 *DI*, vol. 46, 262, 357; vol. 64, 151; 'Catálogo dos Documentos sobre a história de São Paulo existentes no Arquivo Ultramarino, *RIHGB*', vol. 13, 226, 454, 458; DAE, Ofícios Diversos, 879-c84-P01-d39, c84-P01-d21, 99, etc.
87 José Joaquim Nunes, *Cantigas de Amigo*, Lisbon: Centro do Livro Brasileiro, vol. 2, p. 379.
88 Almeida, '142 Histórias Brasileiras', p. 298.
89 Arruda Campos, *Agregados no Tempo dos Capitães Generais*, p. 188.
90 Processo de 1820, cf. Samara, 'A Família na Sociedade Paulista', p. 209.
91 Arruda Campos, *Agregados no Tempo dos Capitães Generais*, pp. 242–6. In table 6.6 the very young babies were the children of maids, but they would start 'helping' at five or six years of age.
92 DAE, Maços, 1804 and 1836.
93 Ibid.
94 Antonio José Saraiva, *História da Cultura em Portugal*, vol. 1, p. 294.
95 DAE, Maços, 1836.
96 Cf. lawsuit of 15 Aug. 1850, where Anna Benedita do Espirito Santo, commonly Cascafina, declares that she 'is keeping some clothes in the room belonging to Rita Maria das Dores in Ladeiro São Francisco'. DAE, Autos Crimes, ordem 3092, cx. 2.

97 That is, 70 young girls out of a total of 192 women living alone. DAE, Maços, 1836.
98 Padre Manuel da Fonseca, *Vida do Venerável Padre Belchior Pontes*, São Paulo: Melhoramentos, 1932, p. 18; Ferreira de Rezende, *Minhas Recordações*, p. 210; Sérgio Milliet, 'A Crise das Mulheres', *RAMSP*, vol. 48, p. 20.
99 Police incidents in Ofícios Diversos, DAE.
100 Cf. Vilhena, *Recopilação das Notícias Soteropolitanas e Brasílicas*, vol. 1, p. 48.
101 DAE, Ofícios Diversos, 870-c75-P01-d74; 869-c75-P01-d67, 75, 63, 96, 97, etc. (29 Apr. 1834).
102 Almeida, *As Elites na Sociedade Paulista*, p. 97.
103 Saint-Hilaire, *Voyage dans les Provinces de St Paul et Ste Catherine*, vol. 1, pp. 271–2.
104 DAE, Ofícios Diversos, 870-c75-P01-d63; cf. lists of incidents and crimes judged in the district south of the cathedral, 870-c75-P02-d45ff. (Aug. 1834).
105 Cf. note 96 above.
106 DAE, Maços, 1836.
107 Ibid.
108 *DI*, vol. 37, 304 (27 Apr. 1822): 'Joaquina Engracia, the accused, having disputes with several people, promises to give up her dishonourable way of life and go and live in her mother's house.' Amador Florence, 'Coisas de Velhos Censos Paulistas', *Anais do IV Congresso de História Nacional*, Riode Janeiro: Dept 2a Imprensa Nacional, 1950, vol. 5, p. 168: 'taking the young girl Madalena from this house of ill repute, warning her to change her way of life and habits, handed over to her mother under penalty of banishment' (proceedings moved by Franca e Horta).
109 Almeida, '142 Histórias Brasileiras': 'A Filha do Pescador', p. 219; 'O Príncipe Lagarto', p. 252; 'Joãozinho e Maria', p. 295. Romero, *Contos Populares do Brasil*: 'O Rei Andrada', p. 43; 'Dona Lobismina', p. 74; 'O Sargento Verde', p. 55, etc.
110 Saraiva, *História da Cultura em Portugal*, vol. 1, p. 66.
111 Theophilo Braga, *História do Theatro Português*, vol. 1, p. 103.
112 Almeida, '142 Histórias Brasileiras', pp. 252, 296; Tereza Margarida da Silva e Orta, *Aventuras de Diófanes (1752)*, Rio de Janeiro: Imprensa Nacional, 1945, p. 38; Bernardim Ribeiro, *Obras Completas*, ed. M. Marques Braga, Lisbon: Livraria Sá da Costa, 1959, pp. 156, 186, 210.
113 Vieira, *Sermões* (Sermon 16, Maria Rosa Mística), vol. 6, p. 31.
114 On the presence of the sixteenth-century stories by Trancozo in Brazil, see Capistrano de Abreu (ed.), *Diálogo das Grandezas do Brasil* (with notes by Rodolfo Garcia), Salvador: Livraria Progresso Editora, 1956, p. 177, note 203; Almeida, '142 Histórias Brasileiras'; Otávio da Costa Eduardo, 'Aspectos do Folclore de uma Comunidade Rural', *RAMSP*, vol. 144, 1951, p. 14.
115 Manuel Cavalcanti Proença (ed.), *Literatura Popular em Verso, Catálogo (1)*, Rio de Janeiro: Casa de Rui Barbosa, 1961, pp. 55, 96, 122, 151, etc.

CHAPTER 7   THE MAGIC OF SURVIVAL

1   In 1804 in districts of São Paulo there were 178 households of women on their own with servants out of a total of 557 (32 per cent); in 1836 there were 110 households with servants out of a total of 589 (19 per cent). DAE, Maços.

2   Letter from the Morgado de Matheus, 4 Feb. 1768, *DI*, vol. 23, 394. The 1810 treaty was a decisive moment increasing the commercial relations between Great Britain and Brazil. It was reconfirmed in 1827 and again in 1844.

3   John Mawe, *Viagens ao Interior do Brasil*, Rio de Janeiro: Hélio Valverde, 1944, p. 193.

4   Among the women living from making lace described in DAE, Maços, 1804, were white women between the ages of twenty and thirty like Ignácia, spinster, thirty-one years old, Maria Joaquina, spinster, twenty-one years old, Joaquina de Almeida, forty-three years old, single mother with three daughters. See Holanda, 'A Província de São Paulo', p. 427; Freitas, 'A Cidade de São Paulo no Dia 7 de Setembro de 1822', p. 33; Gustavo Beyer, 'Ligeiras Notas de Viagem do Rio de Janeiro à Capitania de São Paulo, no Brasil, no Verão de 1813', *RIHGSP*, vol. 12, 1908, p. 288.

5   Manoel Alvares de Azevedo, *Obras Completas de Alvares de Azevedo*, ed. Heliodoro Pires, São Paulo: Nacional, 1944, vol. 1, p. 43. The correspondence of this nineteenth-century Romantic Brazilian poet was published by L. F. Vieira Souto in *RIHGB*, in 1931.

6   Bruno, *História e Tradições da Cidade de São Paulo*, vol. 2, pp. 711, 823.

7   Rugendas, *Viagem Pitoresca Através do Brasil*, p. 179.

8   *Atas*, XII, 499 and 533.

9   Abreu, *Primeira Visitação do Santo Ofício às Partes do Brasil: Denunciaçoes da Bahia*, pp. 278–9, 323, 337, 347.

10   Xidieh, *Narrativas Pias Populares*, pp. 46, 51.

11   It is unlikely that during the initial process of urbanization in São Paulo they worked more than three or four days a week doing salaried work. Cf. as points of reference similar works on parallel themes: Mintz, 'The employment of capital by market women in Haiti', p. 297; Chinas, *The Isthmus Zapotecs: Women's Role in Cultural Context*; R. J. Broomley and R. Symanski, 'Marketplace trade in Latin America', *Latin America Historical Review*, vol. 9, no. 3, 1974; Manning Nash, 'The social context of economic choice in a small society', *Man*, LXI, 1961, p. 186; Sol Tax, *Penny Capitalism: A Guatemalan Indian Economy*.

12   Gilberto Leite de Barros, *A Cidade e o Planalto*, São Paulo: Martins, 1967, vol. 2, pp. 310, 317.

13   Mota, *Do Rancho ao Palácio*, p. 41; Holanda, *Caminhos e Fronteiras*, p. 217.

14   Ibid., p. 217, 226.

15 Ibid., pp. 239–42; Antonio Candido, *Os Parceiros do Rio Bonito*, Rio de Janeiro: José Olympio, 1964, p. 29.

16 Holanda, *Caminhos e Fronteiras*, p. 217.

17 Xidieh, *Narrativas Pias Populares*, p. 45.

18 Kidder, *Reminiscências de Viagens e Permanência no Brasil*, p. 197.

19 Debret, *Viagem Pitoresca e Histórica ao Brasil*, vol. 1, p. 162.

20 *Registro*, XV (1814), 78.

21 APJ, Inventory of Catarina Brau, 1840, Juízo de Órfãos de Santo Amaro, AG. Proc. 56/64 cx. 7 (3 cheeses $600); Custódia Maria de Jesus, executor, APJ, Juízo de Órfãos da cidade de São Paulo (1832), AG. Proc. 01 to 05, no. 1275.

22 Kidder, *Reminiscências*, p. 227.

23 Holanda, *Caminhos e Fronteiras*, p. 77.

24 Maynard de Araújo, *Folclore Nacional*, São Paulo: Melhoramentos. n.d., vol. 3, p. 284; Barros, *A Cidade e o Planalto*, vol. 2, p. 311; Debret, *Viagem Pitoresca e Histórica ao Brasil*, vol. 1, p. 134, fig. 6. In São Paulo in Rua da Cruz Preta, Sinhá Maria, the potter, sold pots of clay made in São Miguel and S. Bernardo. Martins, *São Paulo Antigo*, vol. 2, p. 120.

25 'In São Paulo the colour the houses are painted varies between straw yellow and pale pink.' Kidder, *Reminiscências*, p. 189.

26 Saint-Hilaire, *Voyage dans les provinces de St Paul et Ste Catherine*, vol. 1, pp. 400–1.

27 Debret, *Viagem Pitoresca e Histórica ao Brasil*, vol. 1, p. 179; Carlos A. C. Lemos, *Cozinhas, etc.*, São Paulo: Perspectiva, 1976, p. 50.

28 Mawe, *Viagens ao Interior do Brasil*, pp. 70–5.

29 Saint-Hilaire, *Voyage*, vol. 1, p. 400.

30 *IeT*, XXV, 248; Holanda, *Caminhos e Fronteiras*, p. 217.

31 APJ, Maria Joaquina do Espirito Santo, executor, Santo Amaro (1841), Ag. Proc. 73/3-cx. 9 n. 78; APJ, Antonio Pinto de Andrade and his wife. Ursula Pires de Oliveira, Santo Amaro (1833), Juízo de Órfãos da Capital, Ag. Proc. 6 to 17 cx. 2; José Quaresma da Silva, Partilha de bens, Santo Amaro (1834), Ag. Proc. 18 to 23, cx. 3, no. 1370; Maria Violante dos Santos, district of São Miguel, parish of Penha (1840), Ag. Proc. 56/64 cx. 7; Maria Balbina Ribeiro, Cotia (1842), Ag. Proc. 81/89 cx. 10, no. 351; Custódia Maria de Jesus, Santo Amaro (1832), Ag. Proc. 1 to 5 cx. 1, no. 1275; APJ, Francisca Maria das Chagas (1842), district of Tremembé, district of Santa Ifigênia, Ag. Proc. 81/89 cx. 10, no. 1386; APJ, Maria Joaquina dos Santos, Santo Amaro (1841), Ag. Proc. 73/8 cx. 9 n. 78; APJ, José Quaresma da Silva, Partilha de Bens, Santo Amaro (1834), Ag. Proc. 18 to 23, cx. 3, no. 1370.

32 Antonio Candido, *Os Parceiros do Rio Bonito*, p. 22; Barros, *A Cidade e o Planalto*, vol. 2, pp. 309–10.

33 DAE, Maços, 1804 and 1836.

34 Holanda, *Caminhos e Fronteiras*, p. 259.

35 Bueno, 'A Cidade de São Paulo', p. 25.

36 APJ, Francisca Maria das Chagas, executor, district of Tremembé, district of Santa Ifigênia, Juízo dos Órfãos de S. Paulo (1842), Ag. Proc. 81/89 cx.10, n. 1386.
37 Bueno, 'A Cidade de São Paulo', p. 25.
38 DAE, Maços, 1836.
39 Almeida, '142 Histórias Brasileiras', p. 253.
40 Oliveira Mello, *Minha Terra: Suas Lendas e Seu Folclore* (Patos de Minas), Belo Horizonte, 1970, p. 179.
41 Luís D'Alincourt, *Memória sobre a Viagem do Porto de Santos à Cidade de Cuiabá*, São Paulo: EDUSP, 1975, p. 49.
42 Holanda, *Caminhos e Fronteiras*, p. 258.
43 Alincourt, *Memória sobre a Viagem do Porto de Santos à Cidade de Cuiabá*, p. 49.
44 Oliveira Mello, *Minha Terra*, p. 180.
45 Antonio Manuel de Mello Castro Mendonça, 'Memórias Econômicas e Políticas da Capitania de São Paulo', *Anais do Museu Paulista*, XV, 1961, p. 118.
46 Bueno, 'A Cidade de São Paulo', p. 24.
47 Holanda, *Caminhos e Fronteiras*, p. 262.
48 Ibid., p. 259.
49 Antonio Baião in ibid., p. 260.
50 Contas do Seminário dos Meninos Órfãos São Luís, Ofícios Diversos, 870-c-75-P03-d49 (17 Aug. 1834).
51 DAE, Maços, 1804 and 1836.
52 DAE, Ofícios Diversos, 870-c75-P03-d49.
53 APJ, inventory of Maria Balbina Ribeiro, Cotia (1842), Ag. Proc. 81/89 cx. 10 n. 1215.
54 Bueno, 'A Cidade de São Paulo', p. 24.
55 Ibid., p. 24.
56 APJ, Maria Antonia Pires de Oliveira, Santo Amaro (1834), Juízo de Órfãos de Santo Amaro, cx. 2, no. 1216.
57 APJ, inventory of Maria Violante dos Santos, São Miguel, Freguesia da Penha (1840), Purveyor's office of city of São Paulo, Ag. Proc. 56/64 cx. 7.
58 *IeT*, vol. XVII, 292, 382, 426.
59 Bueno, 'A Cidade de São Paulo', p. 24.
60 Ferreira de Rezende, *Minhas Recordações*, p. 205.
61 Leme, *Nobiliarquia Paulistana*, vol. 1, p. 76 and vol. 2, p. 197; Saint-Hilaire describes the hats worn by São Paulo women, tipped backwards, in *Voyage dans les provinces de St Paul et Ste Catherine*, vol. 1, p. 271.
62 APJ, Antonio P. de Andrade and Ursula Pires de Oliveira, inventory, Santo Amaro (1833), Juízo de Órfãos de São Paulo, Ag. Proc. 6 to 17 cx. 2; also inventory of Maria Antonia Pires de Oliveira, Santo Amaro (1834), cx. 2, n. 1216.
63 DAE, Maços, 1836.
64 Out of 48 there were 28 mulatta, 13 white, 7 black. DAE, Maços, 1836.

65 APJ, civil papers from inventory of José Vieira da Silva, the executor being Maria Joaquina do Espírito Santo, Santo Amaro, 1841, Ag. Proc. 73/8 cx. 9, n. 78.
66 Barros, *A Cidade e o Planalto*, vol. 2, p. 478.
67 Amaral, *Tradições Populares*, p. 169.
68 Debret, *Viagem Pitoresca e Histórica ao Brasil*, vol. 1, p. 274.
69 Saint-Hilaire, *Voyage dans les provinces de St Paul et Ste Catherine*, vol. 1, p. 255.
70 Bueno, 'A Cidade de São Paulo', p. 30.
71 Ewbank, *Life in Brazil*, p. 74; Kidder, *Reminiscências*, p. 97.
72 *Atas*, X, 323; XVIII, 379, etc.
73 Debret, *Viagem Pitoresca*, vol. 1, p. 274.
74 DAE, Maços, 1836.
75 Bueno, 'A Cidade de São Paulo', pp. 30–1.
76 Ferreira de Rezende, *Minhas Recordações*, p. 265.
77 DAE, Maços, 1836.
78 Ibid.
79 Freitas, 'Folganças Populares do Velho São Paulo', p. 25; Almeida, '142 Histórias Brasileiras', p. 71; Fernandes, *82 Estórias Populares Colhidas em Piracicaba*, p. 24.
80 *Atas*, XVII, 1824, 477.
81 Menéndez Pelayo, *Orígenes de la novela*, vol. 2, pp. 119ff.
82 Romero, *Contos Populares do Brasil*, p. 60.
83 Pedro Nava, *Balão Cativo: Memórias 2*, Rio de Janeiro: José Olympio, 1973, pp. 23–6.
84 *Registro*, XV (1819), 465.
85 Fernandes, *82 Estórias Populares Colhidas em Piracicaba*, p. 66.
86 Almeida, '142 Histórias Brasileiras': 'O Cavalo Escuro e o Rei Alemão', p. 326.
87 Ibid., p. 272.
88 Barros, *A Cidade e o Planalto*, vol. 1, p. 244.
89 Romero, *Contos Populares do Brasil*, p. 18.
90 Almeida, '142 Histórias Brasileiras', p. 295.
91 Ibid., p. 217.
92 Amaral, *Tradições Populares*, p. 164.
93 Xidieh, *Narrativas Pias Populares*, p. 56.
94 Ibid., p. 305.
95 Ibid., p. 57; Amaral, *Tradições Populares*, pp. 153, 338.
96 Almeida, 'Contos Populares do Planalto', pp. 335–6.
97 Almeida, '142 Histórias Brasileiras', p. 260.
98 Almeida, 'Contos Populares do Planalto', p. 24; Xidieh, *Narrativas Pias Populares*, p. 18.
99 Bueno, 'A Cidade de São Paulo', p. 23.
100 *Atas*, XII, 404; XV, 379; Abreu, 'Divertimento Admirável', p. 258.

101 DAE, Maços, 1836.

102 Ferreira de Rezende, *Minhas Recordações*, p. 274.

103 Ibid., p. 261; Jacob Penteado, *Belenzinho 1910: Retrato de Uma Época*, São Paulo: Martins, 1962, p. 163.

104 Bueno, 'A Cidade de São Paulo', p. 30; Holanda, *Caminhos e Fronteiras*, p. 64.

105 *Registro*, XII, 614; Bruno, *História e Tradições da Cidade de São Paulo*, vol. 1, p. 307.

106 Holanda, *Caminhos e Fronteiras*, p. 90.

107 Ibid.; Xidieh, *Semana Santa Cabocla*, pp. 80ff.; Hildegardes Cantolino, 'As "Aparadeiras" e as Senderonas', *RAMSP*, vol. 178, pp. 56ff.; Oswaldo Cabral, 'A Medicina Teológica e as Benzeduras', *RAMSP*, vol. 160, 1957, pp. 5–204.

108 Mário de Andrade, *Música de Feitiçaria no Brasil*, São Paulo: Martins, 1963; Roger Bastide, *Estudos Afro-brasileiros*, p. 194.

109 *RAMSP*, vol. 8, 13; Holanda, *Caminhos e Fronteiras*, p. 96; Bruno, *História e Tradições da Cidade de São Paulo*, vol. 3, p. 1146.

110 *Atas*, XXXV (1845), 156, 160, 177; *Registro*, XIV, 293 (regulating the use of the law); XVI, 192, in Santo Amaro; *Atas*, XIX, 454 and 216.

111 Bernardo Guimarães, *Rosaura, a Enjeitada*, Rio de Janeiro: Garnier, 1914, vol. 2, p. 15; Bruno, *História e Tradições*, vol. 2, p. 512.

112 *Atas*, XXXV, 1845, 128; Freitas, *Tradição e Reminiscências Paulistanas*, p. 11; Bruno, *História e Tradições*, vol. 2, p. 556.

113 APJ, Anna Emilia da Silva (1900), testament, Juízo de Direito da Provedoria da Comarca da Capital, Ag. Proc. 1/33 cx. 001; Francisca de Paula Barbosa, testament, 1873, Juízo da Provedoria de Capelas e Resíduos, Ag. Proc. 1/33 cx. 001.

114 APJ, Isabel Ignácia de Jesus, Testamento (1872), Capital, Ag. Proc. 1/33-cx. 001.

115 Ferreira de Rezende, *Minhas Recordações*, p. 259.

116 *Atas*, XXVII, 548 and 559; *Atas*, XXXIV, 195.

117 *Atas*, XLIII (1857), 112.

118 *Atas*, LIX (1873), 5.

119 *Atas*, LXIII (1876), 58; Sud Menucci, *O Precursor do Abolicionismo no Brasil: Luís Gama*, São Paulo, 1938, p. 24.

120 *Atas*, LXI (1876), 83; Henri Raffard, 'Os Núcleos Coloniais', *RIHGB*, vol. 55, p. 159; Caio Prado Jr, *Evolução Política do Brasil*, São Paulo: Brasiliense, 1966, p. 130.

121 Afonso de Carvalho, 'São Paulo Antigo (1882–1886)', *RIHGSP*, vol. 41, 1942, p. 48; Everardo Valim Pereira de Souza, 'A Paulicéia há 60 Anos', *RAMSP*, vol. 111, p. 63; Bruno, *História e Tradições*, vol. 3, pp. 1110–39.

122 Florestan Fernandes, *A Integração do Negro na Sociedade de Classes*, São Paulo: Dominus/Editora da Universidade de São Paulo, 1965, vol. 1, p. 29.

Bibliography

For abbreviations, see the beginning of the notes, p. 168.

Archival Sources

Departamento do Arquivo do Estado

Maços da População da Capital: 1804 – ord. 33, x. 33; 1829 – ord. 37, cx. 37; 1836 – ord. 372, cx. 37a.
Ofícios Diversos da Capital: 1836 a 1850; ord. 864, cx. 69a; 89 cx. 94.
Autos Crimes da Capital: 1840–1859: ord. 3901, cx. 1; 3902, cx. 2.
Crimes da Sé: 1830–1839; ord. 870, cx. 75.
Inventários Não Publicados: 1800–1816: ord. 571, lata 94: 1817–1851, ord. 572, lata 95.
Livros da Barreira da Capital Ponte do Ó: 1826–1836, ord. 2017–308.
Ocorrências Policiais (Capital): 1837–1841, ord. 2436, lata 3.
Querelas (Capital): 1816–1831, ord. 6019, cx. 1.
Escravos: 1830–1883, ord. 5534, cx. 1; 1882–1888, ord. 5535, cx. 2.

Arquivo da Cúria Metropolitana de São Paulo

Livro de Tombo do Braz 1818–85.
Pasta do Bispo Dom Matheus de Abreu Pereira (pastoral enquiries and visits and annulment of marriage).
Processos de Divórcio – estante 15, gaveta 27ff., nos 357 to 386.
Livro de Óbitos da Sé (1830–1844).

Arquivo da Prefeitura Municipal de São Paulo

Posturas 1830–37 CM–1–39–vol. 73.
Papéis Avulsos, 1870–1875.

Arquivo do Poder Judiciário

2ª Vara de Família
Provedoria da Imperial Cidade de São Paulo: Inventários: 1800–1870: Ag. proc.
1/33, cx. 001 to 10.
Juízo da Provedoria de Capellas e Resíduos: Testamentos: 1872–1874: Ag. proc.
1–35, cx. 2.
Juízo de Órfãos: autos cíveis de inventários: 1840–1847: Ag. proc. 56–64, cx. 6
and 7.
Juízo de Órfãos da Capital: 1832–1842: 81–89, cx. 10, nos. 85ff.

Primary Published Sources

Collections

Actas da Câmara Municipal de São Paulo, São Paulo, Arquivo Municipal,
1914– .
Documentos Históricos da Biblioteca Nacional do Rio de Janeiro, Rio de Janeiro,
1928– .
Documentos Interessantes para a História e Costumes de São Paulo, São Paulo,
Arquivo do Estado, 1894–
Inventários e Testamentos, São Paulo, Arquivo do Estado, 1917– .
Registro da Câmara Municipal de São Paulo, São Paulo, Arquivo Municipal,
1917– .
Coleção Chronológica de Leis Extravagantes (1609–1761), Biblioteca Municipal
Mário de Andrade, Seção de Livros Raros.
Coleção de Leis Extravagantes (1710–1822), 'Avulsos' da Biblioteca Nacional, Rio
de Janeiro (with index by M. Weinberger Teixeira).

Books and articles

Abreu, Manoel Cardoso, 'Divertimento Admirável', 1783, *RIHGSP*, vol. 6, 1900,
pp. 253–93.
Alincourt, Luís D', *Memória sobre a Viagem do Porto de Santos à Cidade de
Cuiabá*, São Paulo: EDUSP, 1975.
Almeida, Aluísio de, '142 Histórias Brasileiras', *RAMSP*, vol. 144, 1951, pp. 163–
332.

Almeida, 'Contos Populares do Planalto', *RAMSP*, vol. 147, 1952, pp. 3–50.
—— 'Lendas e Narrativas Brasileiras', *RAMSP*, vol. 178, 1969, pp. 7–35.
—— 'Notas para a História de Sorocaba', *RAMSP*, vol. 183, 1971, pp. 147–66.
Almeida, Luís Castanho de, *50 Contos Populares de São Paulo*, São Paulo, 1947.
Bueno, Francisco de Assis Vieira, 'A Cidade de São Paulo: Recordações Evocadas de Memória', *Revista do Centro de Ciências, Letras e Artes*, Campinas, 1903, Ano II, nos 1, 2, 3.
Cascudo, Luís da Câmara, *Cinco Livros do Povo: Introdução ao Estudo da Novelística no Brasil*, Rio de Janeiro: José Olympio, 1953.
Castro, Antonio Manuel de Mello e, 'Memória Econômica e Política da Capitânia de São Paulo', *Anais do Museu Paulista*, XV, 1961, p. 98.
'Correspondência de D. Lourenço de Almeida', *RAPM*, vol. 7, 1906, pp. 207ff.
'Correspondência de D. Pedro de Almeida, Conde de Assumar', *RAPM*, vol. 3, 1898, p. 263.
Debret, Jean-Baptiste, *Viagem Pitoresca e Histórica ao Brasil*, São Paulo, Martins, 1949, 2 vols.
Ebel, Ernst, *O Rio de Janeiro e Seus Arredores em 1824*, São Paulo: Nacional, 1972.
Ewbank, Thomas, *Life in Brazil, or A Journal of a Visit to the Land of the Cocoa and the Palm*, New York: Harper, 1856.
Fernandes, Waldemar Iglésias, *82 Estórias Populares Colhidas em Piracicaba*, São Paulo: Comissão de Literatura, Conselho Estadual de Cultura, 1969.
Ferreira de Rezende, Francisco de Paula, *Minhas Recordações*, Rio de Janeiro: José Olympio, 1944.
Florence, Hércules, *Viagem Fluvial do Tietê ao Amazonas de 1825 a 1829*, São Paulo: Cultrix/EDUSP, 1977.
Gomes, Lindolfo, *Contos Populares: Episódios, Cyclicos e Sentenciosos, Colhidos da Tradição Oral, no Estado de Minas*, São Paulo: Melhoramentos, n.d., 2 vols.
Kidder, Daniel P., *Reminiscências de Viagens e Permanência no Brasil: Rio de Janeiro e São Paulo*, São Paulo: Martins, n.d.
Lisanti, Luís de (ed.), *Negócios Coloniais: Correspondência de um Comerciante do Século XVIII*, Brasília: Ministério da Fazenda, 1965, 3 vols.
Luccock, John, *Notas sobre o Rio-de-Janeiro e Partes Meridionais do Brasil: Tomadas Durante uma Estada de Dez Anos Nesse País, de 1808 a 1818*, São Paulo: Martins, 1942.
Marrocos, Luís Joaquim dos Santos, 'Correspondência', *ABN*, vol. 56, p. 213.
Mello, Moraes Filho, *História e Costumes*, Rio de Janeiro: Garnier, 1904.
—— *Festas e Tradições do Brasil*, Rio de Janeiro: Fauchon, n.d.
Oliveira, Eduardo Freire de, *Elementos para a História do Município de Lisboa*, Lisbon, 1911, vols 1–18.
Ribeyrolles, Charles, *Brasil Pitoresco: Histórica-Descrições-Colonização-Instituições*, São Paulo: Martins, 1941, 2 vols.
Romero, Sîlvio, *Contos Populares do Brasil*, Lisbon: Nova Livraria Internacional, 1885, 3 vols; Rio de Janeiro: José Olympio, 1954, 2 vols.

Rugendas, João Maurício, *Viagem Pitoresca Através do Brasil*, São Paulo: Martins, 1941.

Saint-Hilaire, Auguste de, *Voyage dans les provinces de St Paul et Ste Catherine*, Paris: A. Bertrand, 1851, 2 vols.

—— *Segunda Viagem do Rio de Janeiro a Minas Geraes e a São Paulo (1822)*, trans. A. de E. Taunay, São Paulo: Nacional, 1932.

Salvador, Vicente do (Frei), *História do Brasil (1500–1627)*, São Paulo: Melhoramentos, 1954.

Trancozo, Gonçalo Fernandes, *Histórias Proveitosas*, Lisbon, 1681.

Tschudi, J. J. von, *Viagem às Províncias do Rio de Janeiro e São Paulo*, São Paulo: EDUSP, 1980.

Velloso, Antônio Rodrigues de Oliveira, *Memória sobre o Melhoramento da Província de São Paulo*, Rio de Janeiro: Typ. Nacional, 1822.

Zaluar, Augusto Emílio, *Peregrinação pela Província de São Paulo (1860–61)*, São Paulo: EDUSP, 1975.

Secondary Sources

Bibliographies

Moreira Leite, Miriam F. et al., *Mulher Brasileira: Bibliografia Anotada*, Fundação Carlos Chagas/Brasiliense, 1979.

—— et al., *A Mulher no Rio de Janeiro no Século XIX*, São Paulo: Fundação Carlos Chagas, 1982.

Books

Alcântara Machado, *Vida e Morte do Bandeirante*, São Paulo: Martins, n.d.

Almeida, Elisabeth Darwiche Rabelo de, *As Elites na Sociedade Paulista na Segunda Metade do Século XVIII*, São Paulo: Safady, 1981.

Amaral, Amadeu, *Tradições Populares*, São Paulo: Instituto de Progresso Editorial, n.d.

Barros, Gilberto Leite de, *A Cidade e o Planalto: Processo de Dominância da Cidade de São Paulo*, São Paulo: Martins, 1967, 2 vols.

Bastide, Roger, *Psicanálise do Cafuné e Estudos de Sociologia Estética Brasileira*, Curitiba: Editora Guaíra, 1941.

—— *As Religiões Africanas*, São Paulo: EDUSP, 1971.

—— *Estudos Afro-brasileiros*, São Paulo: Perspectiva, 1973.

—— *La Femme de couleur en Amérique Latine*, Paris: Anthropos, 1974.

Bastide, Roger and Fernandes, F., *Brancos e Negros em São Paulo*, São Paulo: Nacional, 1971.

Bohannan, P. and Dalton, G., *Markets in Africa*, Evanston, Ill.: Northwestern University Press, 1962.

Boserup, Esther, *Woman's Role in Economic Development*, New York: St Martin's Press, 1970.

Boxer, C. R., *Portuguese Society in the Tropics: The Municipal Councils of Goa, Macao, Bahia and Luanda 1510–1800*, Madison: University of Wisconsin Press, 1966.

—— *Mary and Misogyny: Women in Iberian Expansion Overseas 1415–1815, Some Facts, Fancies and Personalities*, London: Duckworth, 1975.

Bruno, Ernani da Silva, *História e Tradições da Cidade de São Paulo*, Rio de Janeiro: José Olympio, 1954, 3 vols.

Bruschini, Maria Cristina and Rosemberg, Fúlvia (eds), *Vivência: História, Sexualidade e Imagens Femininas*, São Paulo: Brasiliense, 1980.

Camargo, Paulo Florêncio da Silveira, *A Igreja na História de São Paulo*, São Paulo: Instituto Paulista de História e Arte Religiosa, 1952–3.

Costa, Iraci del Nero, *Vila Rica: População (1719–1826)*, São Paulo: FIPE, 1979.

—— *Populações Mineiras*, São Paulo: Instituto de Pesquisas Econômicas, 1981.

Detienne, Marcel and Vernant, Jean-Pierre, *Les Ruses de l'intelligence: la métis des Grecs*, Paris: Flammarion, 1974.

Fernandes, Florestan, *Folclore e Mudança Social na Cidade de São Paulo*, Petrópolis: Vozes, 1979.

Foucault, Michel, *Les Mots et les choses: une archeologie des sciences humaines*, Paris: Gallimard, 1966.

—— *La Volonté de savoir*, Paris: Gallimard, 1976.

Franco, Maria Sylvia de Carvalho, *Homens Livres na Ordem Escravocrata*, São Paulo: Instituto de Estudos Brasileiros, 1969.

Freire, Gilberto, *Casa Grande e Senzala*, Rio de Janeiro: Schmidt Editora, 1936.

—— *Sobrados e Mocambos*, Rio de Janeiro: José Olympio, 1968, 2 vols.

Freire, Paulo, *Pedagogia do Oprimido*, Rio de Janeiro: Paz e Terra, 1977.

Freitas, Afonso de, *Tradição e Reminiscências Paulistanas*, São Paulo: Martins, 1955.

Fukui, Lia de Freitas Garcia, *Sertão e Bairro Rural*, São Paulo: Atica, 1979.

Genovese, Eugene D., *Roll, Jordan, Roll: The World the Slaves Made*, New York: Pantheon, 1974.

Gutman, Herbert G., *The Black Family in Slavery and Freedom, 1750–1850*, New York: Pantheon, 1976.

Hafkin, Nancy J. and Bay, Edna G., *Women in Africa: State and Society in Economic Change*, California: Stanford University Press, 1976.

Holanda, Sérgio Buarque de, *Caminhos e Fronteiras*, Rio de Janeiro: José Olympio, 1957.

—— 'A Província de São Paulo', in *História Geral da Civilização Brasileira*, vol. 2: *O Brasil Monárquico*, São Paulo: Difusão Européia do Livro, 1964.

—— *Raízes do Brasil*, Rio de Janeiro: José Olympio, 1973.

Karrasch, Mary Catherine, *Slave Life in Rio de Janeiro: 1808–1850*, Princeton: Princeton University Press, 1987.

Landes, Ruth, *A Cidade das Mulheres*, Rio de Janeiro: Civilização, 1967.

Leite, Beatriz Westin de Cerqueira, *Região Bragantina: Estudo Econômico Social (1653–1836)*, Marília: Faculty of Philosophy, n.d.

Lemos, Carlos A. C., *Cozinhas, etc.*, São Paulo: Perspectiva, 1976.

Luna, Francisco Vidal, *Minas Gerais: Escravos e Senhores*, São Paulo: Instituto de Pesquisas Econômicas, 1981.

Marcílio, Maria Luisa, *A Cidade de São Paulo: Povoamento e População 1750–1810*, São Paulo, 1968.

—— 'Crescimento Demográfico e Evolução Agrária Paulista 1700–1836', thesis, São Paulo, 1974.

Marshall, Gloria, 'Women, trade and the Yoruba family', doctoral thesis, Columbia University, 1964.

Matta, Roberto da, *Carnavais, Malandros e Heróis: Para uma Sociologia do Dilema Brasileiro*, Rio de Janeiro: Zahar, 1979.

Mattoso, Kátia Queiroz, *Bahia: A Cidade de Salvador e seu Mercado no Século XIX*, São Paulo: Hucitec, 1978.

—— *Être esclave au Brésil (XVIe–XIXe)*, Paris: Hachette, 1979.

Meillassoux, Claude, *Mulheres, Celeiros e Capitais*, Porto: Afrontamento, 1977.

Mesgravis, Laima, *A Santa Casa de Misericórdia de São Paulo*, São Paulo: Secretaria da Cultura, 1978.

Mesquita, Eny, 'O Papel do Agregado em Itu', Master's thesis, São Paulo, 1975.

Menucci, Sud, *O Precursor do Abolicionismo no Brasil: Luís Gama*, São Paulo, 1938.

Morse, Richard, *Formacão histórica de São Paulo*, São Paulo: Difusão Européia do Livro, 1970.

Moura, Paulo Cursino, *São Paulo de Outrora (Evocações da Metrópole): Psychologia das Ruas*, São Paulo, Melhoramentos, 1932.

Petrone, Maria Theresa S., *A Lavoura Canavieira em São Paulo*, São Paulo: Difusão Européia do Livro, 1968.

—— *O Barão de Iguape: Um Empresário da Época da Independência*, São Paulo: Nacional, 1976.

Pinto, Luís Costa, *Lutas de Família no Brasil Colonial*, Rio de Janeiro: Nacional, 1949.

Prado Jr, Caio, *Formação do Brasil Contemporâneo*, São Paulo: Brasiliense, 1962.

Prado, Paulo, *Província e Nação: Retrato do Brasil*, Rio de Janeiro: José Olympio, 1972.

Queiroz, Carlota Pereira de, *Vida e Morte de um Capitão-Mor*, São Paulo: Conselho Estadual de Cultura, 1969.

Queiroz, M. I. Pereira de, *Bairros Rurais Paulistas*, São Paulo: Duas Cidades, 1973.

—— *Cultura, Sociedade Rural, Sociedade Urbana no Brasil*, São Paulo: EDUSP, 1978.

Ribeiro, Coriolano Pinto, *Dona Joaquina do Pompeu*, Juiz de Fora, 1947.

Rodrigues, Leda Maria Pereira, *A Instrução Feminina em São Paulo: Subsídios para a Sua História*, São Paulo, 1962.

Saia, Luís, *Morada Paulista*, São Paulo: Perspectiva, 1978.

Samara, Eni de Mesquita, 'A Família na Sociedade Paulista no Século XIX (1800–1860)', doctoral thesis, São Paulo, 1980.

Sant'Anna, Nuto, *São Paulo Histórico: Aspectos, Lendas e Costumes*, São Paulo: Dep. de Cultura, 1937–1944, 4 vols.

—— *Documentário Histórico*, São Paulo: Col. Dep. de Cultura, 1951, 4 vols.

—— *Metrópole*, São Paulo: Departamento de Cultura, 1953.

Silveira Bueno, A., *O Auto das Regateiras de Lisboa*, São Paulo: Livraria Acadêmica, 1939.

Singer, P. and Madeira, F. R., *Estrutura do Emprego e Trabalho Feminino no Brasil: 1920–1970*, São Paulo: Cadernos CEBRAP, no. 13, 1973.

Souza, Antonio Candido de Mello e, 'The Brazilian family', in T. L. Smith, *Brazil: Portrait of Half a Continent*, New York: Dryden, n.d.

—— *Formação da Literatura Brasileira*, São Paulo: Martins, 1964.

—— *Os Parceiros do Rio Bonito: Estudo sobre o Caipira Paulista e a Transformação dos Meios de Vida*, Rio de Janeiro: José Olympio, 1964.

—— 'Dialética da Malandragem', *Revista do Instituto de Estudos Brasileiros*, no. 8, 1970.

Taunay, Afonso de Escragnolle, *História da Cidade de São Paulo, no Século XVIII*, São Paulo: Imprensa Oficial do Estado, n.d., 2 vols.

—— *História da Cidade de São Paulo no Império*, São Paulo: Dep. de Cultura, 1956, 6 vols.

Tax, Sol, *Penny Capitalism: A Guatemalan Indian Economy*, Washington DC: Institute of Social Anthropology Publications, no. 16, 1951.

Thompson, E. P., *The Making of the English Working Class*, New York: Pantheon, 1956.

Xidieh, Oswaldo Elias, *Narrativas Pias Populares*, São Paulo: Instituto de Estudos Brasileiros, 1967.

—— *Semana Santa Cabocla*, São Paulo: IEB, 1972.

Articles, etc.

Andrade, Mário de, 'A Dona Ausente', *Rev. Atlântica*, Lisbon, 1929, p. 10.

Beyer, Gustavo, 'Ligeiras Notas de Viagem do Rio de Janeiro à Capitania de São Paulo, no Brasil, no Verão de 1813', *RIHGSP*, vol. 12, 1908, pp. 275–311.

Bueno, Francisco de Assis Vieira, 'A Cidade de São Paulo', *Revista do Centro de Sciencias, Letras e Artes de Campinas*, no. 3, 1903, p. 25.

Canabrava, Alice, 'Uma Economia de Decadência: Níveis de Riqueza na Capitania de São Paulo 1765/67', *Revista Brasileira de Economia*, vol. 26, no. 4, 1972, p. 95.

Florence, Amador, 'Coisas de Velhos Censos Paulistas', *Anais do IV Congresso de História Nacional*, Rio de Janeiro, 1950.

Freitas, Afonso A. de, 'A Cidade de São Paulo no Dia 7 de Setembro de 1822', *RIHGSP*, vol. 22, 1923, pp. 3–35.

—— 'Sorocaba dos Tempos Idos', *RIHGSP*, vol. 27, 1930, pp. 97–118.

Friedl, Ernestine, 'The position of women: appearance and reality', *Anthropological Quarterly*, vol. 40, 1974, p. 95.

Hermann, Lucila, 'Evolução da Estrutura Social de Guaratinguetá num Período de Trezentos Anos', São Paulo: Instituto de Administração da USP, vol. 2, 1948.

Hershberg, Theodore and Modell, John, 'The origins of the female-headed black family: the impact of the urban experiences', *Journal of Interdisciplinary History*, vol. 6, no. 2, 1975, p. 211.

Higman, B. W., 'The slave family and household in the British West Indies, 1800–1834', *Journal of Interdisciplinary History*, vol. 6, no. 2, 1975, p. 261.

Kuznetsof, Elizabeth A., 'The role of the female-headed household in Brazilian modernization (São Paulo, 1765 to 1836)', *JSH*, vol. 13, no. 4, 1980, p. 588.

—— 'Household composition and headship as related to changes in mode of production: São Paulo, 1765 to 1836', *Comparative Studies in Society and History*, vol. 22, no. 1, 1980, p. 78.

Lange, Kurt, 'As Danças Coletivas Públicas no Período Colonial e as Danças das Corporações de Ofícios em Minas Gerais', *Barroco*, Belo Horizonte, no. 1, 1969, p. 29.

Lobo, M. Eulália Lahmeyer, et al., 'Estudos das Categorias Sócio-profissionais dos Salários e do Custo de Alimentação no Rio de Janeiro, de 1820 a 1930', *Revista Brasileira de Economia*, vol. 27, no. 4, 1973, pp. 154–60.

Lowrie, Samuel, 'O Elemento Negro na População de São Paulo', *RAMSP*, vol. 48, 1938.

Luna, Francisco and Costa, Iraci del Nero, 'A Presença do Elemento Forro no Conjunto dos Proprietários de Escravos', *Ciência e Cultura*, vol. 32, no. 7, 1980, p. 836.

Luz, Nícia Vilela, 'A Administração Provincial de São Paulo em Face do Movimento Abolicionista', *Revista de Administração*, no. 8, 1948, p. 80.

Mello, Nilva R., 'De Como se Vestia a Gente de Piratininga nos Tempos Coloniais', *Rev. do Atheneo Paulista*, vol. 4, 1967, pp. 63–81.

—— 'De Como Eram os Paulistas', *Rev. do Atheneo Paulista*, vol. 5, 1968, pp. 73–89.

Mintz, Sidney W., 'The employment of capital by market women in Haiti', in R. Firth and B. S. Yamey, *Capital Savings and Credit in Peasant Societies*, Chicago: Aldine, 1964, pp. 256–86.

—— 'Men, women and trade', *Comparative Studies in Society and History*, vol. 13, 1971, pp. 247–69.

Moura, Clóvis, 'Revoltas de Escravos', *RAMSP*, vol. 181, 1970, p. 103.

Pereira, Lucia Miguel, 'As Mulheres na Literatura Brasileira', *Anhembi*, 17, 1954, p. 17.

Ramos, Donald, 'Marriage and the family in colonial Vila Rica', *HAHR*, 55, 1975, p. 200.

—— 'A Estrutura Demográfica de Vila Rica às Vésperas da Inconfidência', *V Anuário do Museu da Inconfidência*, Ouro Preto, 1978, p. 41.

Riegelhaupt, Joyce F., 'Saloio women: an analysis of formal and informal political roles of Portuguese peasant women', *Anthropological Quarterly*, 40, 1974, p. 109.

Sampaio, Theodoro, 'A Cidade de São Paulo no Século XIX', *RIHGSP*, vol. 6, 1900, pp. 159–205.

Sant'Anna, Nuto, 'Como se Vestiam as Paulistas em Fins do Século XVIII', *RAPM*, vol. 11, 1935, p. 156.

Santos, Joaquim Silveira, 'São Roque de Outrora', *RIHGSP*, vol. 38, 1939, pp. 232–57.

Silva, Maria Beatriz Nizza da, 'Sistema de Casamento no Brasil Colonial', *Ciência e Cultura*, vol. 28, 1976, p. 1248.

—— 'Casamentos de Escravos na Capitania de São Paulo', *Ciência e Cultura*, vol. 32, no. 7, 1980, pp. 816–21.

—— 'O Problema dos Expostos na Capitania de São Paulo', *Rev. de História Econômica e Social*, Lisbon, vol. 5, 1980, p. 95.

Soeiro, Susan, 'The social and economic role of the convent women and nuns in colonial Bahia 1677–1800', *HAHR*, 1976.

Taunay, Afonso d'E., 'Festividades Setecentistas', *RAPM*, vol. 15, 1935, pp. 5–25.

Willems, Emilio, 'A Estrutura da Família Brasileira', *Sociologia*, vol. 16, no. 4, 1954, p. 327.

Wood, A. J. R. Russell, 'Women and society in colonial Brazil', *JLAS*, vol. 9, no. 2, 1977, pp. 1–34.

Index